T0356897

CATCH A FIRE

CATCH A FIRE

The Blaze and Bust of the Canadian Cannabis Industry

BEN KAPLAN

DUNDURN
PRESS

Copyright © Ben Kaplan, 2025

All rights reserved. No part of this publication may be reproduced, stored in a retrieval system, or transmitted in any form or by any means, electronic, mechanical, photocopying, recording, or otherwise (except for brief passages for purpose of review) without the prior permission of Dundurn Press. Permission to photocopy should be requested from Access Copyright.

Publisher: Meghan Macdonald | Acquiring editor: Kwame Scott Fraser/Julia Kim | Editor: Russell Smith
Cover designer: Karen Alexiou
Cover image: matchbox: Man_Half-tube/istock.com; cannabis leaf: starline/Freepik;
joint: MicrovOne/istock.com; back smoke: pch.vector/Freepik
Interior: matches: designed by Freepik
All photos courtesy of the author except p. 56, Chris Cowperthwaite/Open Democracy; p. 143,
Peter J. Thompson; and p. 212, Bryan Passifiume.

Library and Archives Canada Cataloguing in Publication

Title: Catch a fire : the blaze and bust of the Canadian cannabis industry / Ben Kaplan.
Names: Kaplan, Ben, author.
Description: Includes index.
Identifiers: Canadiana (print) 2024045698X | Canadiana (ebook) 20240457080 | ISBN
    9781459754652 (softcover) | ISBN 9781459754669 (PDF) | ISBN 9781459754676 (EPUB)
Subjects: LCSH: Marijuana industry—Canada. | LCSH: Marijuana—Economic
    aspects—Canada.
Classification: LCC HD9019.M382 C3 2025 | DDC 338.1/73790971—dc23

We acknowledge the support of the Canada Council for the Arts and the Ontario Arts Council for our publishing program. We also acknowledge the financial support of the Government of Ontario, through the Ontario Book Publishing Tax Credit and Ontario Creates, and the Government of Canada.

Care has been taken to trace the ownership of copyright material used in this book. The author and the publisher welcome any information enabling them to rectify any references or credits in subsequent editions.

The publisher is not responsible for websites or their content unless they are owned by the publisher.

Printed and bound in Canada.

Dundurn Press
1382 Queen Street East
Toronto, Ontario, Canada M4L 1C9
dundurn.com, @dundurnpress

Cannabis, as a moment, was massive, fast, addictive, and insane. When Canadian prime minister Justin Trudeau ended prohibition and legalized pot, he not only changed the culture, he blew up the business world. From 2018 to 2019 — six months before and after marijuana legalization on October 17, 2018 — sixteen Canadian cannabis start-ups had multibillion-dollar market capitalizations.

Fourteen of these companies were led by Canadian originals, risk-takers having the time of their lives.

Marijuana businesses were led by novices in the public markets and by the government, novices in dealing drugs. Big money was made. Big money was lost. And Canada had the eyes of the world on its policy. Israel, Germany, the United Kingdom, Jamaica, the United States, and, yes, countries all over the world have followed, and will continue to follow, Canada's revolutionary clusterfuck.

Profiteers ravaged the sector. And the hype behind weed, which twisted up Drake, Martha Stewart, Snoop Dogg, the Toronto Raptors, and me, created a frenzy that, like a joint at a Tragically Hip show, couldn't last.

Ninety-seven percent of the value of those sixteen Canadian cannabis start-ups disappeared. Every single one of the Canadian founders is gone.

It was a fizzy, fuzzy epoch of whistle blowers, IPOs, Hells Angels, private planes, and edibles; a billion-dollar company in Edmonton with a Gmail account for investor relations. This book will trace the journeys of some of the major players in this heady period of speculation and fantasy — marijuana, from golden goose to smoke cloud, blown away.

For Matthew and Esme, my babies.
DON'T DO DRUGS!

Contents

Part III: Revenge

Part IV: Redemption

PROLOGUE

The First Hit

"Look at what we did, man."

The phrase hangs over our small table at an off-the-Strip Las Vegas steakhouse like a puff of smoke from a Canadian pre-roll. I'm sitting with Canada's two original weed kings — Terry Booth, founder of Aurora Cannabis, and Bruce Linton, founder of Canopy Growth. They are dining together for the first time. Booth is straightening out with a double Ketel One vodka after taking an edible someone had passed him at the cannabis convention earlier that morning.

Booth is the man who put down $3 million to start Aurora in 2013 in his hometown of Edmonton, Alberta. He knew about weed because he used to pinch some from his father in between beatings, smoke it, and sell it to his high school friends. Before launching Aurora, which he'd grow to be worth more than $15 billion and now has a $230-million market cap, he spent three months in the cannabis underground, hitting black market dispensaries, examining grows, meeting patients, watching his back, and getting high.

It's October 2021, three years after Canadian pot legalization, and Booth is fifty-seven years old. He is stumping for his new U.S. marijuana company.

He is bearded, beaming, and coming down. He's wearing a hat and T-shirt bearing the name Audacious, a cannabis company he spun out from Aurora that aims to grow and distribute marijuana in the U.S. He speaks with a mumbled Western accent. Machine Gun Kelly, the pop star, will fly in with his girlfriend, Megan Fox, to meet Booth, smoke weed with him, and perform for Audacious the next night at the Cosmopolitan Hotel.

Terry is magnanimous, spontaneous, funny, aggressive, loyal, cutthroat, and self-destructive. Rumours have circulated that his board at Aurora pulled him back from public appearances after he appeared drunk onstage one time too many. Between the booze, blow, 'shrooms, and edibles, Terry says he was having too much fun to give two shits. "Convincing twenty-five countries to allow cannabis as an alternative medicine was more important to me than what some dipshit at a conference thinks," he says. There were drug rumours, especially about cocaine, but they may have been fanned by businessmen in Toronto making fun of the cowboy from Alberta who looked at Bay Street with spite.

Or they may have been true.

Terry Booth doesn't care. What Booth said onstage at a cannabis conference when his defences were down was that "Ontario and British Columbia shit the bed on the legal marijuana rollout." What he meant was that, as the companies began actually selling legal weed and none of the lofty financial projections proved true, the fault lay with the regulators — not with companies like his own.

He has always been a brash player in the world of legal pot. Back in 2016, rival cannabis executives sent out a joint press release about ending the taxation on marijuana medicine, but they included signatories from illegal cannabis dispensaries, who had paved the way for the legal system. Booth responded by emailing his colleagues at 2:30 a.m., in defence of the early activists: "Pull your heads out of your asses," he wrote. "We've been handed the torch from the pioneers!"

Now Terry Booth is back in weed after getting sacked from Aurora. Back in Vegas, pressing the flesh. Back, in between shutdowns from Covid and proxy battles with dissident Audacious shareholders, making deals, giving interviews, drinking Ketel One, buying companies, wearing company swag, and taking edibles from strangers. Tonight he wants Bruce Linton, who has ordered for the table, to invest in his new American weed brand.

Bruce Linton is listening.

At this stage of his career — fifty-four years old, his hair grown long, his beard hanging an inch beneath his chin — Bruce is restless. For no real reason, he had the American founder of the cannabis company Tilray fly up on his private plane to meet him and walk the aisles of tomorrow's Las Vegas weed expo. They weren't friends. But Bruce thought it would be fun. And Brendan Kennedy, Tilray's founder, worth more than $2 billion in 2018 and now estimated by *Forbes* to be worth closer to $230 million, listened to Bruce.

Bruce Linton is a conduit of action. Another cannabis executive, Sébastien St-Louis, the founder of Hexo, says that when Linton brought the alcohol behemoth Constellation Brands into cannabis, it was "a magic trick." Linton started Canopy Growth in 2012. Like Booth, like Kennedy, like St-Louis, he was white and rich. He had never smoked pot then, but didn't care. He wasn't a stoner. He was an opportunist, a genie, a promoter — a visionary who sensed in weed a product he could sell.

Canopy's market capitalization — the value of all its shares — grew to $22 billion. This was hoisted up by hedge funds and investment banks. "King Kong on cocaine" is how Linton's right-hand man, financier Sean McNulty, describes him during this period. Tireless, spontaneous, hungry, bellicose, having the time of his life — and, heeding a call of his own, from nowhere, building a company selling marijuana once worth more than U.S. Steel.

Linton, bucktoothed, approachable, unpredictable, a father with no time for therapy or books, is an adrenalin junkie. He gets a second bottle of burgundy, and we all order cocktails while Terry talks Bruce up to our distracted waiter. This guy, Terry tells the inattentive waiter, saw a new world opening and, from suburban Ottawa, put Canada at the centre of the global weed boom — a boom, and a bust, that he fostered. It was Linton who took a cannabis brand public with the stock ticker WEED. Linton brought in institutional money and Martha Stewart, CBD soap, Snoop Dogg, sparkling cannabis lemonade, and Drake.

"This is the king!" declares Terry, and Bruce just smiles. It's been a long time since someone called him that. Canopy lost more than $675 million in

2023, a huge improvement from the $3.3 billion it lost in 2022, but, because of how Bruce structured his company, may never be able to turn a profit.

When Linton bought Bedrocan, a medical cannabis rival that increased his market cap by 15 percent, the first thing he did was fire Cam Battley, their spokesperson. Bruce didn't want a spokesperson. He wanted to be the spokesperson for the entire industry.

Cam Battley, a Cub Scout leader, would end up spokesperson for Aurora once Terry was forced out of that role. Cam hated and still hates Bruce, and is hated by, despised by Terry, who thinks Battley badmouthed him to his board at Aurora. Bruce and Terry call Battley a cocksucker and a company stooge. Then Terry pulls out the nuclear diss: the ass-kisser faked inhaling when he pretended to smoke weed.

Because of the stakes, the inexperience, and the money, the degree to which the business was personal, the weed executives feuded like WWE wrestlers: they called the regulators on one another, poached each other's executives, and bad-mouthed one another like teenage girls at a slumber party.

It was all part of the intensity — the emotion, attention, and buzz — of legal marijuana, a business that would grow from a court case involving medical cannabis use to rival oil and gas as a top contributor to Canada's annual gross domestic product. Eventually, cannabis would add $43 billion to Canada's bottom line, at a time when many companies in other industries, from Suncor to Shopify, saw their fortunes sink.

Bruce Linton and Terry Booth made something new from something sacred. They said acquisitions equalled acceleration. They said soccer moms would drink weed. They said marijuana would be a billion-dollar industry and, for a little while, it was. Bruce turned a shuttered chocolate factory in the middle of nowhere into a marijuana Taj Mahal, with sugar-free weed chocolate, tour guides, and more than fifty rooms for growing indoor marijuana. He once gave a tour to former Toronto police chief Bill Blair, asking the straitlaced copper, "When's the last time you saw this much weed without everyone running for the door?"

Terry wanted to beat Bruce bad. He had built a grow op outside the Edmonton Airport so big that pilots complained the reflection from his roof was so bright they couldn't land their planes. Upon arriving in Edmonton, the first thing you smelled was Terry's weed. It didn't matter that Edmonton and Smiths Falls, Ontario, were the worst places to grow marijuana (cold weather, expensive electricity, not many people). They were $800 million PR stunts, and if the goal was to increase their companies' paper value, they worked, for a time.

But time would eventually run out.

Over T-bones in the Golden Steer Steakhouse — talking loudly, finishing each other's sentences, slamming tequila, and having fun — Linton enjoys Booth's conversation. Both men are off the clock and jamming, settling into their memories and hopes, if not fantasies, of trying to become useful in a world in which Canadian cannabis companies with American owners are being brutalized on the stock exchanges in New York and Toronto. Indeed, Aurora has just been dropped from the S&P/TSX Composite Index. To complicate things further, psychedelics — in which both men have money — are today where pot was when they started. Mushrooms, goes the thinking in today's weed world, are the new pot. And both men obviously know how to tell this story.

Even without booze, Terry and Bruce are champion bullshitters. At their zenith, the combined value of the men and their start-ups was over $30 billion, and they had more than six thousand employees. They had facilities from Germany to Jamaica, and all over Canada. Terry made a deal for $1 million on a napkin at Richard Branson's private island resort. Once, at a Raptors game before Bruce Linton and Drake publicly announced their joint cannabis venture, Bruce had to tell Drake to be discreet about it, as photographs of the two men together could influence the market.

In the process, Bruce and Terry drove up the value of their companies and the entire industry, only to see the whole thing come crashing in a fiery heap to the ground, where it lies today. Eight hundred people have just been fired from Canopy. Aurora lost $28.3 million in the three months ended June 30, 2023, and their new CEO framed that number as good news. There are people in cannabis who have lost their life savings gambling on Terry and Bruce — who have been gambling with their own companies the same way.

The Canadian economy is speculative, perfect for hedge funds who would short weed stocks, betting against the very companies they've helped raise money for. As long as they make their commissions and sell before the suckers — Canadian retail investors — the bankers don't care. They're eating expense account steak on Bay Street, following the same template they perfected in the 1990s with junior mines.

What could be more speculative than the size of the first legal cannabis sales? No one had done what Bruce and Terry did. There was no blueprint. No ceiling. And, for lots of it, there were elastic rules. Health Canada was learning right alongside the companies they were regulating. Justin Trudeau, the dashing Canadian prime minister, rode into office as a breath of fresh air. Goodbye prim Conservative prime minister Stephen Harper. Trudeau told *Vice* he had smoked pot as an MP. Justin Trudeau arrived as the Barack Obama of the North. Canada was sexy, hip; marijuana legalization signalled youth, change.

Bruce and Terry, guns blazing, were that change.

The two men now making their way through a second bottle had convinced investment bankers that it wasn't $10 million that a Canadian producer licensed to sell marijuana needed to raise. It was $100 million. More! All Terry had to hear was that Bruce was interested in some company, some seed manufacturer, energy drink, or Dutch vault system, and he'd pay a premium on that asset, whatever it was. A $5 million company could suddenly be worth $500 million because Terry or Bruce would pay that much. Was it worth it? Fuck no. But also … difficult to determine, because the ensuing result — in an industry in which you couldn't advertise — would be that their stock would rise. It was speculative. Marijuana companies had to buy things to get attention, to keep the bubble inflated. Until, of course, the bubble burst.

Eventually, sales would have to come. Profits. EBITDA — earnings before interest, taxes, depreciation, and amortization — became the weed world's metric, rather than vault size or "funded capacity," which determined a company's value based upon how much greenhouse space it owned. Boards would eventually want to see profits. Even the boards themselves would eventually grow up. Booth and Linton wanted to be cannabis's Zuckerberg and Bezos, and they were encouraged by Jim Cramer, Nelson Peltz, and everyone's sister or aunt in Saskatchewan to try. They inflated the value of the legal cannabis market and forced business decisions. It got so that a cannabis executive in British Columbia couldn't work on making their licensed producer profitable in Canada, to grow good weed and build a brand. They had to think globally.

Trevor Fencott, who sold Mettrum, his medical marijuana company with Michael Haines as CEO, to Linton for $430 million before opening a chain of cannabis retailers, says everyone in the industry had to become IBM overnight.

The Canadian cannabis industry, led by Terry and Bruce, artificially created weed companies with bad weed (which Terry refutes) and market values that were one thousand times sales (which he doesn't). Legalization was a groundbreaking, historic end of prohibition that placed Canada (and, strangely, Uruguay) ahead of the rest of the world. It caused a rush: it stoked a market fuelled by C-level investment banks when institutional money — smart money — wouldn't touch the sector. For everyone involved, it was intoxicating. Silicon Valley, if you swapped out computers for blunts.

In 2016, I began working in cannabis and felt a visceral attraction to the scene. I attended the marijuana Oscars — the Lift Awards, which named winners in categories like Top Indica Flower, Top High CBD Oil, and Licensed Producer of the Year — and couldn't get a beer, but there was a room at the award show for cannabis vaping. I hadn't seen a vape before. I was so excited I felt like I was high even before I got stoned. Eager, opportunistic, and desperate for anything, I was looking for mentors, for fun, for money, for bylines — for action — and I found it in Terry and Bruce. I took a hit of a vape pen and felt my mind explode. I can manoeuvre in this environment, amongst these people, this product, in ways other people can't.

Inevitably, for all of us, the momentum could not be sustained: investment around the world dried up, facilities closed across the country, and thousands of jobs and billions of dollars disappeared like so many hundreds on a blackjack table.

Over the course of the evening's vodka, two bottles of red, and shots of tequila at the Golden Steer, Terry Booth and Bruce Linton recount the birth of a Canadian moment: when entrepreneurs and investors in London and Los Angeles had to travel to Edmonton and Smiths Falls to get into the Wild West Canadian sector that banks in America still can't touch. They name names, pick winners and losers, and explain how they came to have a deep affection, a sincere appreciation, for a flower that people have rolled up to feel better since the beginning of time.

Outside the restaurant, Booth has a Rolls-Royce waiting, and when the bottle is dry, we hop in the car. We drop Linton off at the Marriott across the street from the cannabis convention. In Las Vegas, in marijuana, where even junior executives compete to flaunt money, Linton takes the opposite approach: he eats bagels from a strip mall and the only reservation he wanted was at the Golden Steer.

Booth, however, is good for a nightcap — he's still a year away from getting sober — and we walk through his hotel, the Wynn, find a bar for more vodka, and take an edible produced by a young hustler. The kid has a company, he tells Booth, that is going to be big. Terry gives him his number. He tells me, "Ya never know."

This is the story of Terry Booth and Bruce Linton and all the activists, entrepreneurs, and hardworking people who saw an opportunity in marijuana and competed, as Hexo founder Sébastien St-Louis likes to say, like cage fighters: to win.

Earlier in the evening, Linton had a chance to respond to Terry's "Look at what we did, man" comment. Bruce thought about it as he finished his drink, then smiled.

He said, "We changed the world."

Twin Towers: Bruce Linton (right) and Terry Booth at the Golden Steer Steakhouse in Las Vegas. Booth, coming down off an edible, had a Rolls-Royce parked outside.

PART I

RISK

CHAPTER 1

Patient Zero

"Everyone should have access to marijuana."

Terry Parker

This story begins with a sick man in a poor part of town, smoking weed.

Terrance Parker was smoking marijuana in his fourth-floor apartment in Parkdale, a gritty neighbourhood of Toronto, when he heard a bang on his door. Parker, thirty-nine at the time, in the summer of 1996, was already a veteran of Canada's drug war. He was dazed and confused when the police arrived, but he wasn't exactly stoned. Parker doesn't use weed for a buzz. Rather, he uses it to control his buzz, to escape it. He's suffered from violent epileptic seizures all his life and, since he was sixteen, has used cannabis medicinally.

In 1987, when he was thirty, after a bust for simple cannabis possession, Parker was acquitted on the grounds of "medical necessity." This created a cannabis grey zone and a regulatory nightmare: it was a medical necessity that Terry Parker smoked weed, but how was he supposed to get it? Parker used cannabis to control his otherwise uncontrollable fits. Pot makes the volcano not explode. But there was danger in the marijuana underworld.

Hippies, sure. But also criminals. He'd been robbed. Been sold fake weed. Made himself vulnerable.

In the summer of 1996, Parker would become the only person in Canada with paperwork saying he could legally smoke pot. This was the result of numerous court cases fought by Aaron Harnett, Parker's long-time pro bono counsel. In court, Harnett, only a few years out of law school, was prepared, emotional, a bit gonzo, and all in. Like a lot of people who went into law to change the system, there was no doubt this stuff was personal to him. Even today, he tears up when discussing the cause: the activists at the time — all of them smoked marijuana — believed legalization was a cross to die on, an indelible charter of rights that tied into freedom, health, and an almost religious ideal for how the world should be. The plant was sacred, society needed to change, and people were willing, at the time, to go to jail — not for banking irregularities, but for their beliefs.

Terry Parker, Harnett says, was not scared of jail. With his condition, he'd been imprisoned all his life. Outside of court, Aaron Harnett appeared before the cameras, bearded and with curly red hair, looking like Woody Harrelson as Larry Flint, strumming his guitar and espousing the virtues of marijuana. He barely turned a profit at his small law firm, where he worked cases he believed in for free. Harnett, a long-time smoker, was a marijuana guy.

In the Parker case, Harnett, backed solely by his mother, who acted as his secretary, worked tirelessly to defend his client, who was known to go off the rails. It was the lawyer Alan Young who connected Parker to Harnett. The irascible Young, who believed in marijuana as one would believe in Allah, Buddha, and Jesus Christ, represented pornographers and prostitutes and dedicated his life to using the law to grant individual freedoms. He had smoked a lot of weed before going to Yale (and smoked a lot of weed at Yale, too). Young had defended Marc Emery, Canada's BC-based self-described "Prince of Pot," who sold seeds to Terry Parker and was arrested in 1994 for selling *High Times* magazine. Young had gotten Emery off. Emery supplied Parker, and also became the country's first big, bold-faced, money-making, attention-seeking cannabis star, alongside Jodie, his much younger, troubled, and beautiful pot-smoking wife.

Jodie — who appeared nude on the cover of her husband's pot maga-zine — made a more appealing face for the marijuana movement than Terry Parker, who had long scraggly hair covering stitches that formed the shape of a Christmas tree on his skull. Parker, who Alan Young wouldn't defend because he'd made anti-Semitic remarks, needed handling. He was sick.

Aaron Harnett gave me Terry Parker's number, and I walked over to his house.

Parker tells me he took his first pull of a joint on December 24, 1972, with a friend who worked as an orderly at a hospital. It soothed him, like a pan of water ceasing to boil, and, unlike for his buddy, didn't seem to pro-duce typical marijuana effects. He didn't giggle or find the meaning of life in the lyrics of Pink Floyd. Instead, his fingers unspooled from his fists. He says he'd never again celebrate Christmas in pain.

He tried cannabis again and the same thing happened: unlike the experi-mental treatments for his epilepsy that had failed to help him in his teens, marijuana created a sensation in his body like peace. Some people get para-noid. Some get hungry. You can get the giggles, get horny, get the sudden urge to paint. In Parker's case, the pot settled his body down. His muscles, on pot, stopped attacking him. The seizures went away. It's a feeling, he told me the first time we met, in the cold outside his apartment building, that for his whole tortured life he'd been chasing and had been unable to find. And his life has certainly been tortured. Parker's pre-marijuana treatments read like *One Flew over the Cuckoo's Nest*. At fourteen, he had a right temporal lobec-tomy at the Hospital for Sick Children in Toronto, which involved opening his cranium and removing brain matter. Two years later, under only a local anaesthetic — which means Parker was awake while this happened — sur-geons opened his skull and sliced brain material apart, attempting to scrape harmful neural matter away from the brain of this terrified sixteen-year-old.

It was January 2021, and Parker was standing in front of me telling me that these experimental operations didn't help him, but they did make him depressed and suicidal. "If they can cut my head open," he asks, "why can't they give me a joint?"

"Everyone should have access to marijuana," Parker says. He stood glove-less in the grey Toronto pandemic, wearing a camouflage medical mask half off his face, outside the same Toronto apartment where his arrest had set in motion the dominoes, falling, slowly, of marijuana laws all over the world. "Pot stopped my fucking seizures after all the bullshit the hospitals tried — that almost killed me, but definitely didn't fucking work."

Parker was angry, difficult to talk to, and given to impossible-to-follow asides. But he was encyclopedic on the details of his case and recognized that he played an important historical role in changing his country's cannabis laws. The Terry Parker case, which would help end prohibition in this country, was, in Aaron Harnett's words, "about making Gramma not afraid of marijuana." For society to accept medicinal marijuana, the movement needed a sympathetic figurehead. Jodie could've worked. They got Terry Parker instead.

That summer in 1996, Parker was working in construction, living with his girlfriend, and taking care of his mom, who was going through chemotherapy but wouldn't try the medicine her son was legally entitled to consume. Terry grew the pot he smoked in a back closet of his Parkdale apartment. When the police searched the place, they found seventy-one plants. They didn't care when he said he was legally entitled to produce and consume medical marijuana — the police didn't know their own cannabis laws — and he was arrested for possession, cultivation, and trafficking. In court, Parker admitted to giving joints to other people who suffered from his same epileptic condition; he was a one-man compassion club.

Harnett could've gotten the charge thrown out. The courts were loath to press cannabis charges on white men. By the late 1990s, already half a million Canadians had cannabis convictions, and the data states that of that number, Black and Indigenous men and women were disproportionately arrested. While consumption rates are the same among all races, arrest rates certainly are not.

Parker, who is white, decided to fight the case in court, and Aaron Harnett saw his opportunity to bomb the system. He says he had two cases to prove: one to the judge, and the other to Gramma — the court of public opinion.

The timing, Harnett says, for reconsidering marijuana was good. In the 1990s, we were in the midst of the AIDS epidemic. Allan Rock, Canada's minister of justice, had been in Montreal with Yoko Ono and John Lennon at their 1969 bed-in, when they wrote "Give Peace a Chance." Even before hearing of Terry Parker, Rock had visited the 519 Clinic on Church Street in Toronto, in the gay village, and listened when activist Jim Wakeford told him, "I have AIDS and I'm wasting away and the one thing that saves me is marijuana. I can eat and stay alive and you won't let me have access to marijuana. I think that's wrong." It was an image Rock couldn't shake and the spearhead of a movement in Canada that was also happening in liberal parts of the U.S.

In 1996, California passed Proposition 215, known as the Compassionate Use Act, which legalized marijuana as treatment for a limited list of medical conditions. Prop 215 is the precedent that introduced cannabis as a means of increasing appetite; reducing nausea; and helping with sleep problems, glaucoma, muscle spasticity (a common symptom of multiple sclerosis, or MS), and what Terry Parker suffered from, epilepsy. But it wasn't only that. Public perception also was changing.

Alan Young, the crusading Canadian lawyer, says he knew he could go after marijuana legalization when he saw how it was treated on TV. In the 1980s, if Alex P. Keaton were to smoke a joint on *Family Ties*, he'd be in rehab in the next episode. By the 1990s, however, on *The Simpsons*, when Lisa says that Otto's jacket smells funny, it's simply played for a knowing laugh. In 1992, Bill Clinton looked like a loser when he said that he'd tried marijuana but didn't inhale. The culture was changing, at least in the tarot cards as read by Alan Young. Compassion clubs, illegal storefronts that provided cannabis to anyone who flashed a membership card, were popping up in Vancouver, Toronto, and Montreal. These activists set the groundwork for legalization, but they were generals with no army. The owner of a compassion club that was busted in Montreal in 1998 told me, "The police were hating on me, and organized crime didn't like me either."

Terrance Parker, who continued cultivating, imbibing, and dispensing to the sick, was arrested again in September 1997. Again, with Harnett mounting his defence, he told the court that he wouldn't stop doing any of those things.

One day Parker had a seizure in court. His lawyer had established how violent the episodes could be and how, when they occurred on a subway platform or on the street, they could make him susceptible to violent crime. In public, he'd had seizures that had knocked him out and as he lay on the street, he'd been robbed. Harnett told the judge that this had happened to his client more than fifty times. But nothing could prepare the court for what a seizure looked like: Parker falling off the bench, shaking, writhing on the floor.

This wasn't the Hells Angels or hippies. This wasn't college kids reading the Beats and protesting the war. This was human rights. This was Jim Wakeford speaking to Allan Rock about not wasting away.

Harnett told the court that to deny Parker his marijuana was to take away his constitutional right to health and security. In the choice between stability through marijuana or prison — a life where he either experienced upward of ten seizures a day, some life threatening, or jail time — Harnett argued that it was Parker's constitutional right to smoke cannabis. "It was about increasing an individual's right versus the state," Harnett tells me.

Canada, at the time, was becoming increasingly liberal with regard to individual rights. In 1988, it had been established that women were entitled to an abortion. In 1995, compassionate suicide became a new category of crime for adults assisting in consensual euthanasia. The state, on behalf of brave plaintiffs and pioneering lawyers — most, like Harnett and Young, pot smokers working for free — was affording more power to individuals and accepting, grudgingly, that individuals had the right to make decisions that an earlier generation might not choose.

Harnett won Parker's appeal on July 31, 2000. This opened the floodgates to what we have today. During that trial, the Ontario Court of Appeal not only ruled in Parker's favour, but also ruled that the law as it was written forced Parker to choose between committing a crime or succumbing to inferior medical treatment. Criminalizing marijuana put his security at risk. The court tasked the federal government with creating a regulated system for distributing medical marijuana. And there was a caveat in this decision: if the government couldn't figure out a way to administer the medicine that Parker and other Canadians legally needed and were now entitled to, then all of the marijuana laws would cease to exist.

In the time between Parker's arrest and the Court of Appeal verdict, other activists around the country got onboard. Jim Wakeford sued the Canadian government for access to legal medical cannabis in 1998, and Chris Clay, in London, Ontario, was arrested for selling cannabis seeds. Both of these men were represented by Alan Young. Meanwhile, on the West Coast there were Marc and Jodie Emery (today, Jodie goes by Jodie Giesz-Ramsay and has disassociated herself from her ex). Marc, a lightning rod for publicity, moved from aggression to aggression against any authority — including U.S. drug czar John Walters, which eventually got him thrown behind American bars.

Notable potheads on the West Coast also included Ted Smith, who established the Hempology 101 club at the University of Victoria, organized 4:20 sessions, and opened the Victoria Cannabis Buyers Club for medical patients. Buyers clubs administered to the homeless and the sick. They were run by cannabis consumers who distributed edibles and homegrown weed and lived just above the line of poverty. Hilary Black, a pioneer from the scene, says she saw people battling mental health and addiction issues, as well as people, like Terry's mother, battling cancer or AIDS or any of the myriad social and health issues that affect us all. "If no one was going to help these people, we would," Black says, "and we'd help them with weed."

Around the time of Parker's verdict, Hilary Black was riding her bike through Vancouver with a backpack and a pager, administering grams to people in need. "We'd seen what was happening in California and it made sense to do the same thing here," Black tells me. She had once followed the Grateful Dead, but now she adhered to strict codes for administering her medicine to patients (for instance, people wouldn't be served if they were intoxicated), and she kept detailed financial records of the pot she sold. The point was to do everything right. The underground was creating a system that worked.

But the face of the movement was still, for better or worse, Terry Parker.

"Terry was a terrible poster child for the movement, but legally the best litigant because of the facts of the case," Harnett says. Parker had a detailed, documented history of taking every epilepsy medicine on the market. His stints in and out of Toronto's hospitals since the 1960s followed him around like the stink of a half-smoked joint in his blue jeans pocket, as did his cannabis arrests. Parker had tried everything — even those experimental brain surgeries — and nothing produced the effect of weed. His health struggle was as exhaustive as the treatments' results were unfruitful. There was only one alternative, Harnett argued: cannabis. "Terry didn't want it only for himself. He could've walked from the charge of possession — he was licensed! But it wasn't enough for him," Harnett tells me. "Terry had a crusade against the medical world."

Terry Parker was obsessed not just with his case but with the broken system, and Harnett couldn't dissuade him from seeking to make a lasting change. The lawyer was popular around the Scarborough courthouse. Everyone admired his belief, and judges in the building had taken to whispering in his ear: "The Crown will fold, Aaron. Just walk away." He didn't have to fight the case, went the assertion. The government would drop its case.

But, in the summer of 2000, that's not what Parker wanted to do. He could've walked out of the courthouse and gotten high. The court even offered to give him back his seventy-one plants. "As someone who's gone through the medical system, I know what works and what doesn't, and it makes no sense that anyone should be denied the medical benefits of a simple, natural plant," Parker tells me. "You can cut somebody open, who's a minor, without consent, and that's legal, but you can't let somebody have the joint that they need? It doesn't make sense. I'm not special. But I will always fight for what's fair."

When I spoke to him in 2021, Parker had been in his building for forty years. He shovelled the snow from its walkways. He and his brother took care of their mom before she finally succumbed to her cancer in 2011. He was still in touch with Aaron Harnett, and he still smoked, daily, marijuana that he grew in his closet. There was no doubt his life had been hard. At times, Parker rattled off dates of court rulings and pot busts like a cannabis investor tallying EBITDA reports; at others, he spewed the kind of nasty comments that made Alan Young walk away from the case. Still, I found Terry generous. Young says Parker could be anti-Semitic, but every time we met, I, a Jewish reporter, promised him lunch, and every time I stood with him in the cold outside of his building, he turned me down.

———•

This is how the Terry Parker case changed Canadian law: When he was arrested in 1996 and again in 1997 for possession of marijuana, he was legally allowed to grow and smoke pot as a result of earlier rulings. The pot had been prescribed by his physician. Aaron Harnett argued that the same rights afforded to Parker should be afforded to other people suffering from other afflictions. The judge agreed, but the Crown brought the case to the Ontario Court of Appeal. Harnett, defending Parker, won the appeal, and as a result, the federal government had one year to enact medical marijuana laws or else the entire system of cannabis regulations would become null and void. If there wasn't a way for Canadians to legally procure and consume medical marijuana, all marijuana would have to become legal — including for recreational use. As a result, a team led by Minister of Health Allan Rock enacted the Marihuana Medical Access Regulations in 2001. Under the Controlled Drugs and Substances Act, the federal government now stipulated that patients meeting the approved criteria could lawfully use and possess marijuana.

The case had taken four years from Aaron Harnett's life. He lost money changing Canada's marijuana laws. But he maintains the struggle was worth it. It's the reason why he decided to practise law in the first place. In 2001, after the verdict was read, both Parker and Harnett got high. Harnett, in particular, was a coveted interview for media outlets around the world. He says he remembers best one interview that perfectly articulated the moment: he celebrated his biggest court victory drinking champagne and eating chocolate in bed with his wife while being interviewed on the BBC. He was nude.

CHAPTER 2

Government Weed

"It was a dark, deep, cold hole in the ground."

Brent Zettl

If buying pot from the government sounds like throwing a rave in a jail, so was every other element of the rollout of Canada's legal medical marijuana system — including the clunky, obtuse wording of the groundbreaking cannabis law.

The Medical Marihuana Access Regulations, known as the MMAR laws, were implemented on July 30, 2001, a result of the seemingly endless court cases and appeals won by Aaron Harnett for Terry Parker. These new Health Canada regulations would usher in the first legal, government-run medicinal Canadian cannabis program. Under Prime Minister Jean Chrétien, Health Minister Allan Rock, and Justice Minister Anne McLellan, the law stated that denying a patient their medicinal cannabis was to deny them their human rights, and thus the government had to provide licensed patients with medical cannabis. A patient could legally grow their own pot, if they had a licence, like Terry Parker, or they could employ a "designated grower," someone who could harvest marijuana for them. Patients would receive pot prescriptions for up to a thirty-day supply or 150 grams, whichever was less.

Although California already had a similar system, the response from America wasn't good. The Canadian laws were despised by U.S. politicians. "Canada is the centre of the drug problem in the United States," said John Walters, the U.S. drug czar under President George W. Bush (and foe of Marc Emery). Walters threatened to increase Canadian-American border security and warned that these medicinal cannabis laws set the stage for an increase in crime and drug addiction in youth.

Ronald Reagan, during the 1980 presidential campaign, had said "Marijuana is probably the most dangerous drug in America today." The crack epidemic was less than five years away.

Allan Rock, Canada's then Liberal minister of health, dug into the file and disagreed with Reagan, Bush, and Walters. Rock had a history of drawing conclusions for himself. In 1969, Rock had been twenty-two years old and the head of the student union at the University of Ottawa. That May, John Lennon and Yoko Ono were in Montreal staging their bed-in at the Queen Elizabeth Hotel. There were 2,964 marijuana convictions in Canada that year, and Rock, an aspiring lawyer, had questions. Who was being detained, and why? Rock contacted Lennon's road manager and asked if the former Beatle, then deep into his peace and drug phase, would share his message of love and understanding in Ottawa. The manager said, "Ask him yourself," and so our future minister of health, who would later become justice minister, hopped in his yellow Volkswagen Beetle, drove to Montreal, and asked the most famous doper in the world questions about pot.

Lennon, charmed, agreed to come to Ottawa, and he and Ono were good on their word, making a trip on June 3, 1969. Rock describes his time with Lennon as "thrilling," and says that, before there was ever such a thing as *Carpool Karaoke*, Lennon hopped in Rock's Beetle and belted out "Get Back" when it came on the radio. "Those were the adventures of youth," Rock tells me. He describes driving Lennon and Ono to 24 Sussex Drive, where the three of them knocked on Prime Minister Pierre Elliott Trudeau's front door. You could do that in 1969. "A housekeeper answered and said Mr. Trudeau wasn't there, so John Lennon left our prime minister a note," says Rock with a laugh. He's coy about whether or not he got high with Ono and Lennon. All he'll say is "I had my own interest in marijuana and hash." Still, when his counterpart in the States would have had Lennon arrested, the fact that Rock won't deny toking up with him illustrates the different approaches on each side of our cultural divide.

It was under Allan Rock that Terry Parker was allowed to acquire his medical cannabis legally, and it was Rock who then needed to make a system for the cannabis program. It wasn't originally Jean Chrétien's intention to strike down the country's pot laws. However, after the MMARs were passed and Chrétien, after a decade in power, began looking at his legacy — he'd already announced he wouldn't be seeking another term in 2003 — the PM openly mulled cannabis decriminalization, even knowing it would mean a fight with the U.S. Canada was becoming more liberal, and more bold.

In 2002, the Canadian justice minister who succeeded Anne McLellan, Martin Cauchon, was asked if he had tried cannabis. "Obviously," he responded. The Canadian justice minister had obviously smoked marijuana. The United States, in the dark ages, was on its own.

Rock says the Parker case forced the Canadian health system to decide who was entitled to medicinal marijuana. Scientists still couldn't conduct vigorous research because the substance was banned, and most of the best work, on its use since the 1970s for treating soldiers suffering from PTSD, was coming from Israel. Still, the Canadian Medical Association wouldn't endorse marijuana as medicine. There just wasn't ample data. What did pot do to the mind? What were the side effects and how dangerous was it? Was it addictive? Could it alleviate pain? CBD hadn't yet been discovered. What would happen if a sixteen-year-old tried marijuana? No one could produce empirical data on the plant; acquiring it was against the law.

Rock had a difficult job and says that Canada's beginnings as a medical marijuana supplier were scrappy. In the fall of 2001, if you wanted a medical licence to smoke weed, you just had to ask. "Back then, it was an informal, almost back-of-the-envelope system, with my staff getting letters and messages from all over the country from people asking for prescriptions, and we didn't have a rigorous or scientific or professional way of assessing them. For the most part, we just said yes," says Rock. The government approach to awarding licences was, in a word, humane. Rock says, "Who were we to deny someone reaching out to us who said, 'I'm in pain and I need this relief'?"

Alan Young worked with the government of Canada to draft regulations to clarify the system. The pothead lawyer says he'd beat the court on so many cannabis cases by 2001 that the Crown figured it was better to enlist him to help than to have him keep kicking their ass.

A few more words about Alan Young. He is a rebellious malcontent; hilarious, angry. He's divorced, brilliant, pissed off about money: the perfect Aaron Sorkin character. His 2003 takedown of Canadian law is called *Justice Defiled: Perverts, Potheads, Serial Killers and Lawyers*. We meet for a joint near his home in north Toronto, and through tufts of smoke, bewilderment, a thick moustache, ego, and pride, he describes his journey from outsider to insider. He tells me that he first got involved with cannabis as the founder of Osgoode Hall Law School's Innocence Project, where he defended Rosie Rowbotham. Rowbotham, a non-violent veteran of Toronto's late-1970s Rochdale College scene, was, for a time, among North America's biggest pot dealers. Rosie still has the dubious distinction of spending the most time behind bars for dealing cannabis in Canadian history. Rosie wasn't connected, Young says, to the mafia or the Hells Angels, but as a pot dealer, he obviously consorted with unsavoury characters — connections the legal industry to this day hasn't been able to completely shed.

Alan introduces me to Rosie, and we spend time together just north of Toronto. Rosie is bedridden, dying from stage 4 cancer, but lucid; irascible, but strangely warm. He has his shirt off and a kitten in his bed beside his ashtray, and he tells me stories about the 1960s that, if I close my eyes, bring up images of Led Zeppelin, Ginsberg, and big doobies of hash. Rosie talks in whispers, grinning through pain, while he smokes weed, passes me the joint, and conjures the past. "I'm on Yonge Street. It's the summer of 1969 in front of Sam the Record Man and I get a tap on the shoulder. 'Are you Rosie Rowbotham? Are you involved in hash?'" Rosie says that the man who tapped him on the shoulder was a Lebanese pilot, and Rosie — who also dabbled in LSD distribution at nineteen years old — began importing bricks of hashish from Lebanon and distributing it throughout Canada and, with a partner, the United States. He moved fifty pounds of Thai stick in 1970 and something like sixteen thousand pounds of weed, or eight tonnes, using the freight elevator in his dorm, where he kept six stash rooms filled with hash. It's very possible that if Allan Rock got high with John Lennon in Ottawa in 1969, he was burning Rosie Rowbotham hash. Rowbotham tells me that he kept upping the quantities of cannabis he sold, and eventually he got into even more serious weight — over one hundred pounds of Lebanese hash. The founding member of the Hippie Mafia — what Rosie and his university friends were called — has never apologized for his dealing. He says he doesn't know the details behind the people in Lebanon who got him his supply. He didn't want to. He just knows they gave him enough to supply pot throughout eastern Canada, and also own New York, Boston, and Philadelphia.

Rosie Grew from Concrete: Head of the Hippie Mafia, Rosie Rowbotham, vamping in 1971. Rosie would become a friend in the last year of his life and went to his dying day without ever trying legal weed.

He says, "I didn't have all of the United States, but I did have a nice chunk."

Rosie saw himself as Peter O'Toole. He smoked pot in front of the police, rioted on Bloor Street with kilos inside his dorm room, and told Norman Mailer that he didn't read books; he was the kind of person books were written about. He had a vast array of pit bulls and guns. When he was arrested in 1982 after a decade of dealing weed, in a sting called Operation Rose, he addressed the court: "There's nothing wrong with a hippie selling flowers, and as soon as I get out of here, I will do it again." Rosie did just that, and the Toronto Drug Squad, who had been tapping his phone, arrested him again.

Defending Rosie, always, was Alan Young, who became enraptured with his client. In Rosie, Young tells me, he found a symbol for the societal ills he was railing against. "My client, my friend, got fourteen years, while our firm defended attempted murderers who got six? The disparity in the court was wrong and fucking ludicrous — it pissed me off," says Young. Young's ideology was being cemented. The system was bullshit and needed to change.

To do this, in the 1980s and 1990s, Young specialized for his firm, defending what he calls "consensual crimes" like gambling and prostitution, where adults are making informed decisions and both participants (except in extreme cases) are willing. In 1990, he defended Marc Emery after he'd been arrested for selling the album *As Nasty as They Wanna Be* by 2 Live Crew.

"I wasn't convinced that medical use was real, but realized it would be the thin edge of the blade for how you get to full-on marijuana legalization," says Young. In 2003, Young defended Chris Clay, a twenty-seven-year-old in London, Ontario, who was arrested for selling marijuana seeds to an undercover officer. Clay maintained that he sold seeds to people who had medical licences to grow cannabis. The Crown maintained that he also sold seeds to people who did not have their medical licence. As the MMAR laws were being tried across Canada, Young would, pro bono, take every case. Like Harnett, he says the Clay case was about winning public opinion — soccer moms — which would lead to political ramifications. "I used the media in the late nineties and said 'Look, this drug had benefits, it's not as harmful as we previously believed, and it's costing us an arm and leg to enforce,'"

Young recalls, "and the media was a willing conspirator. I never met more pot-smoking people than journalists."

Anne McLellan was the minister of justice from 1997 to 2002. She had her apprehensions about cannabis, as she had spent most of her career on the enforcement side of the law, including a stint as the head of the RCMP. She didn't find Rosie Rowbotham colourful and had mixed feelings about Alan Young. Still, she says, with the passing of the MMAR laws, her department had to listen to the courts. "The Canadian government did not step out here and say, 'Hey, we want to develop a medical market.' It was the court who took us there, so that's where we went," she tells me.

As the daughter of Nova Scotian farmers who cut her teeth in Alberta politics — she tells me she'd never even seen pot before she worked on the file and never tried it herself — she represented rural Canadian values. But, she says, marijuana was never personal; in 2001, when the court ruled that Canada needed to change its drug laws with regard to marijuana, it was her job to enact the rules.

"Allan and his people found a start-up outside Flin Flon, Manitoba, in an old mine shaft where the first legal cannabis was produced," she tells me. This was Prairie Plant Systems (PPS), the Saskatchewan-based biopharmaceutical agriculture company that won the first licence from Health Canada in 2001 to grow, sell, and distribute medicinal cannabis. There was only one problem, and McClellan had to learn quickly: not all pot is the same.

PPS was started by Brent Zettl while he was still a student at the University of Saskatchewan. Zettl pioneered the biosecure underground growth chamber. He specialized in genetically modifying existing plants to have them do new things. In his underground lair, he created yew trees with antibodies that were used in treatments to fight cancer, and he synthesized tobacco plants that created pharmaceutical protein. He created genetically engineered canola and manufactured rice that could work as a polio vaccine. Zettl owned a cutting-edge biopharmaceutical agricultural company, but he didn't know anything about weed.

"We were known as the guys who did the odd and unusual," Zettl tells me. In the summer of 2020, Zettl, in his new company, would isolate the antigen for Covid-19.

In December 2000, Zettl became Canada's first licensed producer of cannabis. Once Health Canada determined that it wanted nothing to do with growing marijuana — Zettl tells me the government tried to grow plants, but each time, the bud was stolen by those it employed — Zettl was given the government's first legal medical marijuana production contract. It was for five years and valued at $5.75 million. It was a single-sourced request for proposal, and Zettl was tasked with growing two tonnes of weed. "I didn't even know what cannabis looked like until I grew it the first time," he tells me. "I grew up on a farm. We drank and that was good enough. We had cows to milk the next day."

People like Rosie Rowbotham — felons — were federally barred from the system. Rosie was by then living in a halfway house and contributing TV segments for CBC. People like Zettl, who knew nothing of weed or the culture, ran the show. "I gave up everything for the cause, for the movement — my freedom, my family — and what did it get me?" Rosie says, blowing smoke toward his television, which soundlessly plays CNN. "I don't even have enough money to pay for my grave."

After its experience growing bud, security was of the utmost importance to Health Canada. Zettl, with a property in Flin Flon leased from the Hudson Bay Mining Company, offered the government something unique: his grow op would be in an abandoned mine twelve hundred feet below the surface of a lake. If someone wanted to steal his weed, they'd need a submarine. And it got better. Electricity — given a subsidy in Manitoba allotted to abandoned mines — would be free, and the cannabis would be grown in a fortified, impenetrable, secret location.

"It was a dark, deep, cold hole in the ground," Zettl says.

In 2002, PPS had 455 medical marijuana patients with prescriptions. There were zero reported cases of pot theft. However, PPS had a different problem. Zettl could do a lot of different things with plants, but, says Anne McLellan, there was an important thing he could not do. In 2002, McLellan, after leaving her post as the minister of justice, became the minister of health.

Planting the Seed: A look at Brent Zettl's Prairie Plant Systems, Canada's first licensed producer, under Trout Lake in Flin Flon, Manitoba. Activists claimed the only paper for rolling a PPS joint was toilet paper.

The medical marijuana program became her jurisprudence, and so the initial feedback from marijuana patients would arrive at her desk. They weren't pleased. "All the people who had medicinal licences said 'Minister, this is the worst pot in the world — this is terrible stuff,' and I'm sure it was," Anne McLellan tells me. "It was grown a thousand feet under the ground in a dark, wet mineshaft. It had low THC. I'm sure it was mouldy, too."

Zettl doesn't entirely disagree. "When the Supreme Court ruled in favour of medicinal marijuana, they just said, 'Make product for the whole country — without any plan!' We did the best we could," he says, "but there were lumps along the way."

Lorne Gertner is a weed guy — advocate, connector, ruffian, and financier. Alongside David Hill at the investment bank Hill & Gertner, he was an early investor in PPS. Lorne has a background in money, branding, architecture, and design. When he was young, his father, Samuel Gertner, owned Mister Leonard, a women's clothing line, and Lorne helped him elevate its value proposition. He turned Mister Leonard into a trend. It could now sell the same slacks for more cash. Lorne is avuncular, with an edge;

sweet, but scary. He might look like Yoda. But no one is fucking with Lorne. He's comfortable around money and marijuana, which makes him a great judge of weed at the annual underground Emerald Cup. He rolls between Bay Street, Los Angeles, and the unlicensed cannabis world and brings a specific aesthetic to his life's work.

Gertner was once gifted a blue polo shirt by the king of Lesotho. He was there on a cannabis sales call, and the men were about to play golf. Gertner told His Excellency that he had to decline the gift. "I haven't worn blue," he said, "since the eighties."

Of all the cannabis characters in this book, no one has gifted me better weed than Lorne.

In Jamaica, as a teenager, Lorne smoked his first spliff. "Most people didn't see cannabis the way I did. They weren't as deeply invested," he says. "I was doing it for the belief that this plant was going to help people and our Canadian system we were building would be a model for people all over the world."

It was Alan Young who connected Gertner and Zettl. By 2001, Gertner had begun a merchant bank and had investments in everything from condominiums to retail displays inside drugstores. "I cold-called Brent Zettl and said, 'Let me see your company.' Brent said, 'Why would I let you?' I said, 'I assume you need money. Well, I'm in the money business … and I know a few things about weed.'"

Gertner took a plane to Saskatchewan, where he'd never been before, to meet Brent Zettl. The two men — the wealthy Jewish pothead investor from Toronto and the farm-raised prairie-boy plant scientist — then drove eight hours from Saskatoon to Flin Flon, with Gertner repeatedly asking Zettl to pull over so he could smoke cigarettes. Zettl reluctantly agreed, but kept telling Gertner they were in a rush. "We had to leave Flin Flon before it gets dark because when it gets dark, they start dynamiting shit around the mine," Gertner says. He describes the descent into the PPS mineshaft as transcendental, like scaling into heaven in reverse. "It's a de-elevating mine and we're wearing the miner shit and we drive into the earth for half an hour, and then you have to get out of the cage and get in this truck, and I'm in the back bouncing up and down, but it's exciting — we can't believe this trip — and I get to this white door, take off all the mining shit, and put on the gowns, and they use blowers to inflate our suits, Hazmat suits or some fucking thing, and Brent opens the door and I step into this room and it's the most incredible, beautiful thing I'd ever seen in my life."

Gertner walked into a ten-thousand-square-foot, $3 million, state-of-the-art indoor grow room, with cameras in the ceilings, lights enough to power a Super Bowl halftime show, and the kind of surgical approach to growing marijuana — what Gertner once saw cut with a machete from a Jamaican bush — to make NASA marijuana green with envy. It was robot pot buried at the bottom of a Manitoba lake. The cannabis stalks were verdant, lush, and uniform in their dimensions, like a terracotta army of *Cannabis sativa*. They looked and smelled so terrific to our marijuana zealot that he thinks of the experience comparably to first laying eyes on the *Mona Lisa*. "I have a picture that I took at that moment and I still look at it," Gertner tells me, "every day."

Gertner bought 25 percent of Zettl's company on the spot and that night enjoyed the deep sleep of a cannabis king. Unusually for Gertner, on this historic evening he was not stoned; he wasn't able to try his own product. A kink in the MMAR program meant producers couldn't get high on their own supply without a medical licence. (Even after October 17, 2018 — the date on which pot became legal in Canada — you couldn't get pot without it first appearing on a government shelf.)

Gertner, upon leaving Flin Flon, got his medical licence.

———

When the federal government spends nearly $6 million to buy two tonnes of weed, people pay attention, especially people like potheads and criminals and weird amalgamations of the two. In 1994, 325 pounds of cannabis were seized at the Washington State border. In 1998, it was 4,000 pounds. By 2004, according to Dana Larsen's incredible illustrated book *Cannabis in Canada*, a total of 20,500 pounds of homegrown Canadian weed were confiscated at the Washington border. Even before recreational legalization, the Americans' nightmare had come true.

Don Briere, the Vancouver-based long-time cannabis activist, tells me he helped move a lot of that illegal pot. Briere is the founder of Weeds, a line of illegal and legal dispensaries and head shops, and the home of a wide selection of rolling papers, pipes, marijuana, and glass bongs. In 1997, he was arrested for trafficking and possessing cannabis, and in 2004, while out on parole, Briere opened Da Kine on Commercial Drive in Vancouver. At Da Kine, not only could you buy illegal edibles, hash, and ounces, but you could also smoke marijuana in the store. Female employees would walk through its tight aisles with "dabs," systems for burning marijuana resin, and at 4:20 p.m., everyone in the store got stoned. Briere says the MMAR laws were good for illegal weed because they introduced an element of doubt into the law. If the government's selling weed, Briere says, drug dealers thought, *Why can't I?* Even the police didn't know what was up.

"At a certain point in BC, there were huge competitions to get operations to grow. People were bidding on houses with acres or with big, big basements, and there were people in the culture teaching other people how to grow — franchises, so to speak. Basically, tons and tons of weed being produced," Briere tells me.

Da Kine was perhaps North America's first out-in-the-open, public-facing, illegal bricks-and-mortar marijuana dispensary. They paid no mind to pot being medicine. They believed, like Rosie Rowbotham, that pot should be legal for everyone, full stop. And they didn't mind being arrested for the cause. Da Kine was hardly an Apple store; it was a hippie enclave. But it was also in stark contrast to what was being produced in the huge industrial operation in Manitoba.

The Flin Flon operation was legal science and medicine. It produced terrible pot grown underground by non–weed smokers. Da Kine was illegal hippies and growers smoking homegrown bud right in the shop. Briere, with his connections to the growers, dealers, and consumers, says he was perfectly positioned, and politically and financially motivated, to profit from and fight against the MMARs, which he believed were bad laws. Pot shouldn't have to hide, he thought.

"A couple I know had three huge tanks from a gas station buried on their property," Briere says, not exactly bragging but still proud of the ingenuity at work. "You opened a locked door to a small shed on their huge private property and move a bale of hay and open a trap door that led to a four-by-four-foot shaft with a ladder down to the tanks. In these tanks, they grew some of the province's kindest bud."

Briere says that in the early 2000s, the big money wasn't in licensed designated growers selling medical pot at Da Kine in Vancouver, or even in selling to illegal dispensaries in Ontario or Quebec. The big money was in selling to the States, where an illegal pound of BC bud worth $2,000 could fetch US$3,000, before the significant conversion rate. This brought out creativity among the "middlers," mules who connected the growers of BC with the American marketplace. These marijuana producers often straddled the laws and found a grey market in which to operate.

The designated grower clause in the MMARs was easy to abuse. Adam Greenblatt, a long-time cannabis activist and grower, opened a medical marijuana dispensary in Quebec that had 1,000 medical patients — perhaps 20 of them, he told me, had licences to obtain pot from their medical growers. What began for Greenblatt when he was a nineteen-year-old stoner on a quest to find relief for his father, who suffered from debilitating MS, became a lifetime of advocacy. He says that those 20 licensed people had prescriptions for enough legal marijuana — far superior to the PPS product — to provide for his other 980 patients.

Allan Rock's licensing approval process began as an exercise in empathy and ended as a path for illegal growers to camouflage their businesses under the cloak of the law. Doctors were selling licences online — to grow and to consume — and Greenblatt says that it became trendy to get a medical cannabis licence and easy to hire a designated grower. Eventually, growers amalgamated their licences and leased warehouses. It wasn't uncommon to find a warehouse with three hundred lights and thousands of plants. Designated growers were setting up operations to rival PPS, minus the headache of dealing with Health Canada regulations. Plus, the growers were crafty: if a stipulation said that a designated grower could only raise five plants, shrewd botanist inventors began producing marijuana plants the size of Christmas trees, sometimes ten feet tall and five feet wide. The MMAR system worked for some people like Terry Parker, and it was radical, progressive legislation. It also, however, opened itself up to abuse.

Don Briere says the proliferation of the designated grower licences fortified Canada's stash of marijuana, and that the work could be dangerous. But the people Briere worked with, he says, were more likely to be middle-aged schlubs challenging each other for the most creative ways to ship weed than Hells Angels, gangsters, or members of the mob. The way he describes his cronies makes them sound like kids at summer camp sneaking out of their bunks. They used simple technology they had lying around. "One guy kept a tire machine in his truck, ditched the machine [heavy steel contraption], and put twelve pounds of hash in its casing and ran across the line," recalls Briere, using the slang of the time to describe the American border. "Another middler I knew would take really, really kind weed, take the spare off his vehicle, and fill it up with marijuana — twelve or fifteen pounds — reseal the tire, and put it back under his vehicle. You throw some dirt, mud, and pepper on it, then drive across the line."

PPS discarded its entire first crop of cannabis. At first, using at least some of Marc Emery's seeds, just like Terry Parker, PPS produced many different strains all at different potencies, which made it difficult to properly dose. You don't buy Tylenol and get a different potency each time. So that first crop was destroyed by Health Canada.

The agreement was that legal pot would be from 5 to 6 percent THC and sell for just over three dollars per gram. Meanwhile, the illegal marijuana had a street price from ten to fifteen dollars per gram and had a THC range, and pedigree, of uncertain denomination.

In August 2003, almost two years after the initial law passed, PPS produced another crop, with only two strains that met Health Canada requirements. And the government had PPS trash its plants — again. This time, the THC percentage was too high. PPS messed up because it did its job too well. "The government had no idea what they were doing, and Brent Zettl had no idea what he was doing," says Lorne Gertner, who, despite his best attempts as part owner of PPS, couldn't rectify the situation. "We tried everything," says David Hill. "Prairie Plant Systems, flawed as it was, was ahead of its time" in terms of operating as a law-abiding successful Canadian cannabis company.

The solution to the uneven PPS dosing, dreamt up by Zettl, was to grind the cannabis plants into a fine green powder. Along with the buds went the seeds and stalk. Coming from a biotech background, and obsessive about producing anti-carcinogen tobacco through cross-pollination at his farm-meets-science labs, Zettl began to make marijuana into something like a smoothie. He didn't smoke weed and didn't know anything about the culture, so, while he may have created a synthetic Frankenstein product, it certainly couldn't compete with Don Briere's stash. "It wasn't completely ineffective," says Adam Greenblatt of the initial PPS product. "I think the less attached you were to the cannabis world, the less you cared about who grew your weed."

Greenblatt didn't stock PPS weed at the compassion clubs he ran in Ontario and Quebec. What he did do was try to run his clubs like legal businesses. These places weren't like Da Kine in Vancouver. They shared DNA with Hilary Black's place in Vancouver: they were insured, paid taxes, and required a licence of all their patients. They didn't allow onsite consumption. Nothing groovy happened at 4:20 p.m.

Greenblatt says he tried the PPS weed at his club in Montreal. At the time, he was still selling cannabis in Ziploc bags, and he found the gold PPS packaging impressive. "I tried Prairie Plant Systems weed," he jokes, "and I survived."

Greenblatt has a grower's analysis of the PPS product. He says it was dried too fast, so grinding it up resulted in the loss of terpenes, which provide cannabis with its distinct properties, like aroma and flavour. It clearly wasn't as good as the cannabis grown by designated growers in BC and elsewhere, which could be among the finest weed in the world. These were growers with acumen and skill and years of practice and patience, who worked hard to source rare seeds and studied up on plant genetics — not to create a durable, replicable, evenly low-THC-dosed product, but to create a craft experience, a cannabis equivalent of a fine wine.

In 2003, Anne McLellan would again switch portfolios, moving from the Department of Health to become the minister of the Department of Public Safety and Emergency Preparedness. This was post-9/11, and the American borders were much more tightly controlled. Again, in the same way that McLellan doesn't think Rosie is cute, she has little time for guys like Don Briere. Violent crime was undoubtedly becoming associated with certain segments of marijuana, she says, and biker gangs would use their marijuana profits to fuel other wings of their business, including guns, prostitution, and hard drugs. With the American borders closed to them, the Canadian designated growers' cannabis certainly reached untold Canadians without a medical licence.

Pot is bulky, smelly, and worth much less than cocaine. It's not a great illegal business, but criminals, says McLellan, began attaching themselves to the nascent legal cannabis industry. Designated growers sent their over-supply of legal marijuana into Canada's illegal black market.

McLellan says the pot file had become more dangerous, not less, after the passage of the MMARs. "When I leave Health and become in charge of Public Safety, what we're really dealing with on the cannabis file is organized crime," McLellan says, adding that in her new role, she was directly responsible for the RCMP and the police in every province. "On the cannabis front lines, you hear the stories. The police would tell me, 'We're dealing with organized crime and transnational crime.' Everyone knows organized crime is moving BC bud across the border."

McLellan says the problem with the MMAR laws was bad and getting worse, and the regulations needed change. These were the last days of Prime Minister Paul Martin. One day, McLellan received a phone call from the attorney general of Mexico. He said that Mexico needed the help of Canadians. Mexico was receiving a massive influx of BC weed.

CHAPTER 3

Recreational Opium

"Hit the man who offers it to you, and if you are not big enough to use your fists, take a club."

Joseph Kehoe

Before BC bud became a problem for Mexico, there was a time in Canada when recreational opium, marijuana, and cocaine were legal. Today, police chiefs in Vancouver and Toronto are considering re-enacting this period in Canadian drug enforcement in response to the opioid crisis. "We're recommending decriminalizing the possession of all drugs for personal use and connecting all people who use drugs with health and social supports," Toronto's medical officer of health said at the end of November 2021. Vancouver's chief of police, Adam Palmer, said the same thing in the summer of 2020. In the spring of 2024, BC recriminalized the use of drugs in public spaces. However, the future of Canadian drug laws looks a lot like the drug laws of the Canadian past.

In the earliest days of this country, the production of hemp was encouraged by the British and Canadian governments. Hemp was used to make textiles and medical tinctures and treat infirmities from menstrual cramps to alcoholism to anxiety. Cannabis itself has cultural roots in Asia, Africa, and China. Some reports say Napoleon introduced marijuana to Europe after discovering and enjoying hash in Egypt in 1801. Cannabis boomed in the nineteenth century, including in 1820s Halifax, where you could pay your land taxes with a stalk of weed and buy pre-rolls of marijuana, like cigarettes, as medicine. (Pre-rolls are already-rolled joints that are sold individually or in packs and were a hit in the early nineteenth century and for the illegal dispensaries in 2015 and basically anytime they've ever been sold.) However, as we crept toward the twentieth century, drugs, both in the U.S. and Canada, were labelled "foreign." Most of Canada's not-yet-banned substances were imported from India and then China, and soon opium replaced cannabis as the medicinal, and recreational, drug of choice.

Dangerous and addictive — a curative, but also a cancer — opium soon became the target of the prevailing Victorian morality. Its prohibition was, in part, racist coding: an increasingly anti-Chinese sentiment became the rule of the land. In 1885, Chinese immigrants had to pay $50 to emigrate to Canada. In 1901, the head tax was raised to $100. Two years later, the price for Chinese people — and only Chinese people — to enter the country was $500 per person. In 1923, with 90 percent of the Chinese population living in Canadian Chinatowns, Canada would ban further Chinese immigration.

The early 1900s were a period of Canadian expansion. The work being done to accommodate this growth — the actual labour of laying down the British- and American-financed Canadian Pacific Railway — was largely accomplished by low-paid European and Chinese workers. The Chinese labourers, in particular, living among themselves and willing to work for low wages, were blamed for the economic hardships of white Canadians. Asian workers would take on jobs whites didn't want, and do them for pennies on the dollar. This infuriated the working-class white population. Opium wasn't prevalent in early-twentieth-century Canada, but because it was seen to be coming from China, it became lumped into the "Chinese problem." Racism, like populist stumping, fear-mongering, and fake news, has always been a huge part of drug enforcement.

"Ideas about the morally degenerate but highly intelligent and cunning Chinese, played a key role in anti-drug discourse in Canada," writes

Catherine Carstairs in *"Hop Heads" and "Hypes,"* an exhaustive discourse on the advent of the 1908 Canadian drug laws. "Men identified as Chinese-Canadians came in for a disproportionate share of police attention for their drug use and many were deported to China as a result."

In 1907, a wick was lit by low-income white rage, and Vancouver's Chinatown became a backdrop for riots. Chinese homes and businesses were under attack. Arson was used as a physical and economic weapon. On September 7, 1907, eight thousand members of the Asiatic Exclusion League marched screaming through the intersection of Powell Street and East Cordova, waving torches behind a "Stand for a White Canada" banner. These rioters set fire to Japanese and Chinese homes and stores. Police were either overwhelmed, stood by and watched, or perhaps even abetted the destruction. The Asiatic Exclusion League, which would grow to forty thousand members in British Columbia by the 1920s, had begun in the United States and helped push Theodore Roosevelt — in 1907, the year of the Vancouver riots — to end Japanese immigration into the U.S. through Mexico and Hawaii.

But it was the Vancouver riots that helped kickstart Canada's war on drugs.

It was three days after Vancouver's fires went out that the provincial government of Richard McBride, founder of BC's Conservative Party, promised to make amends to the Asian residents, including the legally licensed Asian Canadian opium producers. Three Chinese-owned domestic opium manufacturers sued for riot damages, but the result, once this became widely acknowledged, was backlash. Race and political populism were about to fuel the next hundred years of the policing of drugs. On July 1, the Opium Act of 1908, the first Canadian drug law, was enacted by the government of Prime Minister Wilfrid Laurier. It stated that selling, manufacturing, or importing opium for non-medical purposes was against the law. The statute didn't say anything about opium use or possession, but it outlawed the domestic licensed Chinese manufacturers and set a maximum penalty of three years' imprisonment and a $1,000 fine for violating Canada's new drug rules. It wasn't a health issue that created the law. Akwasi Owusu-Bempah, an expert on drugs and policing who started Canada's Cannabis Amnesty group in 2018, calls it "population control."

Canadians, and Canadian law enforcement, have always had a love-hate relationship with drugs. In 1850, there was a tavern for every 450 Canadians. Fifty years later, 75 percent of those bars had closed. At the turn of the century, the mood across the nation was changing and the temperance movement was taking hold. The prime minister was William Lyon Mackenzie King. A teetotaler, and perhaps a virgin — a lifelong bachelor, he was never romantically linked with a partner, even for a fling — Mackenzie King was a man for his puritanical time. The first drug law in the United States was enacted in 1875, outlawing opium dens in San Francisco. London, England, banned cannabis in 1891, twelve months after the *Lancet*, a British science journal that's still the world's leading source of peer-reviewed medical information, raved about the medicinal properties of cannabis. "There may be no better medicine that we know," the *Lancet* declared of marijuana, right before the substance was banned. "With drugs," Catherine Carstairs tells me, "there has always been a disconnect between science and science fiction."

In Canada, opium was outlawed in 1908, cocaine in 1911, and cannabis in 1923. Alcohol prohibition was looser in Canada than it was in the U.S., but bans on alcohol were intermittently enacted throughout Canada from 1901 to 1918. In the 1920s, the province of Quebec enjoyed some of North America's loosest liquor laws. These North American trends from last century still, mostly, abide; the U.S. remains much more punitive than Canada with regard to drug laws. "America is still brutal with weed," says Bruce Linton. "In America, they don't have grey — it's 'Go to jail.'"

During the 1920s, cannabis became a lightning rod for scaring white folks. Opium had been banned, and even though marijuana wasn't widely available in this country, it began to appear in the U.S. Migrants from Mexico, arriving in Arizona, California, and Texas after the Mexican Revolution of 1910, brought with them, according to Eric Schlosser's *Reefer Madness*, "locoweed," as Texas police referred to bud. "Marihuana" was the Mexican Spanish word for pot and replaced "cannabis" to underscore linguistically its dangerous foreignness. This fear of pot, and sensationalized stories of Mexicans going crazy while under the influence, spread to Canada and became part of our anti-drug conversation.

Emily Murphy, judge of the juvenile court of Edmonton, was an influential Canadian author and columnist. She voiced her opinions — from which many Canadians learned about drugs — through a megaphone for fake news. "A man or woman who becomes an addict seeks the company of those who use the drug, and avoids those of their own social status," writes Murphy in *The Black Candle*, her influential book from 1922, which framed the drug conversation as part of an ugly discourse on race, "the Negro Menace," and "the Yellow Peril." "This explains the amazing phenomenon of an educated gentlewoman, reared in a refined atmosphere, consorting with the lowest classes of yellow and black men," Murphy decrees.

With the rise of tabloid media, fear of "marihuana" was a story that sold. This discourse fuelled the growing newspapers, which thrived on outrage and fear.

(I use the word "marijuana" as a way of reclamation. It was only after legalization that "cannabis" became part of the vernacular, mainly as a way for Canadian licensed producers to make their product sound more scientific. "Marihuana" — spelled with the "h" — is archaic, but still used in Michigan; "marijuana" — spelled with the "j" — is the more common spelling. Either way, when "cannabis" re-entered the lexicon around legalization conversations, it was so the pot companies could align themselves with physicians, not Cheech & Chong. The choice of words was for business reasons. Rosie Rowbotham calls weed "marijuana," and Terry Booth and Bruce Linton, in Vegas, talked about how they popularized "cannabis," the word. I like the word "marijuana," and so does Killer Mike, who won three 2024 Grammy awards.)

A representative Canadian story from 1908 covered the exploits of Won Way, a Chinese drug lord photographed in fur coats, who quipped that he owned the largest limousine in British Columbia. Way told reporters that he annually cleared $500,000 from his opium peddling — the same business that Emily Murphy said preyed on young white women.

"Canada didn't really have a drug problem prior to the Opium Act, and we didn't have people getting rich from marijuana in Canada before 1923,"

Catherine Carstairs says. "Scared? Sure. And profiting? Some people did, I suppose, but really what we see is the mood of the country swings wildly in postwar Canada, and fear of immigration — fear of anything impeding on this mostly imagined vision of Victorian Canadian culture — creates this country's first drug laws."

The anti-drug narrative spread quickly throughout the world and, nearer to Canada, in the United States. Both Mexico and Canada, wanting to be seen on the world's stage as virtuous, took legal action. These were violent, transformative times. In 1914, Canada entered the First World War and embarked on what was the bloodiest conflict in the country's history, still to this day. To make matters worse, both domestically and abroad, 1918 saw the arrival of the Spanish flu. Between the flu and the war, Canada lost more than one hundred thousand lives, and against that backdrop, politicians wanted to be seen taking action against movements they had very little power to stop. The Opium Act of 1908 became the Opium and Drug Act of 1911, which became the Opium and Narcotic Drug Act of 1920. Drug laws were getting stronger and spreading.

The new face of the domestic peril in early-1920s Canada was opium. This was exemplified by a sad, tidy narrative: the life of Joseph Kehoe, a First World War hero whose fall from grace caused alarm nationwide. Kehoe, who probably never tried cannabis, would help bring about the demise of legal Canadian marijuana.

"Hit the man who offers it to you," Kehoe advised Canadian youth on how to resist the opium peddler's enchanting temptations, "and if you are not big enough to use your fists, take a club."

By all accounts, Kehoe, a medical student from Nova Scotia, was an exemplary First World War fighter. He commanded his fellow prisoners to break his arm upon his capture in Belgium, lest he be used in a German munitions factory making bombs to drop on his Canadian homeland. It was the dying days of the war, when alcohol prohibition was the law back in Canada, and Kehoe — after being gassed and tortured, beaten and starved during his wartime imprisonment — was eventually sent back home a broken man. In Canada, where the twenty-eight-year-old washed up penniless and alone in Vancouver, there wasn't yet treatment for post-traumatic stress disorder; Kehoe may have been subjecting himself to an improvised medical program. In 2001, Allan Rock would have approved him for grams of PPS's low-THC weed.

It's not known when Kehoe first started smoking opium, which at that time required two people to administer a hit in a huge bamboo pipe. But what happened after he took his first toke was widely reported. Kehoe's descent came hard. Where patriotism once fuelled his actions, he was now motivated by obtaining his next hit. He was a violent opium offender, a "tea head," as the story unspooled in the press, unable to resist the pull of Chinese-made illegal drugs. Slumming in Vancouver's Chinatown district, Kehoe stole to buy opium — he was an addict, defenceless against his urges and out of control. When he was eventually arrested and sentenced to five years and twenty-four lashes, his sensational story mesmerized readers of the *Vancouver Sun*.

Once reformed, and after receiving his lashes, he blamed his condition — his fall from grace — on opium, and this dovetailed nicely with the prevailing anti-Chinese sentiments of the day. The debate was never going to be about what the drugs could do or what they could be used for, or why Joseph Kehoe needed his medicine and what could be done to help addicts get off the streets. Only now, a hundred years later, are we beginning to understand drug treatment, counselling, and addiction. However, after the war, it was prohibition. Lashes. Repentance. And the moral high ground was abstinence.

"Canada's drug laws weren't created in a vacuum, and our country, in establishing its international identity at the end of the war, wanted to be seen as moralistic, especially when it came to leaders like Mackenzie King, an abstaining Christian, who probably saw himself as a leading light," says Catherine Carstairs. According to Carstairs, Mackenzie King travelled the world attending drug symposiums in the 1910s and 1920s, in places like Singapore and France, and learned anecdotally from world leaders about the different narcotics on the street. It would be in keeping with his character to see drug use as black and white and an issue from which he personally felt compelled to protect his people.

Canada banned pot before most Canadians had ever tried it. Won Way didn't sell it. Joseph Kehoe didn't smoke it. And here's the kicker: marijuana was only outlawed in Canada as an addendum to the 1923 Opium and Narcotics Drug Act. Working on the legislation for this drug law, there was no mention of cannabis until its third and final draft — and even then, it was only added as a handwritten amendment. Making cannabis illegal was an afterthought that would, over time, disproportionately impact Black, Mexican, Chinese, and Indigenous lives.

"There's been many studies that have shown that, after its popularity waned from the nineteenth century, cannabis was not only not available in this country prior to 1923, but it barely appeared here even throughout the 1950s, by which time reefer madness had spread through the U.S. — but didn't really wind up here," says Carstairs, adding that Mackenzie King probably first learned about cannabis at the 1909 International Opium Commission in Shanghai. "Through hindsight, we can look back into history and see the errors of our ways — that there wasn't enough global research into the medicinal values of a plant like cannabis, and that instead it became wrapped up with a local temperance movement that said 'Ban everything.'"

Throughout the 1940s and 1950s, there was more fear about weed than actual weed. Drug use in Canada did pivot from opium. But it wasn't to marijuana; it was to heroin. Except for small pockets of North America, heroin wasn't widespread in the Second World War era. A study of 1940s Canadian drug abuse showed that perhaps four thousand people in the country used the drug. They were called "hypes," for their hypodermic needles, and resided in greatest numbers in Vancouver and Toronto. (Montreal drug use centred around cocaine.) In a widespread study of Canadian hypes — especially those behind bars at British Columbia's Okalla Prison Farm — it was revealed that almost none of them, even those imprisoned with drug convictions, were using or had used cannabis. Except in American port cities like San Francisco and New Orleans and in Mexican border states like Texas and Arizona, pot wasn't available in North America. This wasn't the case around the world.

Having grown up in the Mazar-i-Sharif area of northern Afghanistan, Brishna Kamal — a former executive at Whistler Therapeutics, an early Canadian medical marijuana producer that Lorne Gertner helped fund — says that hash was part of the local medical program in her community in her parent's generation, during the 1940s and 1950s, in addition to other forms of medicine and health care. Like aspirin, its medicinal properties were never questioned. Hash helped reduce pain, invoke sleep, and reduce nausea. Kamal says she wasn't raised amid a cannabis stigma.

"I never smoked cannabis until I came to Canada to attend university at McGill in the 1980s, but I wasn't afraid of it and knew it had medicinal abilities," says Kamal. "By the 1960s, most people in our community knew that cannabis wasn't all bad — that it probably was better for you than alcohol and might even be able to help people suffering reduce pain."

There were plenty of places like Turkey and Spain where cannabis was available and seen as a good alternative to morphine or amphetamines, which also became a North American problem in the 1950s. In 1961, Canada's Narcotic Control Act and the Food and Drugs Act came down hard on marijuana. Possession, trafficking, cultivation, and transportation of cannabis all carried serious legal consequences: as much as seven years for a charge of possession. Pot was now a schedule 1 offence. In the meantime, cannabis couldn't be researched because procuring it was against the law. But there was a culture clash happening, between liquor and pot, old and young.

Marcel Martel wrote the book *Not This Time: Canadians, Public Policy, and the Marijuana Question 1961–1975*, and has been a great help in my research. According to Martel, the *Province* in Vancouver was just one paper that began questioning our new drug laws. Writing on May 17, 1968, about two cases in the courts involving nineteen-year-old boys who both had committed crimes while under the influence of a vice, the paper made clear what many people already believed. The editorial compared the sentencing. In the first instance, a boy guilty of marijuana possession received a sentence of "nine months definite and six months indefinite." Real jail time for possession of marijuana. The other boy in the story, arrested for driving without a licence and under the influence of alcohol, killed his two passengers while driving drunk. For his crime, he was charged $200. No prison time. The outrage once heaped on the Chinese opium peddlers and pushers of the Mexican "locoweed" shifted toward the lawmakers, as clearly the punishments didn't equal the crimes. As the 1950s gave way to the 1960s, as jazz musicians shared marijuana with beatniks, and as students at universities around the world began to consume cannabis, pot — like contraceptives, burning of bras, gay rights, divorce laws, and protesting the war in Vietnam — became a generational touchstone.

Nixon could drink bourbon. The kids wanted to free their minds.

"There is no underestimating how seriously the older generation, now in power and who had a little experience with pot, was concerned about their university-aged children facing serious legal consequences for cannabis, something they now knew wasn't as harmful as once thought," says Marcel Martel. "The frustrating concept for scientists is that with every new study enlisted to defang the hyperbolic writings of people like Emily Murphy — or even Richard Nixon — a new wave crashes through that quells the research before it could unpack the plant."

The Shafer Commission was established in the United States in 1970 to help determine whether marijuana should be a category 1 drug under the Controlled Substances Act (at the time, category 1 drugs were heroin and cocaine, substances legally defined as lacking medicinal benefits). The chair, Ray Shafer, was a Republican Pennsylvania governor and had been a navy officer and Purple Heart winner in the Second World War. While the bipartisan commission was formed at the direction of Congress and Nixon explicitly wanted the result to demonize marijuana, Shafer's research proved the opposite of what the president was looking for. Through years of exploration and more than fifty studies, the commission, charged with determining marijuana's classification in America's drug laws — which would affect criminal sentencing for those caught with pot — decided that Nixon's opinions ran counter to scientific research. In a 1972 report titled *Marihuana: A Signal of Misunderstanding*, the commission reported that nobody — as far as medical researchers could tell — had ever overdosed from marijuana and that the biggest concern with pot was that it would make America's populace less inspired to work. Not criminals. Not addicts. Not cokeheads. It found that marijuana wasn't a gateway drug, and didn't provoke insanity, let alone violence. The Shafer Commission advocated for the United States to decriminalize marijuana.

"Amotivational syndrome — that marijuana could lead to lethargy, loss of interest in school and achievement in general — topped the Shafer committee's list of worries," Marcel Martel tells me. "Basically, when the Shafer Commission couldn't find anything damaging about cannabis in terms of a major health scare, they gave rise to the lazy stoner cliché."

The real person acting like a lazy stoner was President Nixon, who flat-out rejected the findings of the Shafer Commission. Upon the report's publication, nothing happened. The entire exercise proved futile. The science was ignored in favour of the stigma, and social norms, operating in systemic racism, impeded data-driven, equitable research. There was no follow-up to the recommendations from Nixon's own committee. A chance to make change was ignored.

In the meantime, Canada was collating its own commission to look at drugs.

Canada's answer to Shafer was the Le Dain Commission, named after its chair, Montreal-based lawyer and judge Gerald Le Dain, which began in 1969. The Le Dain Commission was tasked by the Liberal prime minister Pierre Elliott Trudeau to investigate marijuana. Trudeau, who had backpacked through India and Pakistan in the late 1940s after graduating from Harvard — and insinuated that he'd smoked hash — could have been Canada's anti-Nixon. Elected Canada's fifteenth prime minister, the worldly leader, whose wife would smoke hash in the 1970s with the Rolling Stones, oversaw our Commission of Inquiry into the Non-Medical Use of Drugs. Over twelve thousand people attended and participated in the Le Dain Commission hearings — including Allan Rock's friend John Lennon, who chose Trudeau as his first Canadian elected official to meet. The Le Dain Commission took a serious look at legalizing pot. Its studies would take three years.

"We would be totally irresponsible if we didn't legalize it," John Munro, Canada's minister of national health and welfare, said of marijuana on Canadian TV in 1970, before the Le Dain studies were even complete. Suddenly, Rosie Rowbotham and the Canadian government were aligned. The Le Dain Commission reported that 1.5 million Canadians had tried cannabis at least once. Given that this number was reached by private citizens telling a government body about their usage of illegal drugs, it's probably safe to assume that the actual number — even today, with pot legal, it's difficult to get an accurate tally — was much higher than reported.

Robert Solomon, now a lawyer and professor at Western University with forty-five years of experience studying cannabis and alcohol laws, clerked for Gerald Le Dain on the commission. He says his boss was a decent, studious man. "Le Dain wasn't someone with any personal connection to marijuana, but he took his work seriously and wanted what was best for the country," Solomon tells me, explaining that, at the time, Le Dain was a father of two teenaged girls and was sympathetic to both youth culture and parental concerns. "Le Dain knew very little about drugs or drug culture, but he approached his work with an open mind." Solomon says Gerald Le Dain met students in coffee shops and at their universities. Like Allan Rock, he spoke with John Lennon. However, while he conducted his research in good faith, oppositional forces were also on the move.

Not content with the Shafer Report, Nixon met twice with Trudeau during the years of the Le Dain Commission, in 1969 and 1972, as Martel reports in his book. In both cases, according to the Department of External Affairs, Trudeau had to reassure Nixon that Canada would support the Americans in their war on drugs. Trudeau told this to Nixon before hearing the findings of the Le Dain Commission. Canada was a signatory on the World Health Organization's 1968 and 1969 Expert Committee on Drug Dependence. The WHO's official late-1960s stance was that "marijuana had no medical purpose and control measures were required," according to Martel's reporting. So, against that backdrop and facing American pressure, when the Le Dain Commission concluded at the end of its study that marijuana should be decriminalized, it's no surprise that the final results were ignored.

When Gerald Le Dain tabled his report to his prime minister, Marcel Martel says, no one cared. Robert Solomon doesn't disagree. "I think the culture just moved on without cannabis, and it became less mission-critical in the early seventies," Robert Solomon tells me.

In 1975, Gerald Le Dain's eldest daughter was killed in a car crash in British Columbia. In 1984, Le Dain moved on to the Supreme Court of Canada and became one of the most powerful judges in the country. By that time, however, he was burned out and still grieving. A diagnosis for depression was still rare in the mid-1980s, and he ended up being pressured to resign from the Supreme Court. From his hospital bed, the judge appointed by Pierre Elliott Trudeau left his post. The man who ruled that cannabis should be decriminalized died without knowing the medical marijuana ruling was only ten years away.

CHAPTER 4

Stephen Harper Don't Smoke Hash

"We know what you're doing."

Vancouver Police Department to Hilary Black

The year Stephen Harper became the Canadian prime minister with a tough-on-crime platform was the same year that Lorne Gertner took North America's first medicinal cannabis company public: 2006. Both events foreshadowed a wild ride. Harper, the strikingly conservative PM, was an unlikely steward of Canada's groundbreaking marijuana laws, yet he presided over more influential cannabis legislation than any other Canadian politician (and, ironically, over more Canadian-owned marijuana companies, save for his successor, Justin Trudeau). The Marihuana for Medical Purposes Regulations (MMPRs, like the MMARs before them, spelled marijuana with a tacky "h" for reasons never explained) were enacted in July 2013, and presided over by Stephen Harper's minister of health, Leona Aglukkaq.

To be clear, Harper never wanted to build an industry. The laws regulating cannabis, treating it like tobacco, were written with a prohibition mentality: there was no advertising permitted, and regulations barring differentiation actively hampered the marijuana companies' growth. But cannabis wasn't going anywhere, and private companies were going to supply demand. "Current medical marijuana regulations have left the system open to abuse," said Aglukkaq at a press conference announcing the change from the MMARs to the MMPRs on December 16, 2012. "We have heard real concerns from law enforcement, fire officials, and municipalities about how people are hiding behind these rules to conduct illegal activity, and putting health and safety of Canadians at risk. These changes will make it far more difficult for people to game the system."

Capitalist systems, however, will always be gamed. It was just the rules of the game that were changing. The MMPRs were different from the MMARs because they cancelled PPS's monopoly and allowed new cannabis companies to compete for government-issued pot-selling licences. Patients would still need a licence to smoke pot, but there would now be competition for whose pot they'd be buying. Importantly, the MMPRs also ended the designated grower program. By now, the legal medical system had been dubbed "the over-grower program," because of how much legally grown weed was winding up on the black market. This important stipulation — whether you could have someone grow your weed — would ping-pong back and forth between legal and illegal, and in actuality was only outlawed for two years. The designated grower system is legal today. But the major catalyst of that law change, which gave rise to our cannabis economic moment, was the birth of the marijuana companies, the additional licensed producers.

In the summer of 2013, Stephen Harper, a teetotaling asthmatic conservative accountant, set the stage for today's industry, a place of one-dollar pre-rolls, cannabis pretzels, pop-up 'shroom stores, and legal one-hundred-dollar ounces.

There had been cannabis legalization inroads prior to Harper's years in office. Both Paul Martin and, before him, Jean Chrétien came close to decriminalizing marijuana, which would keep pot illegal, but would ban prosecution of anyone for possessing less than a defined small amount. Chrétien, the Catholic leader from small-town Quebec, had come around on the pot file and in 2002, following his reappraisal of the abortion and same-sex marriage laws, wanted to move Canada forward on progressive issues. In essence, Canada was becoming liberal under his watch. Chrétien, the centrist, was not connected to the counterculture or cool like that beacon of late-1960s flair, Pierre Elliott Trudeau. Nevertheless, in 2003, his government introduced a decriminalization bill that came close to passing — if not for Parliament being prorogued.

"We just needed another fifteen minutes and we had the vote," a former Chrétien Cabinet member tells me, adding that Chrétien's pollsters surveyed the country, and 65 percent of Canadians said they were in favour of decriminalization. Chrétien, swept up in the seas of change, was ready to heed his nation's call. "We would've done it, but we ran out of time," his former Cabinet member says. "Though none of us in the Chrétien Cabinet wanted full legalization, he paved the way for Mr. [Justin] Trudeau."

In 2006, after Paul Martin's government crumbled, Stephen Harper was elected to lead Canada's smallest minority government since Confederation. From the beginning, he presented as an ideologically right-wing prairie-honed conservative, with little interest or love from the county's youth, left, or elite. Harper appealed to blue-collar white people, immigrant communities, and working-class suburbs across the country — the Canadian Tire, *Hockey Night in Canada* demographic and not the downtown climate-change protesters or university hippies or anything remotely resembling the progressive movement.

Harper's team even had a name for the person who'd never vote for them: "Zöe." She was a sociology major in Toronto and liked to smoke grass. "The ironic thing was that our campaign office was full of Zöes, and so when we heard something from one of them like 'This ad you're making doesn't speak to me,' we'd say 'Great!'" says Ken Boessenkool, author of Harper's two election platforms, a Calgary-based policy expert who helped shape Conservative messaging in eleven campaigns — in which, he says, he was victorious seven times. "If you had twenty dollars to spend on the votes of either ten old people or two young people and you're a Conservative, whose vote do you spend twenty dollars to go after?" Boessenkool says. "It's not personal. It's called efficiency."

Equally efficient, at the time of Prime Minister Harper and at the opposite end of the spectrum, was the cannabis ecosystem at work in this country, a loosely cobbled-together conglomerate of activists, growers, and dealers who had supplied Canada with pot since before the laws began to change. Marches for legalization had begun in the 1960s, and most Canadians who wanted marijuana were able to find it — sometimes it could be tricky, but if you wanted to get baked, even without a licence, you could. These people, who either felt personally connected to the plant or were already making their living from it at illegal grow ops or in courtrooms across the country, were trying to change the world, but they sensed their exclusion from the nascent industry when the MMAR laws were passed in 2001. Government weed wasn't smoked by Terry Parker, and PPS had nothing to do with the wellness centres in Vancouver dispensing cannabis edibles to homeless people with mental health issues or cancer patients or people with AIDS. Outside of a friendship with Lorne Gertner, Brent Zettl shared next to nothing in common with Alan Young.

In 2001, when Canada ushered in the MMAR laws, activists felt like the tide was changing. Now that pot was legal as a medicine, how long could it take for it to also be recognized as a pleasant vice, harmless as wine?

The MMAR laws legalized physician-prescribed cannabis. PPS was the only business in Canada licensed to produce government weed. By 2006, however, when Harper was elected, backlash over the PPS product and abuse of the system — doctors selling prescriptions and licensed designated growers in Kelowna driving hundreds of pounds of Canadian homegrown into the U.S. — forced Health Canada to examine the laws.

According to Tony Clement, Stephen Harper's minister of health from 2006 to 2008, the government wanted out of weed. Let private industry deal with the mess. "The government had a monopoly on cannabis production and did it poorly, which birthed the line 'The only way you can lose money selling pot is if the government's the one that's selling it,'" says Clement, who, as the MP for Parry Sound–Muskoka, says he was comfortable with cannabis, though he told me he personally has never tried it. Up in cottage country, he says, his base was a bunch of potheads. "Most people in Muskoka who hire someone to build their docks, they're smoking weed, and I need the people who build the docks to vote for me," Clement said. "I wasn't coming out against marijuana. I know what hills to fight for and when to keep my mouth closed."

Like Anne McLellan, Tony Clement speaks colourfully about the PPS marijuana. "One hundred percent of Health Canada's supply was grown in some mine in Manitoba that grew crap, was over budget, made a product that wasn't good, but was expensive to produce *and* wasn't available," Clement recalls, adding that legalization of cannabis — the ensuing step after the MMPRs — was left out of the conversation in his Conservative circle, but that he believes Stephen Harper had no moral hiccup equating pot with any other pharmaceutical drug. Cannabis was an opportunity for tax revenue, and Harper had a both a bachelor's and a master's degree in economics. Even though weed would never work for Mr. Harper — he had asthma and was a stickler for routine and control — the resistance among his Cabinet members was never personal. The issue just didn't resonate with his base. This runs counter to popular narrative. It's been reported that Harper had strong feelings about cannabis, though aside from a few ignorant comments — on the campaign trail beside Justin Trudeau, for instance, he said that cannabis was more harmful than cigarettes, which most experts agree is not true — insiders have told me that the prime minister held no personal feelings about pot.

"The system was rickety and unsatisfying, but it wasn't in a crisis point and the prime minister never mentioned cannabis to me," says Clement. "We were tackling reduced hospital wait times and HIV/AIDS policies, heroin, cocaine, and MDMA. We had bigger fish to fry."

Still, even if the Harper government didn't go fishing for marijuana, its crime policies resulted in mandatory minimum sentences, so a nonviolent cannabis charge could result in time behind bars. In a five-year period, from 2006 to 2011, Harper introduced sixty-one crime bills and saw twenty of them turned into laws. By following American-style war-on-drugs policing — where stiffer sentences are supposed to scare criminals away from breaking the law — Canada saw its incarceration rate rise 14 percent between 2005 and 2015. According to the Canadian Centre for Policy Alternatives, systemic racism and misogyny was the hallmark of this legal legacy: the number of Indigenous prisoners increased 52 percent; the number of female prisoners increased 77 percent; the number of Black prisoners increased 78 percent.

Do the Right Thing: Akwasi Owusu-Bempah at a Cannabis Amnesty event, pre-legalization.

The number of white prisoners, meanwhile, decreased by 6 percent.

"Mandatory minimums dehumanize the accused, and when these laws are passed alongside law practices such as carding — in which people can be pulled over and asked to show ID at a police officer's discretion — we know certain neighbourhoods, neighbourhoods where Black and Indigenous males tend to live, it's the Black and Indigenous populations who are being over-policed and over-arrested," says Akwasi Owusu-Bempah, who has worked with police departments across the country to mine data on racialized populations and sentencing. Owusu-Bempah says that mandatory minimum sentences take away a judge's ability to contextualize a defendant's life circumstances in applying sentencing. What's more, he adds, while Mr. Harper was prime minister, a drug offence could carry a stiffer sentence than possession of child porn. While Black and Indigenous men were being disproportionately arrested, Mr. Harper also fought against supervised injection sites during the rise of the opioid epidemic, which began surfacing in force in 1999.

His punitive approach to law enforcement, at the very least, says Owusu-Bempah, created an uneasy environment in which to launch a legal medical marijuana program enriching already rich white men. Against a backdrop of this already occurring for the past one hundred years, it made Owusu-Bempah cringe. "So while we have Black and Indigenous men being arrested for pot and forced to serve real time, we also have the government sourcing marijuana contracts," he says. "Who's profiting from Prairie Plant Systems? White businessmen. Who's being arrested for cannabis possession? Black kids."

Ken Boessenkool doesn't see it that way. Mandatory minimums were designed to be colour-blind, and the last thing the Conservatives wanted was to get involved with marijuana. Legalize cannabis, even medicinally? That's something for Zöe. Better to lock her up because she's too busy banging on her tambourines on Queen Street to vote Conservative. "Conservatives would never put cannabis in the front window because of our support within ethnic communities," says Boessenkool, adding that the Conservatives, never the party of the youth, saw themselves as the party of "families." To Boessenkool — "It doesn't matter what the fuck I thought. What matters was what it took to win" — weed equalled drug messaging equalled immigrant parents afraid for their kids. "Tough on crime" didn't discriminate, says Boessenkool. The mandatory minimums were based on votes. The hammer always found a nail. "In the immigrant communities, we were aggressive to say that pot legalization was bad for the future of their children. I can't tell you how strongly that resonated," he says.

His message for Mr. Harper was simple: "The Liberals want your kids on drugs." Boessenkool insinuates that the posturing could have been an act. "Mr. Harper probably had sympathy for medical cannabis patients — if indeed it was used medically — but cannabis wouldn't be the issue for us."

Cannabis became an issue for Stephen Harper because the MMAR program had spawned massive "grey market" legal grows. They were grey market because a grower might have a Health Canada licence to grow medical marijuana. But the licences were being abused, and a licensed designated grower might produce something like thirty thousand plants. Owusu-Bempah says these types of semi-legal operations were all over his Peterborough, Ontario, neighbourhood when he was growing up. So while a kid who looked like him could face jail time for smoking a joint, real criminals began sensing a softening legal marijuana environment.

Under the designated grower system, criminals began growing weed at scale. In 2004, an officer who had spent his entire adult life fighting crime was involved in an illegal-pot bust at a Molson plant in Barrie, Ontario. When his team arrived on the scene, he tells me, they seized property, automatic weapons, and vehicles worth more than $7.5 million. "This is black market cannabis destined for the U.S.," says the officer, who also makes an important point. The twelve suspects arrested at the Barrie grow op, which housed fifty workers and could generate hundreds of millions of dollars in illegal income per year, were not part of an organized gang. They weren't Hells Angels or the mafia, although both groups were involved in legal and illegal weed. Instead, they were a loose collective of entrepreneurs with enough money to buy high-tech irrigation systems and thousands of hydroponic lights and produce hundreds of pounds of semi-legal weed.

"Organized crime isn't always what you see on TV. It can be any group that's banded together to do illegal things," the officer tells me, adding that much of the illegal Canadian pot is smuggled into the U.S., where it gets swallowed by criminal enterprises and helps fund a reverse shipment back into Canada — most likely as cocaine, cash, opioids, or guns. The officer says that illegal Canadian pot was smuggled through the Buffalo, New York, border at a rate of one thousand pounds per run. "We busted hundreds of sites in the Niagara region, Norfolk county, and Leamington," he says. These are the verdant agricultural regions where licensed producers of legal cannabis would soon begin: Redecan in Niagara and Aphria in Leamington.

By the time Harper was elected, the pot situation was becoming a problem. In 2003, the Ontario Association of Chiefs of Police published the *Green Tide Report*, which claimed as many as ten thousand children were being raised in grow houses and that many of them were close to schools. "They're smart, well financed, and ruthless in their pursuit of profits," the report says of the illegal growers. Meanwhile, alongside the number of illegal grow ops, the number of medical cannabis patients buying legal weed continued to rise. There were 500 medical cannabis patients in 2002. In June 2009, there were 4,029 medical marijuana patients. By 2013, there would be 26,000. And by the end of 2016, there were more than 129,000 medical marijuana patients. Working in Ontario premier Dalton McGuinty's office, John Aird saw the regulations changing and realized there was going to be a problem of supply and demand. A third-generation Liberal insider, Aird, California sober — he smoked pot but didn't touch alcohol — became a licensing fixer for nascent medical marijuana companies. "I knew the need for legal weed was growing alongside the rampant illegal growing," says Aird. "Pot would have to be licensed and I could connect the dots, help build cannabis companies, and see pot was going to be a huge industry."

Alan Young explains why the laws changed. "The government couldn't control the illegal grows," he says. "Canadians were legally entitled to medical marijuana and, insult to injury, the legal weed wasn't good."

Young at Heart: Alan Young reads *KIND* magazine in Toronto after smoking a joint and decrying the legal cannabis system.

Because the legal weed wasn't good and the legal growers were despised, the politicians and the activists could finally agree about something.

By law, PPS and Brent Zettl never worked with the designated growers. Part of the MMARs stipulated that a cannabis company couldn't employ anyone with a record. But these would be the people best suited to growing weed and best connected to the culture. What cannabis users might want or, more specifically, might need, didn't enter the equation. It was us against them at the dawn of the legal cannabis market — for medical and, as we'll see later, for recreational, too. Hostilities often boiled over between the nascent legal cannabis industry and the people working in the grey market.

"PPS thought we were illegal gangsters and would never talk to us, but we also led a countrywide campaign against them for years," says Mat Beren, an early designated grower at the Vancouver Island Compassion Society. Beren was a pioneer of the vertical integration concept of dealing pot, whereby a licensed cannabis producer also distributes their product and sells it in a location they own. This way, explains Beren, a single individual or company can be held accountable for — and earn revenue on — every step of the growing and distribution process. Beren was and still is a leading light in the cannabis culture. In 2004, Beren, then thirty, distributed a cartoon of someone rolling PPS weed in toilet paper. There was only one kind of paper, the cartoon insinuated, suitable for PPS weed.

Brent Zettl says that the abuse he took was relentless and that the cannabis underground spread disinformation and lies. "They thought it was their God-given right to grow cannabis and took every opportunity to defame the government's program and ourselves," says Zettl, who explains why his product had its distinctive feel: his cannabis was milled, which means it was ground into powder, because it was designed to be consumed by vapes, battery-operated cigarette-like contraptions that combusted without a flame. A patient with MS, he says, couldn't properly grind a cannabis bud to roll into a joint. It was Health Canada, he says, that stipulated that the PPS product be distributed already milled. It wasn't his fault that a connoisseur like Mat Beren, used to growing fat nuggets, would claim that smoking PPS weed was like drinking a hamburger through a straw. "The pot was never intended for heavy users. It was medicine," Zettl says. "The whole program was never intended to be rec."

PPS also had to ensure that each gram was consistently dosed. If marijuana was medicine, you couldn't have some variations with 5 percent THC and others with 25 percent. But plants aren't tubes of toothpaste, and even with Brent's technology, it was impossible to identically harvest living things. So Zettl's team took the top of the cannabis plants, which had a high THC percentage, and the bottom of the plants, with low THC, and blended them together. Since the entirety of a cannabis plant didn't mature in concert, it was an odd concoction at best. Meanwhile, the rumour mill said that PPS ground the stalk, seeds, and flower into its grams. Continuing with the hamburger metaphor, Mat Beren says this would be akin to grinding up the plate and napkin and mixing it in with your lunch.

"Poor Brent. We made so much fun of him, and the more that the government was inept, the more righteous we became," says Hilary Black, who had started the British Columbia Compassion Club Society in 1997. Black was never arrested at her club at 2995 Commercial Drive, at the corner of East 14th Avenue, not far from where the Chinatown riots led to Canada's first drug laws. She had a wellness centre attached to her store and lived above the unit while earning six dollars an hour. Black says both the local cancer and HIV centres sent her patients and, while her operation was illegal, she required physician-authorized paperwork to administer her medicinal marijuana, edibles, or hash. She knew she was a target for the police, but she was an activist, willing to take the risk. "I had a big dry bag where we'd shove the pound bags and blocks of hash to bolt out the back door when we thought the cops were coming," says Black. She and her cronies were a different kind of marijuana criminal than the folks shipping pounds out in Barrie. They broke the laws as a form of resistance, she says, and by offering her care to all comers, a Florence Nightingale of bud, she was susceptible to burglary, or worse.

One time, she tells me, she had to call the police herself for assistance when one of her patients threatened violence. "This patient, he just kept telling me I'd be lying in a pool of blood, and I couldn't get him out of the building. Very reluctantly I called the police," recalls Black, "but the cops helped us!

One officer even said, 'We know what you're doing here. You have to call us if you get in trouble. We know that you girls are doing good Christian work.'"

Black, like Mat Beren and most of the compassion club operators, used the licensed designated growers to provide pot for her customers, some of whom had medical marijuana licences, some of whom did not. Since Health Canada was still coming to terms with cannabis consumption — and scientific evidence had yet to be produced to a standard high enough to convince the Canadian Medical Association that pot really worked — grey market operators policed themselves and made their own rules. Especially in Vancouver, they were, by and large, ignored by the police.

Black calls it an act of compassionate rebellion. "Nobody had the balls to do what we were doing in Vancouver," she says. She always knew legalization would come with regulation, and her vision since the late 1990s was only to get good cannabis affordably to the maximum number of needy patients. Though her business was illegal, she worked with Health Canada. She sent reports on her operating system to regulators and worked in adjunct with other compassion clubs in Guelph and Montreal. She, Adam Greenblatt, and Mat Beren were friends.

"Shit would go sideways and we'd all get on the phone, and together we published our first set of operating procedures," says Black, adding that when Health Canada announced the first legal system in 2001, it included many of her recommendations. Black, like Marc Emery, even provided Terry Parker with seeds and weed. This would blur the line between legal and illegal. This underground system — flawed, decent (mostly), and run (often) by brave, compassionate stoners — was not designed to last.

Mat Beren had a legal licence to grow medicinal marijuana, and in 2003 he bought a house on Vancouver Island for the job. Authorized to grow eleven marijuana plants, he grew eleven hundred. When he got busted, he says, the RCMP knew nothing about the MMAR laws, then two years old. "The cops didn't even know cannabis could be medical," Beren recalls. "When they showed up, they just said, 'You're growing weed. You're busted.' The RCMP didn't believe medical marijuana was a thing."

Mat gave the police the 1-800 Health Canada number to confirm the country's drug laws, but since it was late in the day, the office was closed.

"The RCMP destroyed the whole facility and we were devastated, but three weeks later, we said, 'Fuck it, let's rebuild.'"

Beren is white, and Hilary Black is white; Rosie Rowbotham, Terrance Parker, Alan Young, Marc Emery, and Jodie Giesz-Ramsay are white, too. Akwasi Owusu-Bempah says the way we distinguish between activists and dealers often comes down to who the medicine is for. He says law enforcement judged rule breakers differently in Black and Indigenous lower-economic urban communities, especially from 2006 to 2013, during Stephen Harper's tough-on-crime platform. Certainly the Black community was using pot as medicine, too. "Whenever subjectivity is entered into law enforcement, it's the Black and Indigenous people who suffer," Owusu-Bempah says.

And there was lots of subjectivity — and abuse — in the system. Harper, when he was elected, had to deal with the MMAR system that Jorg Scott, a medical marijuana OG in British Columbia, describes like this: "There were doctors who opened up their clinics and said 'Pay me five hundred dollars and I'll give you a licence.' There were lineups out the door." Scott mentions that in 2005, another popular way to get a grower's licence was to hire someone with MS or cancer and recruit them to get a medical marijuana licence and make you their designated grower. Scott says the scene, once the domain of folks like Don Briere of Da Kine, Aaron Harnett, and hippies — lawbreakers who, even if they broke the law, were still connected to the plant — began to change. Opportunism brought in a rougher crowd, and this, too, would be a legacy of legal recreational weed.

"Imagine a guy who has spent his whole life not playing by the rules, sitting in a doctor's office or standing in a line, and he might be a heavy — a guy who you don't want to piss off," says Scott of the criminal element that saw an opportunity in pot. Unlike activists such as Alan Young and Terry Parker, dangerous outlaws found a way to cash in. "These early adopters saw an opportunity. They didn't give a fuck about weed."

Like Hilary Black, Alan Young had been consulting with Health Canada. To its credit, Health Canada was talking to the right people. Young says that, in court throughout the early 2000s, he extended patients' rights to grow their own weed and he set the table for new products such as edibles, beverages, and vapes. (Cannabis in all these formats, dubbed Cannabis 2.0, would become legal in 2019.) Young argued that sick patients needing medicine shouldn't have to smoke their cannabis and that edibles and vape pens should be legally allowed. Lorne Gertner, working with media tycoon Moses Znaimer and Joe Mimran, of the Joe Fresh clothing line, was developing medical devices for patients to get their cannabis without smoking: products like vape pens, inhalers, and Listerine-like strips. His company Cannasat Therapeutics, with David Hill as its CEO, had gone public on the TSX Venture Exchange in March 2006, listing at thirty-five cents per share. Hill says he suffered endlessly trying to make the company work. He had Hilary Black and Mark Ware on his board and raised $6.5 million for his venture. He wanted to use that money to fund cannabis research. "You could see how the company should work — it was right before our eyes," says Hill. "The problem was we were just too soon."

The team at Hill & Gertner had taken the first North American marijuana company public. *Maclean's* called Lorne the godfather of cannabis in 2017. And yet, private companies, not the medical community, had to fund their own studies. Gertner estimated that his company could take 10 percent of the $700 million Canadian pain relief market, eventually, but he couldn't get his brand off the ground. Cannabis had no momentum, no spokesperson, no cachet. The Cannasat stock peaked at eighty cents and made history. It just didn't work as a business. "We couldn't raise any money," Gertner tells me, and echoes his partner. "We were too soon."

Alan Young thought Gertner was early, but he also believed that he was onto something and that the medical program needed to improve and expand. "There were rumours out of the West Coast that the Prairie Plant Systems pot was contaminated. It turned out not to be true, but it helped our case with Health Canada," says Young, who spent much of 2010 in meetings with government regulators, proposing a new system. It was clear the MMAR model didn't work. "There were crooked doctors who exploited the program. You gave them two hundred dollars and they'd prescribe you four hundred grams per day," says Young, who also opened a compassion club in Toronto.

In 2010, he brought underground cannabis growers to Ottawa for a consultation. The group explained to Health Canada why the medical system wasn't working: the government needed to hire growers who understood weed. Young also proposed that the government give out multiple licences to multiple companies, so patients could choose the weed they wanted and make the market competitive. There are multiple types of pain relievers. Why wouldn't there be multiple types of weed? Alan Young envisioned a cannabis world in which licensed patients could buy licensed weed at legal brick-and-mortar stores, assisted by knowledgeable attendants. Budtenders, said Young, could manage the cannabis front lines.

On December 16, 2012, the government of Stephen Harper announced new Marihuana for Medical Purposes Regulations (MMPRs). These were the legal result of Alan Young and Hilary Black consulting with Health Canada. By the end of 2012, pot growing was no longer going to fall solely to Brent Zettl.

"They took away all of our patients without any warning," says Zettl. "We had to start from scratch."

These new companies would need to be well financed. They had to build the facilities before they could receive a licence to grow, and the vaults alone could cost $250,000. And regulations would be strict. Despite its intentions, the Harper government now had marijuana in the front window. The changes would usher in Canada's first wave of licensed producers, the Blessed 13.

The medical marijuana program — and the Canadian economy — would explode.

CHAPTER 5

The Founders

"We'd be selling marijuana for cash."

Murray Goldman

The MMPRs created fortunes. They ended medicinal marijuana home-growing and the designated grower system and opened up the sole-sourced PPS licensed producer contract to other companies growing weed. Presumably, this would end Mexico's concerns about imported illegal BC weed.

Trevor Fencott and Michael Haines had been partners since 2002 in Groove Games, which licensed video games for mobile content. They were coming off the successful sale of their company and casting about for something new. Haines, a soft-spoken married father of two, understood marketing and capital markets, and gradually understood that he had a gift for finance. As a teenager in east Toronto, he had had a close relationship with pot. But after university he stopped smoking and never gave it much thought, until his cottage neighbour, Gregory Herriott, a hemp pioneer and MMAR grower, started talking up the new MMPR system. By 2012, Haines, flush with cash after his success in the tech world, was intrigued. He knew marijuana would be stigmatized by Bay Street. He also knew there was already a healthy market for weed. Canadians loved to smoke. And he knew that starting a business that produced pot would require extensive capital and a capacity to read the government's fine print. The system had come a long way from Allan Rock's approval process for an individual's medical licence. A pot company's approval process, says Haines, was like casting about in the dark through a maze.

As for Trevor Fencott, he'd never tried weed. From Scarborough, he was a lawyer by training whose wife worked in pharma and was more familiar with cannabis than he was. He and Haines weren't activists or farmers. They were businessmen who had just sold their company for $20 million. Haines pitched Fencott on setting up a medical marijuana company. There were other partners from Groove Games, but they didn't like the idea. At first this was scary. But there was a flip side: if the partners they'd just made rich didn't want to get into marijuana, maybe Fencott and Haines would have the market to themselves.

"The stigma knocked out most serious businessmen," says Fencott. He told Haines the work was going to be dirty, dangerous, and difficult. Growing Health Canada–compliant weed at scale had never been done before, and Health Canada would be figuring out the parameters the companies would need to follow as the companies attempted to build their multimillion-dollar grows. Gertner's public weed company had been a failure, and the people who really knew how to grow weed probably had police records, so they couldn't join the legal system; farmers, experts in cucumbers and tomatoes, didn't know the first thing about marijuana. Was growing pot the same thing as growing lettuce? From the lights to the vaults to the seeds to the security, nobody really knew. Plus, it wasn't only Bay Street that wouldn't fund these companies — no one would.

"If it was easy," Haines told his partner, "everyone would be in."

To submit a proposal to grow medicinal marijuana at the start of 2013 required 250 pages of paperwork, an extensive background check, a lease on a growing facility — which no landlord wanted to give — and standard operating procedures for a framework that had never been done, legally, with regard to pesticides, seeds, potency, and packaging, at scale. But Haines and Fencott could see the upside in the downsides. People have always loved weed.

Gregory Herriott, sitting out on his dock in the setting sun, told Michael the horizon was wide open for how big this market could be. Haines and Fencott called their company Mettrum — a word Michael made up that could mean anything — and they say that finding an initial location to set up their grow was a quixotic task. "Damned near impossible," says Haines.

In early 2013, Michael and Trevor visited Haliburton, a small town in northern Ontario that could no longer afford its hockey rink, and the guys set up a meet-and-greet to pitch their idea to their potential new neighbours. In their own eyes, they were heroes. They promised to save the rink and to build a yoga centre and to make a positive impact on community life, creating jobs and hiring local. Haliburton had seen most manufacturers close. A rail line now transporting nitroglycerin cut through downtown. Between wealth incubation and job creation, cannabis could signal a small town's triumphant return.

There were three hundred people at the hockey rink when Fencott and Haines pitched their plan. The rink was quiet. Then it wasn't.

"Who do these pot people think they are?"

And "Marijuana capitalists aren't going to take over our town!"

Fencott and Haines knew starting a marijuana company would be hard. People loved weed. But they hated it, too. Emotions were huge. Standing outside the arena after the town hall, they were heckled and booed. "What about the children?" screamed one concerned mom. Fencott's wife, who he'd brought along to witness his moment of glory, buried her face in her scarf. For Fencott, marijuana began as an unlikely economic opportunity and morphed into something personal. He never got high in university and didn't smoke weed at law school, but like for a lot of the first-generation cannabis executives, having to defend his product before hostile crowds day after day buttressed his beliefs.

Across from the arena, not five feet away from an elementary school, in a bit of real estate irony, sat an LCBO — the provincially owned liquor store.

Fencott and Haines got into their cars. "See you later, losers," called out another Haliburton local.

The *Toronto Sun* even caught wind of the debacle. "What are they smoking?" read the next day's headline beside a photograph of Bobby Orr, who had apparently once called Haliburton home. Orr was surrounded by marijuana leaves. Pot wasn't just a joke. It was a scourge.

———•

The Canadian medical marijuana program — the MMPR, the only federal medical marijuana program in North America — was groundbreaking, destigmatizing, restrictive, and opaque. Patients needed cannabis "scripts" from their doctors to consume the substance. These weren't prescriptions, exactly, because the Canadian Medical Association wouldn't back cannabis as medicine. A costly ruling for patients, this meant that medical marijuana, unlike other prescription medicines, would be taxed and not covered by insurance companies. Basically, the scripts were doctor's notes, like the kind a kid would bring into fourth grade for missing school.

Health Canada's request for proposals would be open to new manufacturers from the private sector. Businesses would produce and distribute and profit from medical marijuana under a regulated Health Canada system. The business would be difficult, as Fencott and Haines were discovering, but certain entrepreneurs — heavily capitalized risk-takers who didn't care what people thought — took note.

"How often does a government deregulate an industry, once a decade?" asks Stephen Arbib, a serial tech entrepreneur who submitted a proposal to Health Canada for a company he called MedReleaf. Prior to the passage of the MMPR laws, Arbib published a Canadian newspaper on Jewish culture and Israeli life. Through that outlet he had become aware of Tikun Olam, a pioneering Israeli company in cannabis research. In Israel, Tikun Olam produced medical marijuana for the government, whose patients included members and former members of the military — that is, nearly 100 percent of the adult Israeli population, as every Israeli is mandated by law to do military service. Arbib knew that partnering with the Israelis would give him a huge advantage over any Canadian company looking to enter the cannabis industry without help. Not only were the Canadian regulations on growing, distributing, and securing the cannabis plants severe and expensive, but the intellectual property regarding growing techniques was new and complex;

outside of PPS, which most regulators, patients, and growers agreed wasn't successful, no Canadian company had produced regulated, dose-controlled, pharmaceutical-grade cannabis at scale. Tikun Olam had done this for decades, and, importantly, knew how to handle security, which was one of the government's biggest concerns (remember, the first legal Canadian grow op was started in a mine under a lake).

Arbib, a clean-shaven teetotaler, had a background in aviation and government procurement. In 2012, he raised $2.4 million to complete his government application, purchase a facility, and recruit a skeletal team. Tikun Olam was the first company to isolate the THC from CBD in cannabis molecules and so had valuable intellectual property, including proprietary plant genetics and seeds. Arbib inherited all these, along with facility infrastructure.

It was difficult for fledgling legal medical marijuana companies to honour the rule of the law and not lean on the black market. Since cannabis had always been illegal, anyone with marijuana experience would have been either a designated grower or a drug dealer. But the designated grower profession was being wiped away. Could you trust a designated grower to drive your multimillion-dollar facility, under prying government eyes?

Tikun Olam gave MedReleaf another initial advantage over its rivals: the model of a lucrative government insurance sales program. In Israel, soldiers didn't have to pay for their Tikun Olam bud. Insurance covered it. The MedReleaf payment program imported this idea into Canadian law. Canadian veterans, and veterans only, would have their MedReleaf medical marijuana covered by insurance premiums. The program didn't work the same way for patients with, say, cancer, MS, epilepsy (like Terry Parker), or AIDS (like Jim Wakeford).

Veterans would be marijuana's most valuable patients. They would be consistent clients, and since they weren't paying, they wouldn't care how much their medical cannabis cost. This meant the MedReleaf team had leniency with its price structure. There was no ceiling on the price of a gram. "MedReleaf was and may still be the only profitable cannabis company in Canada," says Arbib, who, given his background, is extremely knowledgeable in how to get things done — especially around governments in a challenging regulatory environment. "We took the science of cannabis seriously, but we weren't shy about hiring people from the black market. We paired scientists with the most talented growers we could find."

In addition to his Israeli partners, Arbib had another advantage over his competition: Tom Flow, a friend since third grade who was obsessed with marijuana. Flow had become enamoured with weed when he was fifteen years old and turned his closet into a grow op. He wasn't interested in making volcanoes explode for his science fair project. He experimented with growing weed like a stoner Mr. Green Thumb: the lights, the soil, the seeds, the growing cycle. In order to be taken more seriously, some medical marijuana entrepreneurs flaunted to investors the fact that they didn't smoke weed. They, like their investors, were above the culture they intended to serve. Tom Flow and MedReleaf didn't think that way. By the time Arbib asked him to lunch to discuss his new company, Flow was already an entrepreneur who'd managed a tech company with one hundred employees. Flow was a businessman, sure. But he was also a pothead, and strains of pot, to him, were as distinct and specific as designer shoes. "Super Skunk, Northern Lights #5 — I was fanatic about strains," Flow says.

While his buddy Arbib, already a self-made millionaire by the time they went into business, was the last person you'd expect to start a marijuana company, Flow was exactly who you would expect to work full-time growing weed. Flow studied *High Times* as a boy the way other kids read *Sports Illustrated* and had been operating a vast network of quasi-legal grow ops around Ontario since 2007. Flow just never got caught. "I was on the black market side, moving high volumes all over the place," he says of the seventeen expansive marijuana-growing facilities he owned. These places did have licences to grow medical marijuana. But Flow would combine individual licences together in order to maximize their output capacity. When his licences limited how many plants they could grow, Flow figured out how to grow plants the size of elm trees.

He won't tell me how much he earned from his business, so I ask him what kind of car he drove. "Oh," he says, "I had lots of cars."

Arbib was offering Flow a chance to take his know-how and apply it to the legal system. As they did for Lorne Gertner, success and the MMPR laws afforded Tom Flow a chance to live out his cannabis dreams. Flow sold off his grey market assets, imported his genetics to MedReleaf, and crossed sides along with the underground team he'd assembled. "The most exciting part was being that researcher/innovator, that scientist, designing the facilities, construction — every little piece," says Flow of the do-it-yourself model of creating high-quality cannabis-growing facilities at scale. From the water to the nutrients to the lights, the MedReleaf production facilities ran like a high-tech assembly line. Adding Tom Flow to the Tikun Olam playbook, plus obtaining the lion's share of veteran prescriptions, gave MedReleaf an early advantage in the nascent industry.

However, there was another entrepreneur, also obsessed with weed, with an inside track: Marc Wayne, who partnered with a Dutch company named Bedrocan.

Importing five hundred kilos of marijuana from the Dutch government requires a skill set of the sort they don't teach in school. Marc Wayne is a Queen's University grad in biological sciences. He became interested in pot while running an IT business. Wayne, who wears a goatee, is perceptive and daring. He and his partner, Mark Ware, are another foundational piece of the legal Canadian weed industry.

It started for Wayne with those Dutch kilos. In 2007, he was recruited by his university buddy Ware to join the Canadian Consortium for the Investigation of Cannabinoids (CCIC), which had begun with a $400,000 Health Canada grant. Cannabis had always appealed to Wayne, both as a consumer and as someone who witnessed first-hand what the plant could do. When he was a teenager, his mother contracted AIDS (he believes it was from a tainted blood transfusion), and together they consumed licensed marijuana from the government, which formed some of the happiest memories of his childhood. Life was better for them both on weed.

"I didn't need a study to know that cannabis was a life-changing drug," says Wayne, who nevertheless, with the CCIC, was tasked with providing evidence of just that.

Eventually, Valeant Pharmaceuticals, which made a synthetic marijuana product known as Cesamet, hired Wayne to speak with pain physicians across the country, attempting to sway them away from prescribing opioids and toward synthetic medicinal marijuana. Wayne was a true believer and thus a natural salesman, and Cesamet's sales increased enough for Valeant to invest more than $1 million into the CCIC. Wayne beat the drum that other cannabis companies would follow: his roadshows across the country introduced a generation of pain physicians to medicinal marijuana.

Wayne also met regularly with Health Canada. Meanwhile, Ware, his CCIC partner — who, incidentally, had a smoking room connected to his lab at the University of Montreal — was trying to deduce how the plant affected the body's endocannabinoid system. Endocannabinoids are neurotransmitters that have a structural similarity to molecules in the cannabis plant; they help us regulate appetite, pleasure, and pain.

Medical pot was legal, but it still prompted sharp reactions. Health Canada, with a Supreme Court ruling, had decided that pot was medicine. The Canadian Medical Association, the largest association of this country's physicians, said it was not. A grey market was baked into the system from day one. Still, the CCIC went about its daily business, with Wayne raising money and selling Cesamet while Ware conducted his research. Ever since the Le Dain Commission, Canadian politicians had stopped just short of authorizing science to look for proof that cannabis had health benefits and was no more harmful than alcohol or cigarettes. But the CCIC was a consequence of the growing acceptance of Canadian pot.

In late 2011, Wayne read a report from Health Canada suggesting that the legal medical marijuana system would be privatized. It was accepted as fact that licensed designated growers in Ontario and BC were flooding the U.S. and Mexico with black market weed, and regulators had heard enough complaints about the PPS product to know there needed to be another way. In December 2012, the system was being re-evaluated, but Canadian medical marijuana patients still needed the weed they were legally entitled to. Conveniently, through his work with the CCIC, Wayne had a connection with executives at Bedrocan, a leading Dutch medical marijuana company renowned for its pharmaceutical standards. (Besides PPS, the only authorized growers in the world were Bedrocan in the Netherlands, Tikun Olam in Israel, and researchers at the University of Mississippi.) So as the Canadian market underwent its first overhaul, Health Canada approved Wayne to import those five hundred kilos of Dutch weed.

"Health Canada was going to be changing the regulations because of the abuse of the personal designated growers in BC. They wanted a commercial system — and needed advice," says Wayne.

Fencott and Haines were still searching for a building for Mettrum while Wayne worked with Health Canada on the new regulations and shook hands with the Bedrocan team for licensing rights to import Dutch genetics into Canada. Meanwhile, Wayne's stepfather, Murray Goldman, built up the budding cannabis tycoon's war chest. Goldman, a legendary Canadian developer who also once ran the brewery industry in Israel, staked Wayne with $16 million to begin. "While all the other companies were out begging for money, we immediately had product," Goldman, ninety-one, tells me. "We'd be selling marijuana for cash."

PPS, which changed its name to CanniMed, received the first Canadian medical production licence under the MMPRs. Peace Naturals, which Gertner helped fund, received the second. Fencott and Haines at Mettrum got the third. Bedrocan came fourth, and a company called Tweed, started by Chuck Rifici, who was deeply embedded in Ottawa, and the wide-eyed entrepreneur Bruce Linton, received licence number five in the country.

Competition, at the start, was fierce. Lorne Gertner says still no one would invest in any of the pot companies. It was difficult to get physicians to move beyond the stigma of marijuana and for licensed patients to differentiate among brands. With the established medical community not buying into cannabis, the new pot companies deployed their own strategies and their own sales agents to meet with doctors, following the path Marc Wayne had set. Slowly, these new companies began to set the parameters of the new legal medical cannabis world.

Hilary Black went to work at Bedrocan. It was a shot fired across the bow of the activist circuit. Black had built her compassion club in Vancouver to service more than ten thousand patients. Whenever the CBC discussed marijuana, it was Black who'd explain why, as a medicine, it worked. She wasn't a drug dealer. She had studied the compassion clubs of California and banged out Grateful Dead tunes on her tambourine. She ran a wellness centre selling vegan, gluten-free edibles and offering psychiatric help and services for people with mental health and substance abuse problems. By 2013, she'd dedicated more than half of her life to marijuana.

Black respected Bedrocan for what the company had done in the Netherlands; she also had strong positive feelings for both Marc Wayne and Mark Ware. Hilary Black was proud to smoke marijuana *and* she liked the health regulators she had grown to know at Health Canada — even the cops.

In her underground career, Black had fostered good relationships with cancer clinics and illegal BC growers and created an ethical model for legalization that prioritized patients and loosely connected compassion clubs across the country. She saw her work as a charity.

However, having lived in Amsterdam, she knew Bedrocan by reputation and had a relationship with the company's founder. She knew the company had produced its first cannabis seeds back in 1992. She wanted a seat at the table in the new power world of weed and also wanted to exit the grey market. Bedrocan, though corporate, looked good.

"Growers couldn't afford to operate in the new legal system, so pretty much everybody was selling weed in the black market to subsidize their work for patients," says Black, adding that designated growers in her scene were often not paid for their work. Certainly, you didn't get into her corner of the weed world to become rich.

When Black crossed over to the legal system, she was lampooned mercilessly by the pot underground. She says she received misogynistic treatment from a community she helped build and certain activists she once counted as friends grew abusive, even threatening. Sexism, like racism, existed in marijuana, both corporate and underground, like it does everywhere in the world. Tom Flow, for instance, a black market legend, didn't receive the treatment Hilary Black did. Maybe it's because he was known to pack a gun. Still, it's tempting for certain activists to proclaim themselves noble and to paint all of the legal medical marijuana companies as heartless, capitalist jerks. But the distinctions are much more nuanced. A banker was no more honest than a dope grower. And an activist could be just as sexist as anyone on Bay Street, Black says.

It wasn't only the market — in cannabis, everything was grey.

"I was getting disgusting levels of abuse, sexual humiliation," Black tells me, describing the underground cannabis community, and though she received support from Mark Ware and Marc Wayne and leaders from her BC network, it was a difficult transition. Not only was she leaving a mission she pioneered, but she felt alone to defend herself on all sides. What kept her going were her values. "Equal access in cannabis as medicine across the country and removing the stigma around cannabis has always been my north star," says Black, who never stopped working with the BC Compassion Club and had written in her Bedrocan contract that she be allowed to advocate on its behalf. "I had earned the right to shape policy. Nothing could hold me back."

———————

Thirteen medical marijuana licences were announced in February 2014. By December 2014, Health Canada had received 1,191 medical marijuana licensed producer applications and was receiving 15 new applications each week. The first companies to be granted licences were Aphria, Bedrocan, Broken Coast, Canna Farms, CanniMed, Delta 9, In the Zone, Maricann, MedReleaf, Mettrum, Organigram, the Peace Naturals Project, Tilray, Tweed (later renamed by Bruce Linton to Canopy Growth), and the Whistler Medical Marijuana Corporation. In June 2014, a medical licence was issued to a company called Redecan, started by the Redekop family of Niagara-based farmers, who would partner with the controversial Montour family — an Indigenous powerhouse who could mass-produce cheap cigarettes and avoid excise taxes by doing so on Indigenous land. Quietly, the Montours had created the fourth largest tobacco company in the world.

Around each of these licensees was a moat. Each company did things slightly differently.

Tilray, started by the smooth Seattle-based financier Brendan Kennedy, was the first American company to set up shop on Canadian soil, in Nanaimo, British Columbia. Kennedy skirted the American laws barring cannabis production by growing his weed in the north. Aphria, started by Cole Cacciavillani, a second-generation farmer based in Leamington, Ontario, revolutionized cannabis production by growing marijuana, a product he'd never seen before, in the greenhouses his family owned. "We put in our application in August of 2013, and I thought we'd be first, but Canopy beat us out — our licence was number fourteen," Cacciavillani tells me, a cigar in his hand and a huge hunk of meat roasting on his grill. "Still, I laughed at the competitors. They didn't have a freaking clue what to do. All these guys growing in garages, barns, warehouses, or whatever. I knew how to grow in greenhouses. Everyone thought I was crazy, but I'll grow radish, I'll grow lettuce. I can grow anything if there's a buck to be made."

In June 2014, Cacciavillani brought his old friend Vic Neufeld in to run the company, and Aphria's low-cost greenhouse production model transformed the industry.

It was a transformation that Lorne Gertner wouldn't watch from the sidelines. After his PPS investment, Gertner began the Cronos Group in the summer of 2012 to help finance these nascent companies. The pioneer had already lost his shirt in marijuana, but if his dream of a legal industry was going to happen, the activist financier who Bruce Linton says is sober only when he first wakes up had to be in. "I had been so beaten up by that point that I really didn't want to do it, but we did a deal with Peace Naturals and invested in Whistler and by the time there were twelve legal companies, I probably had equity in seven," says Gertner, who at Cronos Group would go on to attract outside capital from an obvious, but unexpected, source: tobacco. The Montour family at Redecan weren't the only cigarette manufacturers to anticipate their advantage for the disruption at the door.

These moves by these people would turn a million-dollar industry into a billion-dollar phenomenon.

———•

Other people wanted in. For would-be medical marijuana producers headed by Canadian entrepreneurs like Sébastien St-Louis at Hydropothecary and Terry Booth at Aurora, who had submitted their applications and secured their facilities but were waiting for Health Canada to approve their licences, the process was agonizing, slow, and costly. St-Louis says that during this interval, while his rivals made sales, he almost went bankrupt three times. Meanwhile, Alan Young says the pot from all of these companies was still bad, and the cannabis community wasn't interested in purchasing "government weed."

Terrance Parker, for instance, never stopped growing — and distributing — his own pot. People who smoked weed continued to smoke weed, medicinally or not, and it had to come from somewhere, and you didn't need a licence for that. (Rosie Rowbotham was coy when I asked him if he got back into the weed game after being released from prison, when the MMPR laws were passed. "What are you," he asked, "a cop?")

The cannabis companies had to wait for the regulators while the competition built their client list and perfected — well, iterated — their infrastructure and growth models. Mettrum's Michael Haines was particularly creative.

His company pioneered the "clinic model," which would be copied by every licensed producer, the idea being that patients could visit a pharmacy for a script and physicians there would prescribe that licensed producer's product. It's like buying the No Frills–branded peanut butter at the grocery store, except this product was cannabis, and no one, doctors included, knew how it should be dosed. To solve this problem, Haines created the Mettrum Spectrum, which helped doctors prescribe medical cannabis based on a colour-coded dosage system. Soon his company had 20 percent of the market share.

Haines did what the market needed — he created a language — but the early days of medical marijuana did not see executives sitting in the boardroom alone. Some days they had to pack planes with weed.

The licensed medical marijuana companies that received licences were racing to grow pot at scale. And the brands all had to adhere to a firm government deadline for purchasing their approved licensed seeds and growth material. Brands had until March 31, 2014, to finalize their live cannabis materials to grow their medicinal pot, and Health Canada couldn't supply growers with a list of whose seeds were legal to buy.

How does an illegal industry suddenly become legal? Inevitably, the companies turned to Kelowna, British Columbia, and the legally dismantled designated growers who, though outlawed, would end up supplying the legal medical market with their first starter seeds. It was chaos at every level. Canada Post, for instance, wouldn't allow cannabis shipments, which meant weed executives had to personally handle the marijuana.

First, Michael Haines at Mettrum had two of his partners drive the cannabis root bulbs and seeds from Kelowna to Bowmanville, Ontario, where Mettrum eventually built their facilities. Along the way, this first Mettrum cannabis source material nearly froze. Next, Herriott rented a prop plane and flew the roots and seeds to a private airstrip near the Mettrum grow. The licensed producers couldn't buy actual finished, sellable marijuana from the licensed growers. They could only buy the root material to make their own.

Still, for people receiving cannabis in 2014, the optics would do little to erase the stigma around weed. "I met Greg at the Ajax airport, half expecting the police to show up and half wanting them to because we had all the paperwork and everything was okay. Still, it looks bad," Haines says. If the police had inspected their legal cargo, they would have found cardboard boxes filled with whole cannabis plants and marijuana seeds inside dozens of plastic bags.

"Plus, the plane just reeked," Haines says. "It stunk to high hell."

But the real action was in Kelowna, and on one spring weekend in 2014, Haines had volunteered to make the deal, before the Health Canada deadline expired. He arrived in town to pack up the boxes of root cannabis material, bulbs, and seeds.

"Clearly it couldn't be a big load of pre-rolls, but there was some discrepancy about what was allowed," he says. The buds could have been cut from the plant, but not dried. It couldn't be packaged and it wasn't to be finished: in other words, you couldn't smoke the weed the licensed producers were allowed to import.

Haines was helping pack up the plane with marijuana and moving quickly — because the cannabis couldn't be processed, the clock was ticking before it would spoil, making the whole mission null and void. Dead plants equalled no weed, and Mettrum, thanks to the clinic model and Mettrum Spectrum, already had thousands of patients in the spring of 2014.

So there's Michael Haines, at sunrise in Kelowna, loading 250 kilos of marijuana plants onto his private plane outside the hangar in British Columbia — and that's when the RCMP arrived, brandishing guns. The cops were responding to what they thought was a drug deal. The millionaire had a plane full of weed.

"I'm taking a shipment back to Ontario," Haines told the officers, and he showed them his paperwork. The RCMP, however, were unfamiliar with the MMPR program, and detectives in Kelowna were cracking down on illegal weed. After all, it was largely their bud that required the legal system to begin with. Haines, an expert in the capital markets, loading boxes of marijuana onto a plane in the dead of night looked suspicious. Meanwhile, he was thinking about the precious seconds ticking away.

As the police had done with Mat Beren, the RCMP officers at the airport called the 1-800 number at Health Canada for clarification. But because it was Easter weekend, the office was closed until Tuesday — at which point the cannabis plants would be dead. It was a standstill, and Haines left Kelowna without his marijuana.

Michael Haines met Bruce Linton the next morning. Mettrum wasn't the only one busted that night. Linton, by way of introduction, told Haines that he'd handle the police and the press. Apparently, Tweed had five hundred kilograms of marijuana at their own hangar in Kelowna. Chuck Rifici had just had $500,000 worth of marijuana confiscated. Worse, Chuck's pot was stashed in hockey bags. "The quantities that Bruce had," recalls Haines, "were staggering."

Linton says he called the RCMP and had them come to check his inventory. The *National Post* spent five years uncovering the documentation from that night and filed an access to information request. The RCMP is quoted in internal documents saying that Linton had "harvested buds packaged for resale." The RCMP wanted to make an arrest and send out a press release about their work. In their telling, it was the private airlines who called the cops. "Can we transport 1,500 pounds of weed?" reads one airline's inquiry to the Kelowna RCMP.

"There were no plant seeds or production material," says the unsealed transcript about what was confiscated that night. Tweed, according to the transcript, had 2,071 plants, and Mettrum had 730. "An unfathomable quantity," according to authorities. The RCMP, however, after confiscating the weed at the airport, were told by Health Canada to go home. The RCMP briefing notes read, "The heart of the problem is Health Canada has gone on record saying that they authorized the shipment which has and will continue to cause us grief." The RCMP had always been a step behind Health Canada with the cannabis laws. It is difficult for a police officer to differentiate among buds, seeds, leaves, and flowers, especially when the material is in hockey bags and discovered in a region notorious for its illegal weed.

Change is always hard, and the source material, even if it came from licensed designated growers, was suspicious. What sort of designated grower could provide $500,000 worth of cannabis seeds? How much weed did they have? Responding to the seizure of what the RCMP called "a quantity rarely seen in Central Okanagan," Linton took over the situation. Bruce tells me he remembers the phone call with Haines. "I go, 'Mike, we have twenty-five times more weed than you. Don't cave in, don't do anything,'" recalls Linton, who, on our night in Las Vegas — loose-lipped from alcohol and vibes — also recites his conversation with Rifici:

Chuck: They took all the marijuana.
Bruce: Did you sign anything?
Chuck: No.
Bruce: Are you in jail?
Chuck: No. But Bruce, it's from bikers.
Bruce: Where do you think it's from? Little Red Riding Hood?

The grey area lies in the fact that you could be both a biker and a designated grower authorized to sell Mettrum and Tweed their "root material," which could get very close to being actual weed. What was the specific definition of root material? At what point in a plant's maturation cycle did root material become illegal drugs? Was it the RCMP's job to inspect every bud and, if so, how?

At the time, the RCMP's director of strategic communications said, "This highlights the deficiencies in the new regulations." And the new regulations were designed to replace the old regulations — which also had deficiencies.

The government apparently wanted the Kelowna episode kept quiet because it looked as if the two ministries, health and justice, were working against each other. The newly licensed producers ended up leaving the scene without their cannabis materials. But no charges were filed. Linton sent out a press release. "We have completed acquisition of seeds and plants to offer a wide variety of choices," it read, which further infuriated the police in BC, who were informed by head office in Ottawa to stay mum.

Linton not only bought more product than the competition, but he then sent out a press release after he'd embarrassed the RCMP, who, six months later, had to return the now-dead cannabis to Mettrum and Tweed.

None of this did anything to slow the business. By the end of 2014, Mettrum had more than two thousand patients and had done more than $2 million in sales. MedReleaf had sold $1.5 million of medicinal marijuana and Bedrocan had sold over $1 million.

Young Lion: Linton at the start of his Canopy journey, in Smiths Falls.

Linton tells me that he always saw himself as different from his competition. The competition says that he did this to a fault. Bruce didn't care about patients, they tell me. He only cared about his stock price and used "farm accounting," valuations today based on tomorrow's yields, which, his competitors derisively say, he must have known would never come because the estimates were too high. When that happened, go the whispers, Linton simply moved the goal posts again.

Still, while other weed brands were trying to attract patients, Linton went after retail investors and took his company public.

Bruce Linton wasn't interested in growing marijuana, not solely.

He wanted to grow Tweed into the biggest brand in the world.

PART II

REWARD

CHAPTER 6

Bruce Being Bruce

"In the end I just said, 'Fuck it, let's make a brand.'"

Bruce Linton

"The narrative always needs advancing."

Again, Bruce

Bruce Linton isn't flashy. I had breakfast with Trevor Fencott at the Soho House. Bruce and I got eggs in the basement of a mall. He isn't on social media, and he doesn't obsessively check the market. He's like a scientist determined to see his theorem proved true. He's driven by convictions. Not moral convictions, but ideas, visions — epiphanies, energy, and a lack of self-doubt. Chutzpah, to prove himself right.

"I didn't set out to say, 'Oh, I'm from Canada. Can I please come in sixth?' No. I set out to be the biggest in the world," he told me. "If it's worth doing, it's worth overdoing."

It's not greed that fuels him, but size — ego in seeing his team win. He didn't have any personal reasons to get into cannabis, and he says he had lots of other ideas at the time he first thought of Tweed. Linton, instinctive, who told me he almost certainly has ADHD, had been a serial tech entrepreneur since the early 1990s. He was interested, for instance, in parking meters, and also raw sewage, and, of course, he planned to continue to play the capital markets by launching IPOs in global tech. In 2011, he applied to run the Water, Sanitation, and Hygiene program at the Gates Foundation — the only job he ever wanted, he says, that he was rejected for.

Married with two sons, generous and loyal, book-averse, with a good sense of humour and self-made wealth, today, fifty-eight years old, paunchy, and game, Linton had built a tech company, CrossKeys Systems, which he took public, then launched WebHancer and became CEO of Martello Technologies, which also had an IPO. He read about the pot laws changing in the *Globe and Mail*, and, though he had no experience in the culture, it struck a chord.

"Are you fucking telling me I have a direct-to-consumer marijuana business opportunity where the government is handing out a few licences and you keep all the margin, not Shoppers Drug Mart?" asks Linton in one of the many walk-and-talk interviews we conducted while he was bored out of his mind during Covid-19. "It seemed like a once-in-a-lifetime opportunity."

Linton's house is big, but it's not palatial. Stephen Arbib from MedReleaf in comparison lives like a Roman emperor. Bruce Linton lives like a sub-urban dad whose dental practice, for instance, does very well. His home is at the end of a cul-de-sac outside Ottawa. It's red brick and Victorian and has a longish driveway where he parks his old Ford. He relies on his personality — accessible and outspoken, chatty and shrewd — to provide the pizzazz, not his things. There are three pot plants, grown by his son, in Bruce Linton's backyard, and they're scrawny, almost sad, which is no surprise. Linton says he'd never seen pot, let alone smoked it, before applying for his medical marijuana licence. He simply followed his curiosity. Linton says he got into tech because he didn't understand it. Marijuana would be exactly the same thing.

"I was almost disinterested in the amount of money we might make. It never crossed my mind," he says. His co-founder, Chuck Rifici, is a former chief financial officer of the Liberal Party of Canada, a position he was appointed to in 2011 by Bob Rae. Linton and Rifici started Tweed, the fifth

Canadian company to receive a medical marijuana licence. Given Rifici's political connections, it has always been speculated that Tweed benefitted from favouritism, receiving inside information from the government, especially as Justin Trudeau came on the scene. Despite an introduction from Gertner and trading emails with Rifici, I could never get Rifici on the phone — in 2021, Rifici was rumoured to be in negotiations for the purchase of Pornhub — and Linton, of course, says any rumours of favouritism are completely false.

Linton tells me he first hired Chuck Rifici for a previous business, a Quebec-based company called Sitebrand, as a favour to Rifici's wife. "She was going to get married to Chuck, who was out of work and looking, and so I put Chuck in as CFO over there." That was back in 2007, and Linton says Rifici did a good job as CFO, but after he left the company, the two men lost touch. Linton eventually ran into Rifici's wife again, and they had a similar conversation. "She'd gone on mat leave with their first kid and I bumped into her and said, 'How's things going?' 'Good,' she said. 'Except Chuck's out of work again. Do you have anything?'"

Linton had something: parking meters. But he also had this cannabis thing, and when he met with Rifici in the late fall of 2012 — "I want to fix parking, but this pot thing is obvious, too" — he found Rifici willing to work with him on a start-up called Tweed Marijuana. Almost a year later, on November 9, 2013 — after CanniMed, Peace Naturals, Mettrum, and Bedrocan — the company was licensed to sell medicinal weed. There was no inherent reason why Tweed would be any different from the rest; Bruce Linton being Bruce Linton gave them their edge.

When Rifici was fired in August 2014, he sued for mental distress.

———

Linton's pot thing would prove more valuable than he initially intuited. To grow pot you had to first build your grow house, which was expensive, and you had to do that before you received your licence. You needed capital to enter the market, before you could begin earning revenue, and institutional investors didn't want to touch marijuana. So the field of competitors was thin. Stigma kept the usual executives away from the sector, so there was a lack of professionals in the space. As Michael Haines and Trevor Fencott learned at Mettrum, the people who knew how to grow pot didn't have the money, and the people with money didn't want to touch weed. It was an opportunity if you had money, and could stomach the stigma, and the risk.

From the beginning, medical marijuana companies all had an extremely high burn rate. Facilities cost tens of millions of dollars to build, and there'd be no revenue until the company was licensed to sell pot, had grown its product, and had found people — without advertising, which was restricted — to buy it. Despite being a literal weed, marijuana is tricky to grow, and Health Canada had instituted stipulations on pesticides and tools of the black market trade, where many of the new legal growers would hail from. From the beginning, Linton thought pot as medicine would be huge.

"All you had to do was look at our initial patients, people needing something for sleep or dealing with multipurpose pain," he says, alluding to anxiety, depression, or even aching joints, all afflictions some say cannabis can help mend — and all "diagnosable" for legal Bruce Linton weed. "They needed something to move them through the day and night, rather than another pill."

Linton figured the audience of people who could benefit from a non-pharmaceutical pain medicine was vast. Plus, people loved weed. "I figured if we pay X for a building and grow these crops and sell them, it could pay for itself in less than two years." Linton believed that if he moved quickly, he could have an eighteen-month return on an investment of a few million dollars into his first production facility; if he moved slowly, other people would catch wind of his industry and the prices on assets would increase. "At the time, facilities were almost a free asset," he says, "but you had to move quickly, before the rest of the world caught up."

Linton has an aptitude for press and raising money, and he leaned on his contacts from the start-up world. The Bank of Montreal and the Canadian Imperial Bank of Commerce were non-starters for a marijuana company — the stigma of pot in 2013 was such that even the private equity firms wouldn't invest a penny. "When investment bankers who only get paid by raising you money tell you to bootstrap it for a year and that you shouldn't raise money, it's because they hate you," says Linton.

Lorne Gertner agrees. "If you were looking to raise money for your pot brand in 2013, they showed you the door."

Sean McNulty was thirty years old and working at the private equity firm MMCAP Asset Management when he first met Linton. McNulty was the perfect marijuana enabler. He had a chip on his shoulder, walking around Bay Street with a University of New Brunswick degree.

When Linton first entered the MMCAP office, they took the cannabis sector so lightly they sent in McNulty, their most junior guy, to meet him. Since grade ten, McNulty had smoked pot daily, and he's twice played in the World Series of Poker. Sean, known as "McSalty," is amiable, with an open face, and says he knows how to call a bluff. But as soon as he sat down with Linton, he saw a winning hand. Linton says he never saw someone write as quickly as McNulty taking notes during their first meeting.

"Investing in cannabis was one of the most compelling investment opportunities in the history of capitalism," McNulty says over Zoom, from the castle in the Cayman Islands where he now lives. "You're changing the source of supply on an already super-popular product, and there's no brands, no leaders, and Canada, of all places, is home to the capital markets."

In the United States, the capital markets couldn't invest in American pot companies. But the Canadian capital markets could help finance Canadian cannabis brands. They just needed to be convinced to do so. Linton would be the perfect person to connect the world of money with the world of weed. "I didn't understand why more people weren't instantly able to see what I did," says McNulty. "Literally, there's no other place in the world except Canada where capital markets are financing legal companies that sell weed."

When McNulty heard Linton's pitch, he was all in. He told the Tweed president that MMCAP would finance the company with $100 million and take Tweed public that spring. Sean McNulty saw Linton's dream. It was the deal he'd gotten into finance for, and, unlike Linton, he personally had experienced the healing properties of cannabis, which benefitted his everyday life. He thought the deal was too good to be true.

And to McNulty's bosses, it was. They vetoed his deal. The kid had egg on his face. "I had my tail between my legs, but that was it. I was thirty years old. No one fucking cared what I thought."

But Linton could see how the right audience got the picture. Even though MMCAP was out, McNulty was in, and he personally invested $50,000, half of all the money he had. One hundred million dollars was on the line. Weed could be big. So Linton kept raising money, phone call by phone call, closed door after closed door, until money — sometimes $1 million, sometimes $50,000 — started to trickle into his start-up. Just after Christmas, Linton spent $5 million and bought a closed-down Hershey factory in Smiths Falls, Ontario, to convert into the largest indoor cannabis grow op in the world. The address was 1 Hershey Drive.

"We bought that factory on December 28, 2013," Linton says. "If we didn't close another round of financing, we didn't have enough cash to start work on January 1."

Mark Zekulin was originally pitched to join Linton in parking and had his own business ideas — LED Christmas lights. Zekulin, then thirty-three, was a baby-faced trade lawyer who, in 2012, had grown bored with his work and was casting about for change. Something disruptive. Over a beer in Ottawa, Linton and Zekulin discussed the future. At first Zekulin wasn't sold: "God, am I wasting my time?" However, the idea stayed in his mind after the meeting. Patients would buy from the companies directly. Pharmacies wouldn't sell pot, so the companies would have to package and deliver each product, each gram. You could be vertically integrated selling marijuana. You took all the profit. Like Rifici, like McSalty, Zekulin got hung up on Linton's marijuana idea. He sums up his recollection in two words: "Holy fuck."

He told Linton, "Fuck parking meters — let's talk about this weed thing."

This weed thing grew as Linton perfected his investor roadshow and adapted a singular metric for evaluating the value of his business: yield capacity. There had never been a legal marijuana company beyond PPS. So how much could one of these be worth? Linton did the accounting. A gram cost $10 for a medical patient to purchase and could be produced for $3; Canadians annually spent $15 billion on prescribed drugs; and in 2015, 20 percent of Canadians said they'd smoked marijuana in the past year. So all Tweed had to do was corner a small percentage of both of those markets to be huge. Really, really huge. Yield capacity, accepted over time as the evaluating metric for a company's worth, would drive cannabis businesses to race to own acreage. Yield capacity meant the more space you owned, the more weed you could grow and the more your company was worth. The licensed producers would grow in acreage before they learned how to grow weed. But that wouldn't affect a company's stock price. Not yet. And investment bankers and hedge funds, places that nobody ever heard of, would begin to see things Bruce Linton's way. Pocketbooks began to open.

―――――

At Hydropothecary, Quebec's cannabis juggernaut-in-waiting, Sébastien St-Louis wanted in. He was on the phone everyday with Health Canada to check on the status of his production licence as he watched Linton draw capital to his company. He was experiencing bureaucratic difficulties straight out of Kafka. Not one of the Blessed 13, he was stuck in a queue for obtaining a medical licence, and there was no way to know where in the queue he stood. "It was a nightmare building this thing," says St-Louis, who I interviewed over the course of two crazy days in the fall of 2021. St-Louis, in starting his company, took out a $35,000 line of credit and raised money from every single one of his friends and family members. Following Health Canada's regulations, he plunked down $1.1 million to convert a farm in Quebec into a cannabis grow op before he could apply for a licence. The perimeter had to have cameras recording every angle twenty-four hours a day. He needed indoor and outdoor motion detection alarms. Buying and retrofitting the vault behind a seven-thousand-pound door cost $100,000.

Sébastien, a Bay Street virgin in an Under Armour T-shirt who had never tried marijuana, did all these things. And two and a half years passed before he even knew if he'd be approved to sell medical-grade weed. He read about Linton in the paper, and the then twenty-nine-year-old was undeterred. "I missed the dot-com boom. This, I was not going to miss."

On May 26, 2015, Hydropothecary finally received their licence. They were number seventeen. "I saw the legal medical marijuana business as an industry, not as big as it would become. I thought a billion dollars," he says. He mapped out what he saw for the future of his company. "I wanted to build a cash flow business, not take it public, just build this nice $10 or $20 million business and build it small, run it privately, and generate a ton of cash. I knew marijuana was a cash business and knew marijuana would evolve."

———•

For Linton, evolution wouldn't wait. Just like with those plant materials, whatever they were, from Kelowna, Linton found in cannabis a dog he could run. Unorthodox methods were rewarded in an industry making its rules in real time. Lightning in a bottle, the scale of these first medical weed companies began to grow, fast. It had already been established through the millennia that people liked to smoke weed. And now they could. Legally. For their health.

At Mettrum, Fencott and Haines had five thousand patients by the end of 2015. They had a 60,000-square-foot production facility forecasted to annually produce 3,500 kilograms of weed. Based on their operating metrics and their funded-capacity math — the accepted formula of the time, which equated greenhouse capacity with a potential crop yield and could forecast a revenue figure — the cannabis represented $60 million in sales, plus more with the potential for extracts. Press was coming around on these companies, and that attracted patients and further investments alike. It was momentum for a nascent industry, and Linton introduced a threshold to his PR team: a cannabis story would be incomplete if it didn't include Tweed.

Meanwhile, as the business story took hold and the original hippie cannabis activists grew more irate — the hatred for PPS now finding a focus in

Bruce Linton — there was a parallel reduction in stigma. Whether or not a broken-down chocolate factory in Smiths Falls was a good place to grow marijuana didn't matter. The Hershey factory made pot, and Linton, seem cute. Not criminal. Certainly not dangerous. Approachable. "Hi," read a button Linton wore pinned to his blazer over his Tweed shirt — from Terry Parker to a Hershey's Kiss. The attention taught Linton a lesson in publicity and the public markets. A bad deal can be reframed, or even turned into a good deal, because even if you lost money or your idea didn't work, the attention could boost your stock. Making a name for yourself was valuable when introducing a stigmatized market to the skeptical world.

There was very little to differentiate one medical marijuana company from another. By government design, the industry was not built to create successful businesses. It was designed to take crime out of cannabis and get safe products away from minors and onto legal shelves. Bedrocan, Mettrum, and all the other marijuana companies weren't allowed to advertise their existence, and the Canadian Medical Association still wouldn't endorse pot as a medicine. Despite Linton's efforts, it was entirely possible to live in Canada and not even know we had legal medical cannabis. The other executives worked hard at being inoffensive and mature. Not Bruce. He wanted to be memorable. There hadn't been buzz in the sector until now. Linton was making pot look fun. Get rich quick. And the publicity from the purchase of the Hershey factory and the ensuing narrative — marijuana company comes into Smiths Falls, Ontario, where the old chocolate factory's been closed since 2008 and brings jobs back to a devastated sector on the promise of legal weed — introduced investors, and Canadians, to the new world of marijuana. It was the parking meter dream, only it worked: a marijuana chocolate factory with Linton as Willy Wonka. He was born for the part. He loved it. It boosted his bottom line.

Linton had big ideas. Easy to underestimate, he looked like Gary Busey and spoke quickly. He had gaps in his front teeth and was relentless, passionately endorsing a product he didn't use. Alfred E. Neuman on speed — disarming, charming, and unscripted, a reporter's dream. Bruce was raised on a farm and he had a tiny office at the Hershey factory. He let Zekulin have the big office because Bruce didn't like being cornered. If he got bored in a meeting, he could walk out and not have people in his space. Linton made work for other people as he knocked on the doors of every investor. He spoke to any reporter who requested him. He was a frequent guest on Yahoo Finance and Bloomberg and always, always wore his company shirt. He spoke to Canadians refamiliarizing themselves with marijuana. He spoke to people who invested on Robinhood, the buzzy amateur-investor trading app, people in line at his local Sobeys, and to CEOs of other companies.

The Mettrum team once met with U.S. rapper Wiz Khalifa. They rebranded the back half of the Budweiser Stage as the Mettrum Grass. The Tweed people were in the audience that night — Wiz was performing with Snoop — and Michael Haines from Mettrum took a selfie of Linton's team surrounded by Mettrum swag and sent it to Linton, who was livid. Any opportunity in marijuana had to be his.

Bruce also filled the information gap about weed. Every time he was interviewed, he helped reduce the stigma around marijuana and inform citizens and politicians that cannabis was a legitimate medicine. There wasn't empirical data that said a certain number of drags from a joint alleviated knee pain or a strain in a vape helped reduce anxiety and usher in sleep. Neither the Le Dain or Shafer Commission led to meaningful research, and Dr. Mark Ware still couldn't pinpoint, exactly, what pot did to help quiet the epilepsy in Terry Parker. Meanwhile, Mettrum or Tweed or Bedrocan couldn't legally make claims that their Space Cake or Pink Kush helped reduce nausea, promote creativity, relieve pain, or stimulate appetite. All they had were anecdotes that cannabis did all those things.

But it wasn't the same as Xanax or Percocet, or even a name-brand opioid like Oxycontin. For Oxy, a patient got a prescription and a drug identification number, Health Canada's system for tracking a medicine's ingredients and dose. Pot, even when it was legal as a medicine, wasn't dispensed like that. You couldn't get it at a pharmacy. (Today you can.) How to convince people that the drug of choice of Bob Marley was something you could use for nausea or anxiety while also hosting concerts for Wiz Khalifa and Snoop?

It wasn't easy. Pot remained a pseudo-medicine. You didn't buy Tylenol directly from Johnson & Johnson, but you did buy your marijuana directly from Tweed. The public had to be trained on the new world of cannabis.

Bruce Linton — who didn't use the product — was obsessed with showing the way first to Canadians and then to the rest of the world.

"Publicity would be one hundred percent of our marketing," Linton tells me. While Fencott and Haines focused on clarifying how to sell their pot as medicine, and Tom Flow at MedReleaf studied grow cycles and lights, Linton grabbed the spotlight. He was a businessman, but also an entertainer. His idols include Mark Cuban and Elon Musk. Getting attention led to getting money — even though the disconnect between appearances and reality, then as now, was stark. Every business wants their outward face to seem successful. But when Bruce Linton purchased the Hershey factory, animals freely roamed the grounds. The retrofit would be costly — and would take as long as the money would hold. Mark Zekulin remembers his introduction to Smiths Falls. Unlike the welcome the Mettrum team got in Port Severn, when Zekulin and Rifici met the mayor of Smiths Falls, they found an interested, even enthusiastic, audience. The mayor asked the Tweed executives if they wanted coffee. They said sure. So the mayor ran across the street to Tim Hortons.

Tweed had $7 million in the bank in February 2014, after closing its latest round of investments — Linton still making cold calls and enlisting McSalty to work clients on his end. But construction on the licensed production facility was over budget and Tweed was burning from $2 million to $3 million per month. It also had no revenue because it had no product. From the beginning of medical legalization, there were huge supply constraints.

"As soon as you got your licence, patients started calling, but you had to say, 'We have no cannabis for you, sir,'" remembers Trevor Fencott of Mettrum. The entire industry was in a race against time.

The lack of supply and the abundance of demand lit a fire under Bruce. "We were six months behind on production of a nine-month schedule and spending money like crazy, but the building wasn't going fast enough," Linton says. "We were supposed to have everything rolled out in April 2014, in time for the IPO, and know what we had? Nothing."

Rifici was still CEO and there were construction delays, and also whispers of impropriety. It was reported that Rifici had borrowed money from a contractor he hired in Smiths Falls. Linton says that his nascent pot company faced bankruptcy on Valentine's Day 2014. "I'm about to make a quarterly announcement and I knew the first question I'd get asked: What are you going to do about going bankrupt?" Linton leaned on his network and found a fund in New York willing to invest $15 million if he could produce another $5 million. It ended up being a "bought deal" for $22 million, a Canadian special, which diluted Bruce's company — and set the industry standard.

A bought deal means the investment bank commits to buying the entire offering from a company on the understanding that it will purchase all the shares made available on such an offering at a discount. This usually happens around an IPO, but not always. And the broker usually has the deal sold before launching the IPO, to hedge their bets. After a bought deal is finished, the investment bank now owns the company's shares, which it becomes their job to sell. The company becomes liquid, which is great for the brand and the bank; the bank earns commission every time someone buys or sells shares. This creates a financial story, and also creates hype, and moves a company away from fundamentals. Demand is being manufactured. The public, meanwhile — the retail investors, the marks — only gets their price after the funders have been paid. It was this first bought deal that gave Tweed the runway they needed for the $89 million valuation they received that April. McSalty's $100 million appraisal had been pretty close.

Tweed became the first legalization-era cannabis stock listed on the public market.

On April 4, 2014, Tweed shares opened at $4.60. Amanda Daley was brought in from Pfizer to head up medical sales for Tweed in August 2014; she remembers touring the facility in Smiths Falls in June. Linton told Daley he wanted to see the stock trade at $10. It seemed to her like a stretch. "They only had a small quantity of cannabis and were sold out and when I toured the mother room, I remember thinking, 'That's not a ton of plants,' and then they showed me the forty-two-hundred-square-foot vault — it was this big, cavernous room with shelf after shelf of nothing."

Linton fired Rifici after the company went public. His plan was to out-spend and outrace MedReleaf and Bedrocan. "When you're building assets, you can spend twice as much money as anybody else if you have a long-term plan," says Linton. "I thought long-term. So if I spend now, over the next three years my costs will be a third of the price to operate and my short-term pain of giving the stock away cheaper will be mitigated by higher margins and a competitive advantage. You're going to win, win, win if it costs your competitors three times as much to produce as you — aren't you glad they bought that shitty, cheap system?"

Now public, Linton was influencing the entire industry. Investment banks, Anson Funds, MMCAP, and Canaccord (not the big banks like Scotiabank, BMO, and RBC) saw a financial lever they could pull for an industry built on hype with inexperienced retail investors. Bought deals, assuming the investment banks could unload the weed stocks on the public, fuelled the industry's growth.

"Tweed was much more aggressive than us, with everything," says Mettrum's Michael Haines. "Even in Kelowna, we were importing hundreds of kilos, which I thought was a lot, but they had five times that weight. But that was Bruce, and I don't mean that as a compliment, not entirely. We had a shortage of product and problems with the product, as an industry, but he had stars in his eyes and brought capital into our market."

Trevor Fencott says that, even back in 2014, Linton knew there was no way his company could ever make profits on the millions of dollars he raised and spent. "But the bankers didn't care," says Fencott. "They kept flushing money into Linton's coffers, and he kept spending, getting bigger. At one point, they had enough funded capacity to give weed to every medical patient in Canada — absurd, because they were just one of thirteen Canadian weed companies, and if their product wasn't the same as everyone else's, it was much worse."

Still Linton looked for ways to expand his operation. In the late fall of 2014, Bruce toured the Canadian Cannabis Corporation (CCC), which hadn't yet received its licence, but was beginning to build its facility and was well capitalized — apparently. At the time, CCC had a larger market cap than Tweed. The CCC team came to Smiths Falls to see Linton's operation, and then he went north of Toronto to see theirs.

"They had no plants, no lights. They had nothing. On paper, they could claim their worth was over $100 million, but its actual worth was no more than zero," Linton says.

Bruce began sussing out the marijuana environment with a new ethos: he would acquire companies, but he wouldn't partner with them. The CCC team made him uneasy. Cannabis still attracted bad seeds. In a market as regulated as legal weed, it was imperative to bend, but not break, the rules. Things slipped through the cracks, but the whole system was predicated on companies following the minutiae of the new MMPR laws. Bruce knew this. And unsavoury characters were drawn into the business, whether it be drug dealers or investors looking to pump and dump stocks. But above all else, a marijuana company had to protect its licence. Lose that, and you could no longer sell weed. This is why Linton wanted to handle the RCMP after the bust with Mettrum in Kelowna. The licence to sell marijuana was the entry stake to experiment, bend rules — make money.

It could be lost in a million big and little decisions every day.

———————

After the IPO, Linton instituted a company policy: his employees couldn't invest in other companies in the sector, but every Tweed employee would receive equity. In two years, formerly out-of-work manufacturers in Smiths Falls would grow rich. But they had to grow weed first, and it would've been easier, they were discovering, just to sell the designated growers' shit from BC. The licensed producers, as a block, discovered that pot remained expensive and tricky to grow.

Linton spent his way toward a solution. Every six months, he says, Tweed bought acceleration. "If you're not super strong, you have to make moves to show strength," he says. "You need to continue momentum, and if you feel it slipping, you catalyze energy because the narrative always needs advancing."

It's the *narrative* that needs advancing. A nascent industry is like a shark; it needs to keep swimming, or it will die. The worst thing Tweed could've done was to quietly keep building. Bruce didn't want to be everyone else. So Linton needed to buy something to stay in front of investors and send out a press release saying that bought deals were now being offered to him.

Bruce began eying Marc Wayne's Bedrocan. Bedrocan was a European medical cannabis company, and Marc Wayne directed its operation in Canada. Bruce's interest was opportune because the young CEO was beginning to feel the shackles of his corporate parent on his wrists. Canada was moving quicker than the Netherlands, and having an out-of-touch boss in Europe was frustrating to an executive who'd spent so much time getting to this moment, from his first joints with his mom.

After considering a deal with Mettrum, Wayne met with Linton, and the two former competitors sat with Wayne's stepfather, Murray Goldman, the real estate tycoon. They hatched a plan: join forces with Bruce and together attract all the capital. Wayne says, "I didn't want to be the Canadian arm of Bedrocan. They were handcuffing me on so many things."

Wayne wanted to hold more clinical trials and hone in on the medical properties of marijuana that had been restricted for so many years. This had been his interest since joining the Canadian Consortium for the Investigation of Cannabinoids with Mark Ware in 2008. Now, as founder of his own medical cannabis company, he wanted more. "The CEO in the Netherlands was closing this door and that door. I didn't want to be a bit player in this industry I'd already been working in for so long," says Wayne. Bedrocan was one of the most respected cannabis companies in the world, but Wayne knew, even back then, there were too many companies in Canada doing the same thing. Better to partner with Bruce Linton. The winning Canadian cannabis company would be whichever one had the most scale.

Linton scaled first. He saw the industry as a game of Pac-Man, and he could become more powerful eating up other companies, like ghosts. He says the decision to acquire Bedrocan — which he did by selling 33.9 million common shares, worth a paper $61 million — was instinctive, fast. "I gave up forty-five percent of the company and people said, 'Holy shit! You gave away half of your company to buy a company that's one-twelfth the size of you. Why the fuck did you do that?' Well, a lot of people said that was a bad move, but we needed it for the brand position."

The brand position Tweed achieved from Bedrocan was valuable because its Dutch pedigree helped book clients otherwise unable to differentiate among weed strains. "There wasn't anything particular about the process or product — it was the same stuff — but Dutch cannabis had that allure," Linton says. Allure being the most valuable commodity of the day.

After Bruce Linton made the deal for Bedrocan, two other things quickly fell into place. The first one began with a phone call from the TSX. Companies could now move to four-letter ticker symbols and they wanted to know if Linton wanted "WEED."

"We were calling on life insurance companies to put some of their funds in us, and though they ignored us, I wasn't jonesing to call us 'WEED,'" Linton says. "But also, fuck it — there was zero institutional money behind us, and of course, I couldn't let someone else have 'WEED.' In the end I just said, 'Fuck it. Let's make the brand.'"

———

The deal for Bedrocan was announced in the summer of 2014 and made Tweed Marijuana the largest medical marijuana company in the country. Tweed's stock rose 15 percent on the deal, and though Bedrocan's shareholders would receive 33.9 million shares in their deal, Linton cemented his early legacy and the template for Canadian weed companies. It's like when two celebrities hook up. Their popularity is squared. Linton's new market cap was over $150 million. He had combined the market caps of two rival companies and, in doing so, raised the value of the entire enterprise by 15 percent. He was catalyzing energy at last. "What you're buying," he told me, "is acceleration."

After the Bedrocan deal, Tweed would need a new name. With Linton's jockeying and laissez-faire approach, the Tweed brand was beginning to seem stoneresque, a strange bedfellow for Bedrocan, which was scientific and pristine. "The companies Tweed and Bedrocan had to be sisters, and I was fussing with the idea of an umbrella, but that's a rainy-day instrument. Canopy is a pleasant environment — let's go under the canopy and have iced tea."

On September 21, 2015, Tweed officially became Canopy Growth. The company now had a funded capacity of 573,000 square feet.

Mark Zekulin moved his young family closer to Smiths Falls, and after Linton fired Rifici, he made Zekulin CEO, while he became president and chairman of the board. But, to put it mildly, the company was still working out kinks. Canopy Growth may have been worth a paper $150 million, but operationally the business was green. The previous year, when Rifici was still CEO, Tweed Marijuana was licensed to sell its first gram. At the Hershey factory, the head of operations put the bud in the jar. Zekulin, then the president of the company, and Rifici, the CEO, drove the jar to the post office. Heading back to Smiths Falls, they received a phone call from the head of operations, worried that the size of the THC sticker was too small on the packaging. "I might have screwed something up," he said. "Don't send the weed."

Rifici and Zekulin turned the car around and raced to the post office to retrieve their bud.

Health Canada was incentivized to crack down on rule breakers to establish its governance of the sector. Episodes like Kelowna had embarrassed regulators, so now the approach was "Lose your licence, you're done." You might have to wait two years to be licensed again, and there was already a queue of new companies waiting for their licences. Zekulin stepped on the gas. You couldn't send out a jar with wrong labels. An inch could cost your whole company.

"We could just see the headlines: After First Gram Sold, Tweed Marijuana Experiences First Recall," Linton recalls.

The first fulfillment of a legal gram of Canopy Growth marijuana required three members of the company's C-suite to deliver. It took the three of them to affix the sticker. Into this climate things were about to super-size.

CHAPTER 7

Justin Time

"I'm in favour of legalizing it."

Justin Trudeau

"This is fucking batshit crazy."

Amy Weinstein

Justin Trudeau began planning his run for the Liberal leadership in 2012, a year after NDP leader Jack Layton succumbed to cancer and a year before Stephen Harper introduced the Marihuana for Medical Purposes Regulations. Trudeau, forty on his ascent, was the anti-Harper and the Canadian answer to the Obama wave. Obama, in his memoir *Dreams from My Father*, says he has used weed "and maybe even a little blow." Harper, faced with slogans of "Hope" and "Change" galvanizing North America, was seeing his popularity plummet. In addition to his punitive crime policies, under which prison populations increased and 3.8 million Canadians were convicted of a criminal offence, there was a sense that the country was moving forward without him.

In September 2015, a viral photograph of the body, washed up on a Turkish beach, of Alan Kurdi, a two-year-old Syrian refugee who had family in Canada, became emblematic of Harper's immigration rules. These weren't all Harper's problems, but his whole ethos — setting up a hotline to document "barbaric cultural practices," praising "old-stock Canadians" during a leader's debate, and banning the niqab during citizenship swearing-in ceremonies — seemed to confirm that Harper was a man out of time.

Pierre Elliott Trudeau once rolled with John Lennon. Now his son Justin was our ascending Obama. A feminist, in 2017 he was on the cover of *Rolling Stone*. Pierre had backpacked the world and spent time in Morocco, and gave off the impression that late 1960s peddlers wouldn't mistake him for a narc. Meanwhile, Margaret Trudeau, Pierre's wife and Justin's mother, was a famous and beautiful sophisticate, enjoying the Studio 54 nightlife and probably smoking hash in 1977 at the El Mocambo in Toronto with the Rolling Stones. Whether that story is true or not, certainly those kinds of whispers weren't gravitating around Stephen Harper's mom. Justin Trudeau was cast as a daisy to Harper's stone.

Conversations about cannabis legalization had stalled after Paul Martin resigned. Many thought if there was going to be an end to cannabis prohibition, it would be the handiwork of Jack Layton during the NDP's moment of popularity, known as the Orange Wave. But Layton never supported full recreational legalization. Instead, like Jean Chrétien, he only went as far as "decrim," which would make possession of up to fifteen grams of cannabis a ticketed, but not arrestable, offence. Layton didn't want the NDP to be the opposition party. He wanted to be the party in power, and the marijuana platform would not, in his estimation, put him on a path to victory. He already had Zöe — Harper's imaginary leftist voter — voting for him. His job was to get the vote of her stepmom. Layton turned out to be wrong.

When he declared his bid for leadership, Justin Trudeau had spent four years as a Liberal MP in Papineau, Quebec, and he was left of the NDP on the cannabis file. Like his parents, a member of the in-crowd, Justin Trudeau even went further in disclosing his personal drug use than Obama, in 2013 telling *Huffington Post* reporters that, while in office, he'd puffed on a joint that his friend sparked at his house when the kids were away with their grandparents. For the Liberals, the third-place party, he became Man of the Moment, trouncing Joyce Murray and Martha Hall Findlay in the leadership election. There were other factors, but cannabis was to become an important wedge issue that separated Stephen Harper from power.

On July 23, 2013, Trudeau announced a key pillar of his election platform, cannabis legalization, at a campaign stop in Kelowna — so many pot-growing, pot-smoking, pot-everything moments happen there. Fresh-faced, his hair skimming the collar of his purple short-sleeve shirt, Trudeau saw a man in the crowd with a sign calling for the legalization of marijuana. "I see my friend waving a sign about decriminalizing cannabis. I'll take that as a question," shouted Trudeau, looking like a summer camp counsellor with a day pass in the bright British Columbia sun. "I'm actually not in favour of decriminalizing cannabis. I'm in favour of legalizing it.… It's one of the only ways to keep it out of the hands of our kids because the current war on drugs, the current model, is not working. We have to use evidence and science to make sure that we're moving forward." Mr. Trudeau knew what he was doing that morning. Unprompted, he announced a campaign promise that would place Canada alongside only Uruguay in its approach to marijuana: the end of prohibition — federal recreational legalization, full stop. Not a business story, but a story about public health.

Legalizing recreational pot had always been the goal of the medical marijuana movement. Alan Young says legalization for medical purposes was just a Trojan horse — a way of moving toward full legalization. Trudeau, by 2013, was seeing massive changes take place in how weed was being treated to the south. In the U.S., Colorado and California had already legalized medical marijuana, and their dispensary model and licensed distributors were seen as a tourism- and tax-generating success. America's system was governed by the states. Pot wasn't federally legal, and the weed brands couldn't bank or ship their weed across state lines. But a legalization experiment had been started. And there had not been a *Reefer Madness*–like increase in debilitated drivers or a youth drug epidemic in either state. Instead, there was an economic boost, favourable publicity, and an orderly road map for a progressive end to prohibition.

Meanwhile, across Canada during the Harper years, we already had public companies on our stock exchange selling weed. For most of the Canadian pot pioneers, the activists and the growers, the promise of recreational legalization felt like a victory, like a lifestyle validation. They had been right about weed all along.

There was only one problem: assuming Trudeau was elected and his campaign promise proved true, where would Canada get all its weed? With only the medical system in play, there was already a scarcity of supply. If Canadian producers couldn't grow enough marijuana for 20,000 people, what would happen when legal recreational weed arrived, when 20 percent of the population might want a doobie, more than 7 million people trying to get stoned? In the second quarter of 2014, Canada had 7,914 medical cannabis patients. By the end of 2016, there were 129,876 medical cannabis patients.

The compounded annual growth rate was more than 15 percent. Health Canada data said that the licensed producers should have been distributing 18,087 kilos of dried marijuana, which should have been more than enough. Yet patients ordering from any of the legal companies often found strains were sold out. Of course, delivery discrepancies could have been — but were not — a red flag for the valuations of the public Canadian cannabis companies. Investors were looking at the numbers and seeing what the salesmen wanted them to see. Would Canada be able to produce enough marijuana? To find out, Trudeau was going to have to pass his groundbreaking bill.

———

Andrew Leslie is a retired lieutenant-general in the Canadian armed forces who fought in Bosnia and Afghanistan and was recruited by both Prime Minister Harper and Prime Minister Justin Trudeau to represent their sides in federal politics. After leading troops abroad, Leslie headed up disaster relief programs in Manitoba and Montreal. It's Leslie who said, regarding his intended transformation of the Canadian military, "more tooth and less tail."

According to Leslie, who had no moral qualms about cannabis and, as a father of two teenage children, believed that kids — "a staggering number of Canadian youth" — were already smoking unregulated pot, legalizing marijuana wasn't a radical policy platform. He joined the Liberal party after Trudeau announced his plan to legalize cannabis during his first term if he got elected. Leslie says his Liberal colleagues in the House of Commons fell in line with Trudeau's mandate. "Anybody who aspired to be a Liberal candidate in 2014 had to sign a statement that they supported three of Mr. Trudeau's key objectives — one of them being legal pot," Leslie said. The only opposition to the bill came from the oldest 10 percent of the caucus, but Leslie figured those who were unhappy bit their tongue, recognizing that it was a societal trend that wasn't worth trying to disrupt.

In November 2015, after the election, Leslie would become the chief Liberal whip, and it was his job to make sure Trudeau had enough votes to pass the Cannabis Act, Bill C-45, which would legalize marijuana.

For the Conservatives, during the election campaign, pot became a wedge issue that they hammered home, as the Conservative political operative Ken Boessenkool explains, especially in immigrant communities. In attack ads translated into Mandarin and Punjabi, Prime Minister Harper decreed that the Liberals want your kids on drugs. In response to this messaging, Trudeau's team smoothed out their own marijuana value proposition; rather than an issue of societal advances, legalizing pot became a matter of protecting Andrew Leslie's teenage daughters. The Liberals don't want to give your kids drugs, they assured voters. Your kids are already on drugs. What the Liberals want to do is make sure that the drugs they're using are safe.

Kelly Coulter was the national campaign director of NORML Canada — the National Organization for the Reform of Marijuana Laws — and became the first woman on their board in 2010. According to Coulter, NORML Canada first set its sights on Jack Layton. "Jack was a pretty groovy guy," she tells me, but admits being frustrated by his approach to this file. Despite appearances, Layton just wouldn't go in on legalization. He even worked to silence fellow NDPers who wanted to push the legalization, not decriminalization, objective. Dana Larsen, cannabis book author and former BC politician, ended up relinquishing his NDP membership when his cannabis views were deemed outside the Jack Layton party line.

So Coulter began courting Trudeau, even before his campaign speech in Kelowna. Coulter says Trudeau was initially onboard only with decrim, but she helped him reframe the issue. She met with him in 2012 in his office on the Hill. "It was a tiny MP office, very intimate, and he's quite tall, and I remember that when we were sitting, our knees were bumping," Coulter tells me. "The first thing he says is 'Oh, don't worry. I'm all in favour of decriminalizing,' and as he's saying that, I have a bad poker face, I feel my head shaking: NO. His eyes look at me like, 'Are you disagreeing with me?'"

Coulter didn't want decrim. She wanted an end to cannabis prohibition, and she produced an encyclopedia's worth of handouts in favour of legalization: pamphlets that described the safety of the legal medical marijuana market, the Canadian companies working in the space, and the rigour of the entire manufacturing and distributing process. She said something that caught Trudeau's attention and that he'd repeat in his own interviews down the road: "Al Capone would love decriminalization." Decriminalization creates a grey zone, she told him. Organized crime thrives in the margins. Confusion creates a bad-guy revenue stream.

"I saw the change in him: I can sell this," Coulter recalls, with considerable glee. Trudeau had a legal pad and, like McSalty when he first met Linton, took ravenous notes: If we make a safe, legal recreational market, we will hurt criminals while we tax their products and reinvest the harmonized sales tax into drug education. Investing in the country while protecting your kids. Trudeau smiled. He was going to use the drug laws to create a new Canadian revenue stream, from weed. Coulter was going to walk down Sussex Drive smoking a jay.

"I felt like the Cheshire cat that had just swallowed the canary," she says. "We got him."

In the run-up to the elections, Trudeau discussed the marijuana file with the *Huffington Post*; Harper and Thomas Mulcair both refused to have that conversation. In the interview, published on August 22, 2013, the future prime minister mentioned his meeting with Coulter: "That line of argument did [go] a long way towards convincing me," he said.

He also disclosed his family's cannabis history. Michel Trudeau, Justin's youngest brother, was the most carefree of the Trudeau children and the one most familiar with weed. Trudeau said that when his brother fell to his death on a rock-climbing expedition in Kokanee Glacier Provincial Park in 1998, he was awaiting trial on a cannabis conviction. He'd been in a car accident, the future PM said. The police arrived. "One of the cops cleaning up the scene found a little cigarette box with a bit of pot in it," said Trudeau. At the time, 475,000 Canadians had criminal records because of marijuana possession. His brother could've been months away from receiving his own, and if he happened to avoid being convicted, it would be due to his privilege. Black and Indigenous men had more than three times the odds of conviction than white men, even though research shows that all races enjoy the same rate of pot smoking. Trudeau's brother just happened to get caught.

Akwasi Owusu-Bempah says the Black and Indigenous populations are targeted. Expungement of non-violent cannabis convictions, he believes, should have been part of Trudeau's original Cannabis Act. The case against his brother was one of the reasons he was in favour of decriminalizing pot in the first place. Trudeau was building his election platform. But unlike what we would later see in American cities like Oakland and New York, which made special efforts at reparation to give business opportunities to communities directly affected by disproportionate cannabis policing, there were Canadian communities Trudeau was leaving behind.

"Trudeau and his policy makers didn't even think about us," says Owusu-Bempah, adding that legalization in Canada still hasn't done enough to make amends with the communities most punished by biased criminal policing around marijuana. "There's no doubt the Cannabis Act was a good piece of legislation and cost Trudeau a good amount of political capital — it was always a risk. I just wish his staff had been more diverse and race had been thought through."

Indeed, Trudeau, though seeing the world through privilege, was taking a risk with marijuana legalization. In his biography on the prime minister,

Promise and Peril: Justin Trudeau in Power, author Aaron Wherry said something that was repeated by Andrew Leslie: Trudeau, when he puts his mind to something, is fearless. Once he locked into legalizing pot, there was no turning back.

"He's a risk-taker. It surprises people," says Andrew Leslie, adding that Trudeau's team in charge of the file, Jody Wilson-Raybould at Justice, Jane Philpott at Health, and Bill Blair, the former head of Toronto's police force, heading the cannabis task force, covered the sector with the Liberal's best minds. "Justin Trudeau has a switch in him, and when it's activated, as it was with marijuana, he goes all in," says Leslie. "It's impressive."

Justin Trudeau defeated Stephen Harper in the Canadian federal election on October 19, 2015. Legalizing marijuana was a first-term priority. Anne McLellan, former minister of justice and former minister of health, was appointed by Trudeau's newly formed cannabis task force to lead the revolution. She still had never tried cannabis. But for a second time she was tasked with overhauling her country's cannabis laws. "I hadn't thought much about cannabis other than seeing developments happening, but I got this call: 'Anne, we'd like you to lead our task force.' My initial response was 'I'm not the right person. I keep telling you guys.'"

McLellan had been on the enforcement side of the cannabis file and, though her view had swayed toward legalizing pot — like Andrew Leslie, she had no moral qualms with the concept — despite overseeing both the MMAR *and* MMPR laws, she still had no personal connection to the plant. McLellan is the Forrest Gump of weed: by accident, she keeps showing up in pot history. She says that by the time she accepted the appointment, legalization was a *fait accompli*.

"Mr. Trudeau made the promise of legalization in November 2015 and wanted that promise delivered by the election in 2019," McLellan says. Her job was to figure out how to turn the MMPR laws into a system through which Canadians could get pot gummies in the same way they got light beer.

Hilary Black, now working at Canopy after Bedrocan's acquisition by Bruce Linton's company, helped McLellan meet with a vast array of people and organizations on both sides of the law, including police chiefs, cannabis activists, Indigenous Elders, and the Canadian Medical Association, which wanted to end Canada's medical marijuana program and have all patients consume their cannabis recreationally. Black thought the medical program needed to be saved. People like Terry Parker who used pot to fight epilepsy shouldn't pay a tax on their medicine. Pot should be legal just like wine, but for soldiers smoking MedReleaf bud to combat PTSD, it was not recreational. It was important to Black that the task force understand how marijuana could be both things.

Meanwhile, in Black's activist circles, Canopy — the biggest pot company in the world — represented the very worst of corporate marijuana. "Working with Canopy is like working with the devil," read one typically brutal tweet. Jodie Giesz-Ramsay (formerly Jodie Emery) took to calling the company Canopy Gross. Activists barred from the industry heard of Rifici's Ottawa connections and the incredible cannabis market caps, tried their terrible weed, and no longer saw themselves reflected in the culture they loved. Rosie Rowbotham said, "What the fuck had these rich kids ever done for the culture?"

Hilary Black, meanwhile, defended Linton's company — and thus government weed — because she believed government weed was better with activists inside the corporate boardrooms.

"We circled the wagons around the task force and made them consult patients with the Canadian AIDS Society [and] Canada Arthritis Society, and Anne really did meet the patients," says Black. "She'd never seen cannabis work directly as medicine, but I was in the room with her and she's hearing from a twenty-year homicide detective who, from PTSD, lost his family and lost [his] house. He had serious psychiatric issues, he told Anne McLellan, and had his life saved by cannabis."

McLellan says that, as important as the cannabis file was to her prime minister, she was granted autonomy. "I made it clear: if I was going to do this, I was in charge," she says. She had five months for her task force to render their verdict on what the Cannabis Act should include. "Shows what you can do when you put your mind to something," McLellan tells me. "Marijuana produced the fastest task force in Canadian history for such a major public policy change."

That major policy change — the end of cannabis prohibition — determined that provinces would decide their own approaches to point of sales and distribution and that the edible market wouldn't begin on day one of legal weed. There was a possession cap of 30 grams of legal marijuana per individual, and all attempts at advertising cannabis would be banned. Cannabis, with regard to marketing, would be regulated like tobacco, not spirits or beer. McLellan neither expunged cannabis convictions from people with marijuana arrests nor got rid of the medical program.

While legalization wound its way through the government, illegal cannabis wound its way through the streets. First in Vancouver and then in Montreal and Toronto, underground retail dispensaries began popping up around the country when Trudeau took office. It was big business. It was brazen. It was stores selling weed and edibles in plain sight, despite pot still being against the law, and the police, by and large, leaving these storefront weed shops alone, as they had with the original medical dispensaries in Vancouver.

Some illegal operators even franchised. Marc Emery and Jodie Giesz-Ramsay, who had maintained their spokesperson status through the years, had a chain called Cannabis Culture that operated nineteen illegal weed stores across Ontario, BC, and Quebec. They had now the type of business that legalization would usher in: shops where you could buy marijuana and marijuana products. None of it was licensed, and the pot (and hash and edibles, but not mushrooms or coke) for sale was outside the Health Canada system. You couldn't buy Canopy weed at Cannabis Culture. But Marc and Jodie had a name brand, and sold their Cannabis Culture naming rights to entrepreneurial, risk-taking shop owners for $25,000.

With legalization coming, cannabis sellers concluded that they would no longer be arrested for selling pot. If Jodie and Marc could do it, why couldn't they? Clusters of illegal pot shops — places where dogs roamed freely and strains were distributed in film canisters and Ziploc bags — erected sandwich boards on the sidewalk, advertising discounted pounds. The pot was untested. The stores were unlicensed. Rumours circulated that a shop could bring in more than an untaxed million a week. The weed was really good.

"This is fucking batshit crazy," says Amy Weinstein, who worked at one of Toronto's first grey market pot shops in 2016. She was twenty-four years old and had just spent the summer following Phish on tour. To Weinstein, the shops were a natural stop along the path of legalization, and she figured the operation she was running would be grandfathered into the legal market for the price of a licensing fee, which is what ultimately happened in Vancouver. Instead, the illegal dispensary system in Toronto vigorously grew from three shops to thirty and then, just before a huge police bust in May 2016 dubbed Project Claudia, to more than one hundred illegal stores openly selling illegal weed. On the streets, it was hard to know that the Cannabis Act had not passed yet. It was hard to know that these stores were against the law. Some people, however, knew. The pot stores were being robbed. Criminals, even pre-legalization marijuana criminals, couldn't call the police.

It was all very chaotic and another of marijuana's famous grey zones, because it became common practice for an illegal pot shop to be shuttered by the police one day only to reopen the next.

Dealer's Choice: Illegal dispensary weed. A cop in Toronto would confiscate then consume an edible from a store like this and later call for backup when he found himself up a tree.

"I couldn't believe what I became involved with," Weinstein says, because she was an activist hippie. But the culture was pivoting from activists to gangsters to bankers to some kind of weird amalgamation of all three. Even the police couldn't tell who was who. Hilary Black sold pot at the BC Compassion Club from growers she knew. The new dispensaries, mostly, were more like parts of a criminal syndicate, says Weinstein. Before Project Claudia, when a shop got busted, it wasn't rare for police to find, in addition to cash and weed, guns and hard drugs.

The climate lent itself to lawlessness, as drugs always do. The whole legalization gambit was designed to create a regulated system. And yet, when there were four weed stores between my house on the west side of Toronto and my daughter's daycare two blocks away, it was hard to know what the rules were: for consumers, for companies, for cops. The shops were illegal, the marijuana wasn't Health Canada tested, but there they were. There *I* was, buying pot — good pot, illegally — in broad daylight right beside another daycare dad.

Lorne Gertner had a different vision for his pot store. He'd been waiting his whole life to stake a claim in the cannabis movement and had invested in half of the legal pot companies before market data proved out if the product he loved would catch on in the mainstream. But he knew how to build a brand, was connected to the entire industry, and gave many of the first-wave founders money or, at the very least, connections or investment advice. His dream was to make the legal pot shops look like Apple stores, Lululemon boutiques. He believed that cannabis had to shed its stigma — the antithesis to what the current crop of pot shops had done — and that marijuana could be an upscale, curated experience. He wanted to do for pot what he had once done for his father's line of women's clothes.

"We would walk to work every day and pass by lineups outside these illegal dispensaries," says Alan Gertner, Lorne's son, who left Silicon Valley and Google to co-found, alongside his dad, a new retail concept. In 2016, father and son opened a boutique art shop called Tokyo Smoke on Adelaide Street in Toronto, dispensing coffee with panache, style, and design. Lorne wanted to mix marijuana with art and fashion and create a new look for cannabis: bespoke, expensive, chic.

The thuggish, self-righteous hippies who went after Hilary also wanted Lorne's head. Gertner says he received death threats when he introduced a $2,000 solid gold bong. In Toronto's Kensington Market, windows of a legal, upscale pot store would later be smashed. It could be dangerous changing the value proposition of weed, and Tokyo Smoke generated a lot of attention, good and bad. Pot went from the business pages to the style pages, but even in this strange in-between time — when pot was illegal and yet everywhere — Gertner still couldn't legally sell any of Bruce Linton's marijuana. While he waited for the Cannabis Act to take effect, he sold double doubles surrounded by illegal weed stores.

"We were fascinated watching this experiment, but were excited to have our day in the future," says Alan Gertner. His dad echoes the sentiment.

The Godfather: Lorne Gertner, who invested in Prairie Plant Systems, helped launch Cronos Group and sold Tokyo Smoke to Canopy Growth for more than $500 million. Gertner first smoked pot in Jamaica in his teens.

Lorne says he was never tempted to sell illegal weed because he aimed to educate consumers about marijuana. He wanted Prime Minister Justin Trudeau to succeed — a mission he still believes in today. And for the legal market to succeed, eventually police would have to close the illegal shops because the black market pot would affect the legal companies' bottom lines. Gertner trusted the process, smoked legal weed with his medical licence, and opened Tokyo Smoke stores in Manitoba and Toronto, before legalization. It helped that he was well capitalized.

"We believed legalization was going to happen," says Gertner. "It's where we parked everything."

CHAPTER 8

Rolling

"Do I think we're overvalued? Fuck no."

Terry Booth

The Bedrocan deal and the birth of Canopy Growth helped kick off a flurry of public offerings, mergers, convertible debentures, and acquisitions — with market valuations based on narratives, not profit margins. Investment firms like the one run by Sean McNulty's bosses at MMCAP — who'd turned away deals in the sector prior to the Canopy IPO — had a change of heart after Bruce's IPO and Trudeau's election promise.

Soon, retail investors wanted weed stocks on the public markets, which made bought deals easy money for investment firms. Michael Haines at Mettrum says he couldn't play a round of golf without somebody wanting to make a deal. Pot went from "no can do" to "no can miss," and it was retail investors, especially the pot-smoking ones, making the bulk of the trades. The Robinhood Market was fire. Pot stocks were liquid. Liquid stocks moved up in worth.

Canopy opened at around four dollars on the Toronto Stock Exchange on April 4, 2014. Bruce Linton says the IPO was the best publicity his company could receive. But it was more than that. It was good PR for the sector. Canopy, using the WEED ticker, was over eighteen dollars by the end of 2015. What Linton had promised Amanda Daley, the former sales rep from Pfizer, turned out to be true. Linton was a prognosticator. The Canopy cannabis vaults were still empty. The secret sauce was this: it didn't matter. In a speculative economy, attention was more valuable than weed. But the investment banks weren't really making investments. They were doing cannabis bought deals, selling their stock, and recycling the capital into another brand. In a sense, it was just as sketchy as the illegal pot stores. Illusions. Recycled capital is how Aphria, Aurora, and Cronos grew and also how a company could be worth over $1 billion and still have trouble making payroll. Value was much different than cash.

The number of patients in Canada's medical cannabis system was increasing as the big pot companies prepared for recreational legalization. But product availability remained a problem, and so, while the licensed cannabis companies expanded their production facilities, Health Canada began expediting its licensing. The moat, slowly, was being drained, and young hustling entrepreneurs got their chance to enter the game.

Hydropothecary, Sébastien St-Louis's company, submitted its licence request on July 13, 2013. It would be June 2015 before it was approved. The company received the first medical marijuana licence in Quebec. "Very quickly I learned the art of the possible," St-Louis told me. He and his brother-in-law, Adam Miron, were originally going to be a small private company. They were green and they knew it; they had gumption and pride. "Neither of us come from wealth. My parents were teachers, very middle class. Nobody in my family knew how the stock market worked."

When St-Louis arrived on Bay Street, he was in for an awakening: cannabis had grown. "Nobody was interested in a $10 million plan. 'Do you have a $100 million plan?' they asked me. I recalibrated quickly. 'Yeah, I have one,' I said. 'Let's go.'"

Terry Booth at Aurora Cannabis, the first Alberta-based licensed producer, emerged as a different kind of cannabis executive: rougher, brasher than Bruce Linton. Michael Haines and Trevor Fencott at Mettrum had cited paperwork as their superpower. Booth's superpower would be volume.

He wasn't afraid to be impolite. He hadn't grown up with a silver spoon; he had been an electrician. And from the beginning, studying the moves of Bruce Linton, Booth emerged as an executive hell-bent on liquidity and size. From greenhouses to hydroponic light companies, from dispensaries to rival weed brands, he bought something new every week, and his Canaccord bankers, especially Graham Saunders, legally milked this capitalist tool. In a sense, Booth was a vessel from which other people's money could be made. Saunders was a master of convertible debentures, which are a financial tool for raising money. A debenture is an unsecured loan from a company — that is, it is not backed by any collateral — but it can be turned into stock shares in the company if the debt hasn't been repaid at the agreed-upon time. In other words, it is a loan with a ticking time bomb attached. Saunders not only helped Booth at Aurora raise money, but also advised on his acquisitions, thus getting paid twice: as a financial adviser and taking commission on acquisition. Raising more money, buying more things, bigger things, selling more shares, and then doing it again and again.

It was the cocaine approach to building a company: aggressive short-term moves that felt good fast and produced results quickly. Acquisitions and rounds of investment boosted Aurora's share price while million-dollar losses became normal, and rival weed brands were forced to follow Terry Booth or risk being left behind.

Out in Edmonton, Terry Booth thought the competition, who didn't even smoke weed, was soft. He wasn't intimidated by the black market, or by Bay Street, where he felt like he was looked down upon by the moneyed Toronto- and Vancouver-based nucleus of weed. He didn't care. It was motivation. Starving for power and recognition, Booth — foul-mouthed, lavish, a player-coach who really did care for the plant — was an arsonist: loved by his employees, tearing down tradition with glee. In 2013, Booth invested $3 million to start Aurora. Three years later, Yosemite Sam had nine hundred employees. Aurora was worth $5.2 billion in 2016, with less than $50 million in revenue; according to the *Globe*, $779 million came from investors. Terry's plan, influenced by Bruce Linton and thirsty tier-three bankers, was working — his market cap was growing — and he opened production facilities in Quebec, Ontario, Alberta, and Saskatchewan.

Investment bankers like Saunders and retail investors online were pumping his stock, and that made his company valuable, even if it couldn't quite do what it was supposed to: grow good pot. Booth says that whenever any of the investment bankers wanted to raise money for Aurora, he was in. He sat back, appetite growing, and accepted their phone calls. "Take the fucking money" was his approach to growing the company at the time, he tells me in the back seat of his Rolls-Royce in Las Vegas. The more money he spent, the more Aurora was worth. Booth cursed in his emails, and at cannabis expos he drank with fans at the bar, and onstage. He smoked pot, threw lavish parties for Aurora employees, and signed back-of-the-envelope deals for a million bucks. It was not a time for due diligence. At a 4.20 celebration in Vancouver, Booth, the CEO of a billion-dollar company, took an edible that somebody gave him. Edibles were illegal. Booth didn't know the person. Drinking, smoking, travelling, spending millions, and taking toots — he was having the time of his life.

"My dad was anti-drugs. Almost psychopathic. He used to kick the shit out of my brother for ever having any pot, but dad met a guy on his dart team — Dad started smoking weed," Booth says. He was seventeen at the time of his dad's cannabis awakening, living alone with him, "and the entire tiny apartment was filled with blue smoke." Eventually, Booth found his dad's stash: a quarter pound in a plastic container. He was already entrepreneurial. "I sold weed through my dad," Booth says, "in grade eleven and twelve."

Before getting involved in the legal medical marijuana industry — before cutting his $3 million cheque — Booth toured the illegal dispensaries in BC, wanting to understand how the current market worked. He went into the Kelowna underground. He had threats made against him and learned how to remain calm among police and dogs. He says he'd never before thought of weed as medicine. But after three months of exploration, he was convinced.

"This is a safe medicine that should be allowed and never should've been illegal to begin with," concluded Booth, who not only toured the black market, but also hired away a top person from Jodie Giesz-Ramsay to help him build Aurora — a legal answer to black market pot.

Booth says that the illegal operators he met looked down on him as a corporate suit, but he stood his ground. "I didn't give a shit," says Booth. "I grew pot before you were out of your mammy."

By 2016, medicinal cannabis companies like Hydropothecary and Aurora operated side by side with illegal dispensaries and illegal wellness clinics, which had been selling pot out in the open for years. The three sides could work together, but also clash. Hilary Black was just one of the activist pioneers who had crossed over from illegal to legal. Growers like Tom Flow, who didn't have a record, were in demand. Still, the legal medical industry, nascent and already stigmatized due to quality issues that didn't help their valuations, needed to remain at arm's length from the illegal growers, at least publicly. But it was very hard for the legal system to exist completely apart from the previous culture, and it wasn't entirely clear how distant the two universes should be. Even the cannabis executives couldn't reach a consensus.

In the spring of 2016, pot was the only medicine taxed like booze. So Hilary Black attempted to send out a press release from the Canadian Medical Cannabis Industry Association about the need for marijuana patients to not pay excise tax. The statement included signatories from the illegal market, prompting an email conversation among executives at the twenty-five major medical marijuana companies. These included CEOs at Mettrum, Bedrocan, Tweed, MedReleaf, and Aurora. It was Terry Booth's second meeting as a member of the association. CannTrust, which had received its licence on February 23, 2015, Mettrum, and Emerald Health were all onboard with the messaging. At first. The conversation turned when Marc Wayne, for whom Black worked, wrote to the group: "To be transparent, this will include some NGO, other associations and even a few compassion clubs."

Neil Closner, the CEO of Stephen Arbib's company MedReleaf, took immediate offence: "I don't see any value in lending them one ounce of credibility or validation." Quickly, Aphria agreed with Closner. Eric Paul, CEO of CannTrust and son of founder Norman Paul, who'd spent forty years running a mail-order pharmacy, also wanted his company distanced from the compassion clubs. Cannabis was trying to gain respectability, and while some of the compassion clubs were indeed furthering the medical marijuana cause, it was too risky to align the legal companies with their illegal forebears. Trevor Fencott at Mettrum wrote, "Compassion clubs are unequivocally illegal and absolutely buying product from illegal sources — it doesn't help us to then be seen to be aligned with them in any way."

Marc Wayne told the group that the idea for the press release came from the grey market. Closner replied, "The Canadian Association of Medical Cannabis Dispensaries might as well be called the 'Band of Illegal Criminal Pot Sellers of Canada.' They are breaking the law and they are directly infringing on all of our businesses today."

Booth had different ideas. He hadn't yet met any of his peers in person, but he established himself — and Aurora — in the email chain. "I am proud to have the Aurora logo aligned with the compassion clubs," he wrote. "I wonder if any of the naysayers have ever been in a dispensary and spoke with the patients that are members? Bizarre how some of these LP's [licensed producers] don't get what this all means, where this was born, how this fight began. Pisses me off."

He let it rest at first, and then he didn't. Terry toured the illegal dispensaries before starting Aurora. He actually smoked weed. That night, he continued, "This petition has the best interest of the patients in mind, ask yourselves the same question. Do you have the best interest of cannabis patients across this country in mind when you bail on a simple no-brainer initiative because the pioneers of this cannabis industry are participating in the support of this initiative? Holy shit, if your answer is still yes then have another hit. Shake your heads, and pull those heads out of your asses."

Sébastien St-Louis at Hydropothecary wasn't on the email thread. His company was still too small. But he calls those first days of the medical marijuana industry "steel cage matches being fought to the death." The founders had risked their reputations and often, as in Sébastien's case, their life savings. They'd had to work so hard and spend so much money to get to the starting line — with laws changing quickly, cash recycling, and stock prices rising and falling in the industry as a block — and tensions flared. The legal pot companies competed for patients and source materials. Competed for press and competed for cash. The men leading these companies — rich, white, non-marijuana-smoking men — all sought investments from the same financiers. They travelled together to the same conferences and visited the same legal shops in Denver and Los Angeles. They competed for growers and sourced lights and construction permits from the same places. The industry was brand new, intellectual property was worth billions of dollars, and everything was a race. But with the influx of capital, the industry was growing at such a clip that little attention was paid to the details. The guys were street racing Ferraris at night with their eyes closed. And the response from the market was "Speed up."

"No one cared about fundamentals," says one investment banker, who we'll call Chip because he still works in the industry and doesn't want to get caught telling tales out of school. Chip moved to Toronto from New York and wound up managing an independent bank's health-care desk. Companies like GMP Capital, Canaccord, and MMCAP Partners, where McNulty stayed close enough to Linton to earn his first big score on the Canopy IPO, operated outside the institutional banking system, and competed against them. But it was more than that. The investment banks didn't like the conservative Canadian big five banks: Royal Bank of Canada (RBC), Toronto-Dominion (TD), Bank of Nova Scotia (Scotiabank), Bank of Montreal (BMO), and Canadian Imperial Bank of Commerce (CIBC). And the brokers, the independents like McNulty, especially the young ones, the risk-takers — the ones who smoked weed — had something to prove. Outsiders, much like the weed executives they worked with, thought the big five banks were risk averse, slow, stodgy, afraid of betting on themselves, afraid of pulling the trigger, old.

Chip, who is baby-faced just like McSalty, hard working, and always on the clock, says no one cared about fundamentals. But he saw his dividends pay off right away. Before marijuana investing, Chip annually earned $200,000. After cannabis investing, based on commissions, Chip would pocket that in a month.

In 2016, Darren Karasiuk was working at Deloitte in analytics and modelling, and he wanted to attract cannabis clients. He studied the legal cannabis market in Colorado and produced a document that would become the most-viewed report in his company's more-than-175-year history. Obviously, his company was paying attention. The first accountants in the space, Deloitte handled the accounting at Mettrum and Canopy Growth. According to Karasiuk — an ultra-marathon runner with an imperial air — recreational cannabis would be worth over $20 billion. After surveying five thousand Canadians, and discovering that one thousand identified as marijuana consumers, Karasiuk forecasted Canada's annual consumption volume in grams per consumer and price per gram to discover a revenue figure of $4.9 billion to $8.7 billion. As he added in tourism potential, security, testing labs, and taxes, Karasiuk's numbers kept heading north, landing at $22.6 billion.

So, one side of Deloitte produced research. The other side sold cannabis shares to its clients. Nothing illegal; everything grey.

Karasiuk typed up his report. Then he typed his resignation letter.

Darren Karasiuk was taking a job with Stephen Arbib and Tom Flow at MedReleaf. By the end of November 2016, *Vice* reported that the number of veterans getting insured medical weed had jumped from 112 in 2013 to 1,762, in three years. The cost to the government increased from $400,000 to $20 million. A $4 gram from Aphria for a medical patient, according to *Vice*, would cost $12 per gram for a veteran. A veteran could be prescribed ten grams per day. Grey? Absolutely. But finance operates in loopholes — Darren Karasiuk would be working in weed.

"If I made five cents of every dollar raised on the back of that report, I'd be a billionaire," says Karasiuk, adding that when retail investors saw that billion-dollar figure, it was almost irrelevant what number you put before it. Two billion or two hundred billion, Deloitte and Darren made a hot industry burn like a forest fire out of control. Weed was going to be massive, and people — young people, boomers, people who thought it was funny, people who thought they'd get rich — wanted to invest.

Bruce Linton says that in 2016, every licensed producer had that Deloitte number as slide three in their deck. He certainly did. And, like pot dealers with product in a drought, the investment bankers expanded their client lists. Everyone wanted in. Chip says that after making his $200,000 in 2014, he was introduced to cannabis through the deal between Bedrocan and Tweed. Interesting, he thought. A pot company was worth more than $100 million. Then Chip helped raise another $60 million from institutional and retail investors for Canopy in 2016 and $57 million for Organigram in 2017, using the same sales pitch: you couldn't lose money investing in the cannabis space. After the $57 million, Chip tells me, things picked up. He did a lead deal with Cronos, which Lorne Gertner co-founded, and worked closely with its brash young CEO, Mike Gorenstein. The deal was for $100 million.

Chip thought, *My kids won't ever need to work.*

"On my first deal with Cronos, I made over $150,000 — for a day of work," says the banker, adding that his biggest single-deal payday in cannabis would top $1 million. Also, the bankers wouldn't make money like the cannabis executives and retail investors. Chip's money wasn't just on paper. "The best thing about where I was," the banker says over Scotch one night in Toronto, "is that we were not taking home stock. These were not paper gains. It was cash."

The Americans caught wind of the Canadian hustle. In February 2016, Ted Chung, Snoop Dogg's business partner, was in Toronto at the NBA all-star game. Snoop, in addition to being one of the best rappers ever and an entrepreneur lending his fame to Skechers, Corona, and his own brand of wine, had started the cannabis brand Leafs by Snoop that December in Denver, where pot was legal.

The problem with owning an American pot brand, however, even if you're Snoop, is that American cannabis launched in a system that was not federally regulated, which made it impossible to scale. The U.S. was regressive regarding its weed laws. Every state had its own regulations, and the one thing that most of them shared in common was that nearly all of them still couldn't sell Snoop Doggy Dogg weed. In the U.S., pot is a schedule 1 drug, which means there's no accepted medical use and it has a high potential for abuse. Other schedule 1 drugs are cocaine, ecstasy, acid, and heroin. So while the federal American regulations proclaimed cannabis had no medical value, thirty-seven of the states adopted their own medicinal marijuana programs. Each state in America operates as its own country. Even if every state in America legalized overnight, for Snoop Dogg to sell Leafs by Snoop across the U.S., he'd need a partner in each one.

Chung, a laid-back Los Angeleno with a style accrued from making a mint with Snoop, sat with Mark Zekulin, Linton's president at Canopy Growth, at the Shangri-La Hotel that all-star weekend and didn't talk numbers. Ted and Mark talked about the dream of legal weed.

"We met with everybody, but only Mark and Bruce talked about job creation, talked about the people they'd help," says Chung. Zekulin passed Ted Chung's initial audition, and the young lawyer was taken upstairs to a hotel suite to meet Snoop Dogg. The suite looked like Terry Booth's father's apartment — you needed a machete to cut through the smoke. The Doggfather, wearing sunglasses and a fur coat, wanted to get high.

"Despite all my time at Canopy, I didn't smoke weed," Zekulin says of the culture clash. But Snoop had a way of converting the unconverted. There's a reason he's one of the most popular musicians of all time. Zekulin came prepared for the moment. He pulled out a medicinal CBD Canopy joint. Snoop is tall and thin. He's been smoking marijuana since he was eight. He smokes daily. One of his most famous records is *The Chronic*. Zekulin had no hip hop records. He's a lawyer. A nerd. He doesn't know how to dance. At thirty-seven, the affable operations expert lived outside Smiths Falls, Ontario, and had two kids. Still, even non-smokers smoked around Snoop.

When Zekulin produced his Canopy Growth CBD joint, the rapper smiled. Snoop generally smoked blunts, hollowed out cigars refilled with hydroponic California weed. It would take one hundred Smiths Falls CBD joints to get Snoop stoned. Still, he appreciated the executive's gumption. He smoked with the young Canadian and, even though celebrity endorsements were banned by Health Canada, Linton acquired Canadian rights to Leafs by Snoop. The biggest weed smoker in the world now worked alongside Bruce Linton. LA was coming to Toronto. And the press lapped it up. Zekulin says the momentum, if not the revenue — because recreational cannabis was still illegal — set off a cascading series of even more deals. It didn't matter that the cannabis companies were still only earning revenue for medical marijuana sales. The hype was more valuable than cash.

"What these cannabis companies were doing in terms of revenue was completely irrelevant," says Chip, our banker, who describes the market as "retail mania," in which he could invest in any public Canadian cannabis stock on a Friday at 3:30 p.m., thirty minutes before the market closed, and watch how the stocks rose, as a block, on Monday morning — by as much as 20 percent. The stock moved on word of mouth. On FOMO. The bankers knew the price wouldn't hold. "On Monday, about an hour after the open, we pull our money out of whatever cannabis company X at a profit. This happened for about a year."

Trevor Fencott says there was nothing illegal in how the investment banks played the markets. He says, "The investment bankers never cared if the stock went up or down, because if it tanked, whatever — the investment bank shorts the companies and they earn their commissions, but they do this while the business goes down in flames."

While the cannabis companies kept growing in terms of market cap and number of competitors, Bruce Linton wasn't alone in battling skyrocketing construction overruns. The need for capital to increase the size of production facilities was intense. Valuations were still determined by yield capacity. Using Karasiuk's formula for pot's expected $22.6 billion value, a company's worth was based on how much marijuana it could (hypothetically) grow.

Terry Booth and his peers were like Jack from "Jack and the Beanstalk": country boys who trade the family cow for a handful of magic beans, which grow into a massive, towering beanstalk reaching up into the clouds. In the clouds, however, instead of meeting a giant, the cannabis executives were meeting architects who could build out their production facilities, which could cost as much as $250 per square foot.

To build a one-million-square-foot property in Edmonton, Terry Booth needed endless supplies of Canaccord money, because a fairy tale like the one Booth and Aurora spun required lots and lots of money, which Graham Saunders was only too happy to raise. A year out from recreational cannabis legalization, Canaccord saw its net income increase by 500 percent.

The only thing that mattered was growth.

"To some degree, you knew it couldn't last, so the idea was to move quickly," says Sean McNulty, whose Canopy shares were issued at sixty-five cents. They opened around four dollars in 2014 and hit ten dollars a year later. McSalty had scored his first payday. And he did it while getting high in his twenties. Still, if his bosses had only listened, the profits would have tallied hundreds of millions of dollars, just on that one deal — let alone all the companies that would have followed Linton to McNulty's door.

After the Tweed IPO in the spring of 2014, MMCAP experienced a change of heart. Now McNulty's bosses wanted him to invest in weed brands, and as the cannabis companies attracted more attention, they all wanted to go public, all wanted to expand. And amateur investors were ready to buy shares. Marijuana companies became trendy.

"Everyone knew someone who had made a million dollars on weed stocks," says John Fowler, a lawyer and cannabis activist and founder of the Supreme Cannabis Company, adding that the sector began to attract sharks looking to exploit the nascent market.

McNulty was dismayed at the cannabis executives he met. "These people were on a different planet. Plans, budgets — no one had any of these things," he says. "But it didn't matter. The market was worth hundreds of millions of dollars. Billions, actually."

Many of the growers had come from the black market; we know this. And many of the executives didn't smoke pot, also true. So while cannabis executives took up arms against each other over email and in the press, the growers and executives at these companies also squared off from alternative backgrounds. Meanwhile, demand for pot kept growing, but the pot didn't grow quickly enough. This added additional pressure to an already pressurized scene.

"We started off spending money like crazy, but it wasn't going fast enough," Linton says.

Stephen Arbib, who started MedReleaf in February 2013, recalls visiting Michael Haines and Trevor Fencott's medical cannabis producer, Mettrum, in 2016. Fencott and Haines wanted $40 million for their company. Arbib believed that the facilities needed to be rebuilt and that, while they had a few thousand patients — the entire medical market was eighty thousand people, a number hypothetically served by any one of the legal growers — Arbib believed the highest he could spend was $12 million, and even that was a stretch. The MedReleaf deal fell through. But the Mettrum founders weren't mistaken. Two weeks after deep discussions with MedReleaf, a series of calls with Organigram, and a thought of their own purchasing of Broken Coast, Bruce Linton made his sixth offer for the company. This time it stuck: he spent $430 million on Michael Haines and Trevor Fencott's company.

Haines didn't want to sell. He tells me he couldn't walk his dog without someone approaching him about weed stocks. Haines is a quiet guy, a laid-back Aussie, but everyone likes feeling special. He says it was the most exciting time of his life and, cool as he is, self-made and comfortable around money, he still got high off the attention.

"I was no Bruce by any means, but I couldn't go anywhere without getting cornered all night," he says. "It took me a year to realize how annoying to my wife I was. I think she preferred me when I was quietly getting rich."

In the end, the people involved in Mettrum wanted to be richer than Haines had already made them. He was feeling pressure from the board, which wanted to see Canopy-style earnings per share. John Fowler at Supreme says the same thing. Michael Haines says he didn't really have a choice. "Between activist investors and tired partners, it seemed like Canopy had won," says Haines, who sometimes regrets that his company wasn't promotional enough. But then his regrets get brushed away when he stares out over the ocean from the palace he owns in Mexico. Fencott says the $430 million Bruce paid for Mettrum was fair. "Arbib always had a private company, and consolidation in the industry had to happen. All Bruce did was pay a percent premium on the market," he says, adding that it wasn't $12 million offers he'd refused, but offers in the $250 million to $350 million range. "Maybe we were actually worth something like $12 million, but that's a tough case to argue when our market cap was 175 million bucks."

Bruce Linton wasn't worried about the Mettrum price tag. For Bruce to keep being Bruce he had to hold the biggest microphone in town. Mettrum, he tells me, changed the value proposition of Canopy, so despite the cost, it was a good deal. He was defending his crown. After the Mettrum acquisition, Canopy could now count 39,730 patients, half of the Canadians licensed to buy weed (Mettrum brought in 20,000 patients thanks, in part, to Haines's clinic program, which helped steer clients to physicians prescribing their product), and Mettrum shareholders would own 22.3 percent of the new company at a price per share of $5.92. The stock went to $8.42 per share after the deal. From the sidelines, Arbib couldn't believe his eyes.

"That was my first oh-shit moment," Arbib tells me. "The people negotiating have no idea what they're doing and the market doesn't care. It only could end one way."

———————

Chip cared, about money. He would continue to recycle cash into the sector — on paper — while the world followed Snoop into Canada to make deals. This, Chip says, would last for two years.

One afternoon in April 2018, still months before recreational legalization, Chip was in a meeting with a Swiss CBD company when he received a call from Mike Gorenstein at Cronos.

Cronos grew out of the bones of Peace Naturals, one of the original Blessed 13, and Gorenstein, a lawyer with a bachelor's degree in finance, was one of the first Americans to control a Canadian cannabis company (and the only one of the original founders still ruling today). Gorenstein was young, fit, and relatively sober. He would sit with Chip at cannabis conventions and laugh at Terry Booth making unceremonious trips to the bar. His company, Cronos, would grow to an $11 billion valuation in 2019 (and was accused by the Ontario Securities Commission of overstating its revenue figures by $7.6 million, for which they paid a $1 million fine).

Back in April 2018, Gorenstein told Chip he needed $100 million. It was understood that Cronos was being courted by Altria, the parent company of Philip Morris USA, makers of Marlboro cigarettes, and if a deal transpired, Cronos would need to go dark on the capital markets; it could be half a year with no capital raised while regulators studied the deal. And there was only so much money on the street. Times were booming, but there was still a ceiling, and a pecking order. If seven cannabis companies wanted $100 million in the same month — because there was a land grab and a race to grow production space — that would be almost $1 billion investment bankers would have to raise for weed stocks. Pot was popular, but Bay Street wasn't Qatar. Chip says the weed brands played the investment banks against one another. There were commissions on the line and no one wanted to be cut off from the money tap.

"It was like five scorpions in a box," Chip explains, recalling how all of the young, aggressive money men knew each other and all of the cannabis companies worked with each of them. The young bankers would wine and dine the rookie executives. Chip took CEOs to New York for dinner or to the Raptors game, with seats on the floor. Everyone was arrogant in the new world of weed money. In Las Vegas, Chip was spending $10,000 a day. He says he lived in strip clubs. In 2016, he earned $500,000. In 2017, his expense account was $300,000.

Chip says that when Gorenstein called him, he excused himself from the Swiss CBD team and ran across town, screaming into his phone. The weed companies were massive, but it was all on paper. Stock shares couldn't pay salaries or electricity bills, and Chip says that, though Cronos was valued at over $1 billion, without the $100 million they wanted, they were facing bankruptcy. Cannabis companies burned money like the police used to burn fields of weed. No one — the market, the investors, the executives — knew how to value anything. In the spring of 2018, despite the Cronos valuation, they were hard up for actual operational cash. Marijuana companies were spending tens of millions of dollars a month. Hard money. Real money. Chip had to get the financing to Gorenstein. And he did. There was no way he was going to let the good times stop. Chip tells me that, after several screaming phone calls, he eventually got his company to invest $100 million into Cronos. It was on the same day that Gorenstein asked for the cash.

"It was the scariest thing I ever had to do in my life, but it was the right move," he says, explaining how, on this deal, it wouldn't be his retail investors on the hook for the money. It would be his own firm. And Chip took his bet all the way to the bank. In December 2018, Altria announced their deal with Cronos: they were going to buy 45 percent of the company for $2.4 billion. Altria got 146 million new Cronos shares at $16.25 — a 41.5 percent premium to share price pre-announcement. The deal helped the stock reach over $17 per share in the days following the announcement. Gorenstein was thirty-three. Chip was twenty-nine years old.

"The first thing I thought after the deal closed was that's my $6 million dollar fee," says Chip, who had already begun thinking about his next deal and about European expansion for medical cannabis companies. The brands were moving beyond Canada, promising, and perhaps even believing in, a limitless blue-sky potential.

Now the value of pot stocks was determined based on opening production facilities all over the world. This made international licences valuable, and the cannabis executives looked at the globe like children playing a game of Risk. Aurora had lined up an account to sell medical marijuana in Germany. Rumours spread that the entire European Union could legalize medical marijuana next. Italy, Greece, Malta, Britain, Portugal — the medical marijuana system in Canada was working, and each year it expanded in the U.S. Soon it would take over the world.

"We did a deal for Aurora.... Five thousand hectares of hemp in Lithuania?" says Chip. "I didn't even know where Lithuania was on the map."

Bruce Linton says his ability to raise money and acquisition hunger for rival weed companies caused industry-wide repercussions. The price he paid for Mettrum, blowing MedReleaf's offer out of the water, helped determine what things were worth. Stephen Arbib says that all you had to do was tell Terry Booth that Bruce Linton was interested in an asset, and Terry would seek to outspend Bruce's bid, without even seeing the asset, let alone checking its books.

This makes Linton laugh. "There are at least three transactions in which I believe the parties that made purchases spent between fifty percent or even three times more than they needed to, because I acted as if I might buy that asset," says Linton, who strategically sized up companies and got the rumour wheel spinning to jack up the price of something he didn't want. "If I make you pay twice as much for something than you should have, it means you've increased share count, and eventually, when you start reporting earnings per share, it's harder to beat me on my number." Linton means this: if he makes you dilute your shares to pay a premium on something he doesn't want, his own value per share looks even rosier to his stockholders.

Linton got companies he wasn't working with on his side in the charade. "If you asked the CEOs of those companies, they'd say, 'Bruce laid this shit out for us.' I'm one hundred percent not buying you, but if you get twice as much as you think you should get, we both benefit. That was fun!"

John Aird, who had previously worked in the Premier's Office of Ontario and the Ministry of Economic Development and Innovation, remembers spending most of that time on a plane. An expert in licensing and regulations and part of the marijuana subculture, Aird introduced me to half of the characters in this book and initially helped me lay out the legal cannabis timeline. Aird's family is connected. For instance, he has a photo of his grandfather, a senator, with Prime Minister Lester Pearson, beneath which is a handwritten caption from Pearson, who went by "Mike" to his friends: "To John — the Senatorial Hercules, from Mike — the Weary Titan."

Aird travelled to the States so often around that time — to Florida, California, and Colorado, places with legal medical marijuana industries that wanted to invest in the Canadian market — that eventually American airport security wouldn't let him cross the border. "Customs didn't understand that I didn't grow cannabis — I was in the permit business," says Aird, who nevertheless knew law enforcement was behind the times when it came to cannabis legalization. Aird's family co-founded Aird & Berlis — a tony Toronto law firm — and he could've had a team of lawyers argue his case. On principle, he says, he chose to confront the Americans on his own.

"I wanted to be on the front lines. It was absurd the way the legal cannabis industry was viewed as this outlaw work when we were already worth billions of dollars."

Aird helped Newstrike, a mining company that didn't bother changing its name when it decided to get into weed, obtain their medical marijuana licence. In a bizarre world of upside-down chicanery, Newstrike struck a chord all its own. Through the personal connections of CEO Jay Wilgar, the company soon had a differentiating factor no other licensed producer could match: the Tragically Hip. Wilgar's relationship with the band began in the summer of 2016, as they performed their Gord Downie farewell tour. The band wanted to be involved in the medical cannabis movement. Newstrike made their ticker on the Toronto Stock Exchange HIP.

"We had no trouble sharing a jay," Rob Baker, guitarist of the Tragically Hip, told me, adding that he worked with Wilgar to bring the group into the fold. Gord Sinclair, the bassist, named the strains that Wilgar would sell after the Cannabis Act was enacted, and Newstrike created a recreational brand called Up Cannabis; each individual strain was named after a Tragically Hip song. The company hosted a dinner for investors at the band's studio in Bath, Ontario, and the group appeared with Wilgar at a Bay Street event targeting investors. Justin Trudeau attended the group's last show, in Kingston, on August 20, 2016. Gord Downie, who was dying of aggressive brain cancer, had become the most beloved figure in the country. Canadians watched Downie sing his poetry onstage in a metallic leather suit, and those lucky enough to score a ticket cried over their soon-to-be Tragically Hip–branded joints. Downie's cancer was advancing quickly, but in 2017, he was able to tour Wilgar's facility in Brantford, Ontario, where Wilgar grew BC bud in earnest, especially a strain called Ghost Train Haze. Wilgar took Downie and his brother through his facility and very carefully instructed his director of operations to score the guys some weed.

"There's six thousand cameras, but there was one little area in the sorting room that, if you stood at just the right angle, it was possible to not be seen," recalls Wilgar, who then led the brothers outside into the parking lot, still in their lab coats from their tour. "I was CEO of this company and under my lab coat I had a hundred grams of weed."

Wilgar told Downie to meet him down the road at Tim Hortons. He then followed the brothers to the spot and threw the big bag of weed into their car.

Gord Downie would pass away three months later, on October 17, 2017, exactly one year before recreational cannabis legalization. Before he died, it's quite possible he smoked Jay Wilgar's weed.

Rolling

Newstrike became a red-hot commodity. In November 2017, Brent Zettl and CanniMed began pursuing Newstrike for an acquisition. Rec, as recreational legalization was known, was coming and CanniMed wanted to get into the market. Newstrike had the Tragically Hip, and thus was arguably the most appealing brand in an industry where there was little to differentiate one company from another. The two bosses worked through the details. After the deal, Wilgar would handle the recreational line and Zettl would be CEO. Everything was settled.

Until, that is, Terry Booth from Aurora came in and kicked ass. In an act of extraordinary aggression, Booth acquired CanniMed in a hostile takeover for $1.2 billion. To this day, all of the parties are aggrieved. Booth said it was CanniMed's board who first approached him on the deal. Zettl denied this and immediately responded to Booth by filing a $725 million lawsuit against Aurora, claiming Terry's board had insider knowledge of the CanniMed operations. And here's where things get hazy. Canaccord, Booth's investment bank, which he had been enriching, had also been working with Newstrike (the investment banks worked with multiple cannabis companies at the same time). However, Wilgar says that Cannacord, after spending weeks in his data room, told him that their relationship on this deal was terminated. On Friday afternoon, Wilgar was fired by his bank. On Monday morning, Cannacord announced it was representing Aurora in the hostile takeover. Wilgar points out the legality of such business shenanigans in this way: "This is Canada. What do you expect?"

Terry Booth says he didn't see anything wrong with the deal. He didn't care about Newstrike, or Brent. Terry could be hostile. It was his job. "They used to value [cannabis companies] by the size of our growth and our funded footprint, and when we got to our market cap, [Aurora] was way higher than our competition, but our competition [CanniMed] was way bigger than us — that's when you acquire," says Booth, explaining that he had the money in his war chest to act as he pleased. It was what was best for his company. "[The industry] became a sprint, a land grab, and we jacked our funded capacity, but not everyone was in it for the long run. With CanniMed, their shareholders initiated that transaction."

Wilgar and Zettl were pissed, but they were mad at the wrong people. For more than $1 billion, their board, Booth claims, had sold them out to Aurora for a huge payday. And that's when the retail investors really got screwed.

Wilgar had a $10 million clause in his contract should the CanniMed deal crash. At the time, his stock was trading around thirty cents and the company was worth $300 million. In early January, Newstrike received a sales licence. Within four days, the company was valued at over $1 billion. Institutional and retail investors bought shares, but the hedge funds in Toronto knew the price couldn't hold.

The smart money said, "No way." The dumb money said, "Sign me up."

Newstrike became the ideal company to short, and hedge funds bought Newstrike shares just to sell them, hoping the price would go down so they could buy them back at a lower price and profit on the difference. If you were a retail investor holding Newstrike paper, you lost your shirt. It had little to do with building a company and everything to do with destroying one. "The stock traded thirty million shares in a day, and that week, we got a $90 million bought deal from a hedge fund covering their short position," Wilgar tells me. "All of the sudden, we had $100 million in cash when we were down to our last two million in December." Aurora now owned CanniMed. Terry Booth fired Brent Zettl. Newstrike suddenly was flush with cash and Jay Wilgar knew there was only one play. He says, "We spent a fortune!"

Sean McNulty — McSalty — recently told me over beers before a Maple Leafs game that he loved every moment of the marijuana gold rush. McSalty, by the time of the Newstrike deal, was working for himself, rich and proven correct about weed. Bruce Linton's right-hand man on mergers and acquisitions, who had put half his life savings ($50,000) into Canopy's IPO, left MMCAP to start his own operation, at Linton's insistence. He said his new company, XIB Asset Management, with Linton in his ear, had different operating instructions from when Linton had first walked through his door. McSalty, who met me between appearances in Las Vegas at the World Series of Poker and his new home in the Cayman Islands and was still smoking weed, said it wasn't funded capacity, international licences, or cutting-edge science that attracted investors to cannabis companies in late 2017. Anything in the sector was valuable. Everything marijuana was hot.

McSalty had a new and widely shared mantra with regards to cannabis investments: "Buy 'em all."

CHAPTER 9

Growing Pains

"Nick, we just need to take some pictures."

Cam Fletcher, operations manager, CannTrust, to Nick Lalonde

Nick Lalonde never invested in weed stocks. But Nick has smoked plenty of weed. A hobbyist from Pelham, Ontario, he knows strains and seeds and can suss out terpenes and recognize rare breeds from the Netherlands. Growing up, he read *High Times* and collected the centrefolds of lush marijuana plants, just like Tom Flow. Before seeking employment in cannabis, also like Tom and like Terry Parker, Nick turned closets into gardens. He can smoke weed and be high without anyone knowing it. (But if you know it, that's also fine.) He's been part of the marijuana counterculture all his life and was raised hard. He was bullied as a kid, came from a broken home, and learned to sell coke and rob dealers before getting out of that life. With a chin beard and most likely a hoodie, Lalonde went straight and eked out a living selling seat cushions, T-shirts, and the odd dime bag to friends before landing a job at the licensed producer CannTrust in July of 2017. At the time, the company started by Norman Paul was heading towards a billion-dollar valuation and a listing on the New York Stock Exchange.

That summer, a year after Project Claudia shut down a wide swath of illegal cannabis dispensaries around Toronto, the police, Health Canada, and the medical cannabis companies were working hard to get their houses in order before the federal government legalized recreational cannabis. Legal weed had never happened before in a G20 country and there was pressure from every level of government to get it right.

CannTrust was Lalonde's first job with direct deposit and an HR department. He got the job through a family friend and found CannTrust to be like a family. The team, minus the executives, drank and smoked weed together after work. He was personally competitive, in terms of cannabis quality, with the other licensed producers and looked up to Brady Green, the CannTrust master grower, as a mentor and an idol. A CannTrust jack of all trades, he was proud of his work and dedicated to the company. "Master of Destruction" read his business card — his first ever. Lalonde, handy in construction and physically strong, took direction from Cameron Fletcher, senior manager of greenhouse operations. He earned $45,000. He was twenty-six years old.

"This is where I'd be for the rest of my life, part of something I believe in — which also happens to be the most exciting industry in the world," he says. "I was inside."

In 2018 CannTrust was led by chairman Eric Paul and CEO Peter Aceto, former chief executive officer of Tangerine, the online wing of Scotiabank. CannTrust differentiated itself from its peers by portraying itself as serious, business-minded, with a rare-in-the-industry grown-up approach to its dealings.

Aceto was a suit, and he had the industry's most vaunted professional experience: banking. He was seen as the executive the industry needed. Bruce Linton was a promoter, Vic Neufeld at Aphria was seen as an accountant, and Aurora's Terry Booth was portrayed as a cowboy, but none of them had ever led a company of the magnitude of the weed brands they founded. Very few Canadians have led billion-dollar companies, and even the ones with experience in the public markets have never led anything like the juggernaut start-ups these men were steering now. Meanwhile, many other cannabis companies had young CEOs or even connections to the black market. But CannTrust was different. At least it was supposed to be.

Even Walls Fall Down: A look inside the CannTrust facility, before the exposure by Nick Lalonde would lead to its billion-dollar demise.

Nick Lalonde, CannTrust's new hire, showed up enthusiastically to work, even though it was grunt work. The kid was happy to be working amid weed and buzz. He helped break down the original greenhouse in Fenwick, Ontario, and schlep the waste material to the dump. He also carried the cannabis plants from the trucks to the grow rooms. Like in any big business, at a company like CannTrust, with a staff of 800, or even Aurora, with a staff of 1,700, only a very few people were executives. Most of the employees in marijuana worked like Nick did, as growing cannabis was labour intensive and there was equipment that needed to be hauled and things that needed to be fixed. When Lalonde started at CannTrust in 2017, the eight biggest cannabis companies were trying to recruit thousands of new people. These people, people like Nick, followed instructions, made minimum wage, believed in the cause, and, generally, smoked weed.

At the Fenwick CannTrust facility in the summer of 2017, there were twelve growing rooms, seven of them licensed by Health Canada to produce and sell medical marijuana. The five that weren't licensed were fully operational and were in the Health Canada queue to be inspected. From fifteen to thirty people, Lalonde tells me, worked in these unlicensed rooms each day, growing pot, which roused his suspicions. Lalonde says he often worked late — though he was never paid overtime — and he remembered the night, at perhaps around 7:30 p.m., when his manager, Cam Fletcher, made an unusual request. His boss wanted him to hang a wall up around the unlicensed plants. "Nick," he said, "we just need to take some pictures."

Lalonde says he understood Fletcher's choices. Fletcher is a weed guy — not a suit — who was taking instructions from his boss, and everyone wanted their company to win: grow the most pot, grow the best pot, have the highest stock price, get rich. There was not enough cannabis in the legal market to meet demand, and the weed in the unlicensed rooms was the same as the pot growing in the licensed facilities. It was all from the same seeds grown by the same people with the same equipment. The problem was that you couldn't speed up the growth of a plant. And it was still illegal to sell cannabis to medical patients from unlicensed grow rooms. Until Health Canada inspected each room of a licensed facility and granted a licence, it was illegal to sell medical marijuana grown in unlicensed rooms. Nick, however, did what he was told to do. But he didn't like how it felt.

"I'm not stupid," he tells me. "I realized we're hiding all these plants and moving cameras around and it's just, 'What the hell?' Something's wrong here," he says.

That summer, Nick spent a few weeks requesting a word with his boss, but was routinely ignored. Finally, Nick and Cam sat down. Nick says he told his boss, "I don't have a criminal record and I don't want anything to do with going to jail. Fuck that, I like my freedom."

———

George Robinson is a long-time cannabis insider who has worked with companies like Tilray and Aurora to ensure their greenhouses are up to Health Canada regulations. Burly and sporting a silver goatee, he's a fan of Formula One racing and a long-time security analyst whose clients include Corrections Canada, the Bank of Canada, and the Canadian Security Intelligence Service. Robinson, basically, is a fixer. He helped Brendan Kennedy at Tilray receive its medical licence in 2013 and brought Aurora's facility in Alberta up to code in 2015. Specializing in zoning bylaws and quality assurance — he can read the Health Canada playbook and give the agency back what it wants to see — Robinson helped design the huge early cannabis grow ops to create Health Canada–approved workflows and processes.

In 2018, he got a phone call. "I think we're in trouble," said an executive at Bonify, a Winnipeg-based privately held medical cannabis company. Four years earlier Robinson had helped start Bonify, transforming a meat-packaging plant into a state-of-the-art, Health Canada–approved licensed facility. Robinson had great affection for the company, and he caught a flight to Manitoba from his home in Vancouver.

Bonify was accused of repackaging cannabis purchased from the Hells Angels and selling it into the licensed medical cannabis system. At the behest of the company and in order to help it become Health Canada compliant, Robinson studied the company's books. His research was enough to force the termination of the entire C-suite and ultimately bring down the company. Robinson, with deep connections in Ottawa and government contacts from his time with CSIS, believes the Hells Angels — and their marijuana — are rampant in legal cannabis, even today. Many insiders dispute this claim, but it lingers around the industry.

The criminal lawyer Alan Young, who has worked with Health Canada and defended illegal growers for forty years, thinks the biker gang is not involved in any large way. Weed is smelly. And bulky. It needs a lot of room to grow and doesn't sell for much money. In other words, it's not as good an illicit product as other illegal drugs. The police officers and detectives I've spoken with tend to agree with Young. There is crime in marijuana, but my source with Ontario's Organized Crime Enforcement Bureau believes it's not that the Hells Angels are actively involved, but rather that the illegal market consists of groups of loosely cobbled-together packs of unaffiliated individuals. Neither the grow ops nor the illegal dispensaries, my source believes, are the handiwork of organized national biker gangs.

Yet George Robinson wasn't sure what was happening at Bonify, and he thought there were many bumps in the road in the transition from an illegal to a legal system in Canada. This wasn't surprising. Pot had been against the law for more than one hundred years. It's hard to shut down an illegal economy. Robinson, however, says that the Canadian industry has been plagued by illegal connections from the outset and points to Chuck Rifici being detained by the RCMP in 2014 at an airport hangar in Kelowna with his hockey bags of weed. Legalization has always been a grey zone.

At the time Rifici was detained, raw materials from licensed designated growers' seeds could be grandfathered into the legal medical market. Still, hockey bags? Not a good look. Back then, Canopy's pot was confiscated, but they didn't lose their licence. The accusations against Bonify, which Robinson was now investigating, were that 441 pounds of unlicensed cannabis had been sold into the legal market from undocumented sources.

Canada didn't have a cannabis shortage, says Robinson — the legal industry did. Since the licensed producers needed more pot than they could grow and since their growers stemmed from the underground, where many still had connections, it was not difficult to find pot if you were desperate — even if you had a legal licence — and knew where to look. Smaller licensed producers needed revenue to keep the lights on.

Pot, says Robinson, was coming into Bonify's facilities without documentation and was arriving not in Brink's armoured trucks, but in pickup trucks driven by guys with tattoos. "It didn't require Columbo to ascertain where marijuana was arriving from in Manitoba," he says. It was coming from the black market. Further, Robinson discovered that, without any documentation, the Bonify CEO had approved the product and its head of finance had approved the payment. The payment, to say the very least, was uncommon. "If everything else wasn't red flagged enough," Robinson tells me, "it sure as hell should've caught someone's attention that these invoices had to be routed through Mexico."

Robinson says that Bonify's problems were writ large for the industry: they'd entered into supply agreements for thousands of kilos of pot, which they had no way of growing, but which was their only revenue option, and there were bills to pay. Bonify, says Robinson, needed to deliver the illegal weed to get the money to continue to grow the legal weed and secure additional funding.

It was similar to the mess unfolding at CannTrust. When you overpromise, there's a reckoning when it's time to deliver. To counterbalance the lack of product, cannabis companies have always bought and sold each other's weed. And for a lot of mid-tier companies, it was more lucrative to sell their cannabis wholesale, white labelled — which means you're giving your product to someone else to sell as their own — than it was to try to achieve their own market share. It was easier for a smaller company to sell its weed in bulk to a more established company that had production and distribution networks secured. For the bigger company, market share was worth more than the money it would lose paying too much for pot. They weren't chasing profits; they were trying to pump their stock price and eliminate rival brands in a race to become the Coca-Cola of weed. Having the biggest patient list was valuable, as Mettrum proved. It was the perfect thing for a press release. The problem was, though they faced very different accusations, CannTrust and Bonify, according to Lalonde and Robinson, didn't cut corners — they broke laws.

"These people didn't care. To them, because they had no connection to the culture, weed was money," Nick Lalonde says. "It's almost like there was this attitude that somehow they thought weed was dirty or quasi-illegal anyways, so what's the big deal about doing illegal things? I don't know if they thought that weed gave them an illegal licence, but it was a fucked-up thing to see for someone who always wanted to work at a big, legal weed brand."

———

There was a suspicion in the air that things were amiss.

Gabriel Grego was head of Quintessential Capital, an activist investment firm in New York that studies markets and companies and seeks to question their leadership and poke holes in their business claims to make money. Our banker Chip calls Grego "a short seller on crack," meaning that if all short sellers are pit bulls, Grego was a *Tyrannosaurus rex* in terms of his aggressive methods. A former Israeli paratrooper, Grego became interested in Canadian weed. When he looked at the industry, he saw a market fuelled by enthusiasts with little hope of meeting market valuations; their expenditures went well beyond the rosiest expectations for revenue. Grego didn't think too highly of Karasiuk's projections at Deloitte.

"It's not bubbles that catch my eye — it's corporate malfeasance," Grego tells me from New York. At the end of 2017, he was studying the Canadian cannabis market. He believed Canada was too cold for inexpensively harvesting marijuana and had a population too small to match the Deloitte consumption projections. He also thought Canada's first-mover advantage was slipping. By the start of 2018, nine U.S. states and Washington, DC, had legal recreational marijuana, and thirty-five of the fifty U.S. states would have legal medical marijuana by 2020. Why would Germany, Mexico, or Jamaica buy Canadian weed?

The gossip in investment circles, much of it fanned by Bruce Linton and other Canadian companies hell-bent on expansion and by Canadian media hungry for a scoop, was that Europe, South America, and Israel would be the next to end cannabis prohibition. Grego, however, didn't think so and began investigating the investments of Canadian weed brands. He believed that Aphria, started by Cole Cacciavillani and now led by Cacciavillani's friend, CEO Vic Neufeld — and valued at more than $2 billion in the summer of 2017 — had made self-serving deals.

Grego tells me he wanted to explore whether management had profited on unethical, perhaps illegal, mergers and acquisitions. He believes there were circular transactions with a company Neufeld once led called Scythian Biosciences and that there were attempts to hide names on corporate registries. Executives, he alleged but never proved, were paying exorbitant sums for shell companies they owned. "A lot of the companies Aphria was buying had applied for a name change shortly before the transaction," Grego tells me. His investigations into Aphria's dealings — inspired, he says, by spy movies — took him to Argentina, Colombia, and Jamaica. He was reliving his paratrooper days as a banker. In Colombia, he says, he discovered an abandoned building that was supposed to be the headquarters of Colcanna, a pharmaceutical distribution company that Aphria bought.

Grego also went to Jamaica to see Aphria's assets on an outdoor grow, part of an acquisition that cost Aphria $300 million, but Grego couldn't find the farm. Later, reporters from Bloomberg went to Kingston, Jamaica, themselves and were able to locate the production facility. Clearly some of the problems Grego was uncovering were rooted in the difficulty of determining anything's value. Even if a farm in Jamaica wasn't yet producing grams of marijuana, how much were a greenhouse, staff, and a production licence worth there, a country where everybody in cannabis wanted to own property? Jamaican ganja could be sold at a premium. It would be like selling wine from France. Lorne Gertner had made it his personal mission to set up a Canadian shop out there. Bruce Linton made several trips to Jamaica and definitely wanted in.

Plus, if you bought something, anything, generally, your stock would rise. Companies still can't advertise in 2024. So in 2017, whose pot should you buy and which company should you invest in? It was not hard to do the math and say, "I like the company that's growing weed in Jamaica. They're spending big money and are doing big things." So what was that Jamaican company worth to Vic? Vic says he never did anything wrong. However, on the ground in Jamaica, Grego says, it was easy to dismantle the hype. As proof, he says, he discovered that a Jamaican cannabis-growing licence wasn't hard to obtain. "All you need is the will, five hundred dollars, and a bunch of Jamaican board members. That's it."

Aphria executives wanted to point out that Grego's "short report" — a document laying out why he believed the company was overvalued — was self-serving. Grego intended to profit from it. The nature of Grego's business was to borrow shares from current stockholders and then sell them at their current value. He then issued his short report, after he'd sold his borrowed shares, sending the stock down. Then, when he'd sunk a stock, he bought the shares back, at the lowest possible price. He profited, but all of the other investors lost their shirts.

Aphria promised a furious rebuttal to Grego's report. But it never came.

Perhaps the industry was due for a correction anyway. The company would lose more than $1 billion in value from their encounter with Grego. In biblical terms, marijuana had its first burning bush.

"It was like somebody took a knife and turned it in my heart," says Cacciavillani, adding that he'd never heard of a short report until one was issued for his company. Cacciavillani says Grego was full of shit, the report was all lies, and even if his company was overvalued, as many of the Canadian cannabis stocks were at the time, it had never engaged in anything against the law. "The report basically said the stock is worthless, but it's far from being worthless. The $800 million we spent building the place is all there and worth every penny of it," he tells me. "How can these fucking guys make shit up and lie and I have to defend it? Gabriel Grego tells lies."

Grego would receive death threats after issuing his report, which only added to his allure, while the Canadian market hemorrhaged based on his claims.

"Instead of a rebuttal," Grego says, "they sacked their CEO and entire board."

Meanwhile, legislators in Canada were still working behind the scenes to make recreational legalization occur. In Ottawa, Eric Costen, the lead at Health Canada who would usher in the Cannabis Act, had his sleeves rolled up. Regarded fondly by activists and cannabis executives, Costen speaks about recreational legalization with humour and grace. "When young Mr. Trudeau declared his intentions, we could see the groundwork had been laid by Mr. Harper," Costen explained. Marijuana legalization was pushed forward after Trudeau's election win, and it was Costen who turned so many people's dream into a plan. As the executive director of the Office of Medical Cannabis, with a staff of one hundred people, Costen took the Harper MMPR policy and updated it for Prime Minister Justin Trudeau. Costen told me that, while cannabis valuations broke through the stratosphere and Aphria's Vic Neufeld dealt with Gabriel Grego, he kept his focus on the patients and the plants. He believed the Cannabis Act was important, and he consulted far and wide to understand the needs of the community.

"We had a foundation already for a regulated market," said Costen. "Pot wasn't being grown in somebody's dank basement. We could show senators what these grow ops looked like — people walking around in hazmat suits in safe and secure locations. The message at Health Canada became 'We're going to legalize cannabis to better protect our children.'" It was the inverse of the Harper message, updated for Trudeau. "Our job was to frame legalization not as an absence of controls, but a set of new controls," said Costen, "and that message was delivered by Mr. Blair."

Blair, Toronto's former police chief, could polarize. But according to Eric Costen, Bill Blair carried weight. He reaffirmed nervous constituents that an adult was watching over legal marijuana — even as Bruce Linton and Project Claudia made the news. But if Blair appeased nervous voters, like Canopy and Lorne Gertner, he also rankled activists countrywide. He'd arrested so many people for marijuana — especially a disproportionate number who didn't look like him. Alan Young hardly wanted a cop in command, but for legalization to succeed, there had to be a decrease in marijuana stigma. Bill Blair was part of the team whose first order of business was getting the Cannabis Act passed for Trudeau. So, while Costen worked to hammer the rules in place at Health Canada, Trudeau's best people — Jody Wilson-Raybould and Jane Philpott, with Blair acting as secretary for both officers — worked to execute the Cannabis Act, Bill C-45.

In the Senate, the job to bring the bill home fell on one man. Tony Dean, an independent senator appointed to the chamber on November 10, 2016, did not smoke marijuana, at least when his pot journey began. An independent lifelong public servant, Dean volunteered to shepherd the cannabis file. Like Anne McLellan and Trevor Fencott, he had no personal cannabis beliefs, but he saw a chance to make history. "It was enormously rich in terms of policy. It had the health component, the social justice element, and the economic window in terms of tackling an estimated three- to five-billion-dollar illegal market," says Dean, who learned everything there was to know about marijuana and worked tirelessly to open minds among his Senate colleagues. Finally, once Anne McLellan's cannabis task force report became Eric Costen's bill, it was introduced by Jody Wilson-Raybould to Parliament on April 13, 2017. Tony Dean's job was to wrangle enough votes to see it through. It was by no means an easy job. Dean says that some of his peers scoffed at reading the material he prepared — "We don't do things like that around here," said one colleague about reading. However, there were others, especially newly appointed independent senators like Dean, who were ready to dig in.

"We wanted to do something not done often in the Senate, which was to answer the question, 'What problem are we trying to fix?'" says Dean. The answer, of course, was "How do we legally sell marijuana?" The file had been a judiciary exercise for Dean, until it became something different. At the start of 2018, he received a diagnosis of cancer. Medicinal marijuana became personal. Dean began using cannabis medically to help him sleep, stimulate his appetite, and relieve post-surgery pain.

He was sick. But he was also reinvigorated to fight for the cause. "Some people thought it might have been wise for me to take the year off, but this was the biggest, best distraction," says Dean, who would travel to Ottawa from Princess Margaret Cancer Centre in Toronto between bouts of chemotherapy and radiation, lugging his big bag of cannabis research to his Senate colleagues.

On June 1, 2018, the Senate approved an amendment to Bill C-45 with a vote of 34 to 28. (One Conservative MP, Scott Reid, voted in favour of the bill in the House of Commons. He said that, for this action, he was "sacked" from his role as critic of democratic institutions by his leader, Andrew Scheer, and demoted to the backbenches.) The recreational cannabis market was coming. But, as ever with Canadian marijuana, a trouble-free period wouldn't even last long enough to give Dean time to enjoy a celebratory joint.

⁓

On September 27, 2018, less than a month away from the end of prohibition, the first Canadian pot producer to have its licence suspended was Ascent Industries — not CannTrust, Aphria, or Bonify. Ascent Industries had been started by two weed guys in their twenties who learned the trade on Vancouver Island, growing medical pot legally under the MMAR laws. James Poelzer, head of business development at Ascent, was twenty-six years old when he began working with Philip Campbell, Ascent's CEO, and he says Health Canada kept them in the queue for a licence to cultivate recreational cannabis for nearly three years, from March 1, 2015, to January 1, 2018. In the interim, and in possession of their medical cannabis licence, the company had four additional Health Canada licences and eight hundred plants.

Poelzer, who told me he sold weed sparingly in high school and has a business degree, wrote standard operating procedures for his company and maintained, he says, vigorous record-keeping. Like most cannabis producers, the company was bleeding money as it waited for Health Canada approval on their recreational licence, spending $1 million on a vault, among other things, and pioneering unique product offerings for their patients. They set up an ethanol extraction lab in Maple Ridge, BC and began selling their patients concentrates.

On a research trip to Colorado, they discovered an early cannabis vape pen and produced their own, which they believed was legal for medical patients under the MMAR laws. They assumed that their medical business, like Canopy's or Aurora's, would have no bearing on the verdict of their recreational licence. Ascent also had an effective medical e-commerce site, Poelzer's baby, and business began booming. They consulted with Bruce at Canopy and Vic at Aphria and hobnobbed with the biggest cannabis companies.

Poelzer says his favourite cannabis executive was Terry Booth. "We used to have big parties at the Aurora head office in Vancouver and every year, take their big yacht out. We smoked the whole harbour out, it was a lot of fun."

Poelzer, however, didn't like any of the legal weed. "The legal medical pot was garbage. It was a disgrace," Poelzer says, adding that the medical side of cannabis was shortchanged by the big licensed producers as they turned their attention to the bigger market of recreational marijuana.

Poelzer kept stringent records of all of his medical weed sales and says, even when revenue topped $10 million in 2016, everything he did was legal. "There was too much at stake for us to ever cut corners, and we didn't want to risk everything that we built," Poelzer tells me, then adds that the success of Aurora and Canopy impacted the thinking at Ascent Industries. Poelzer says he wouldn't have taken Ascent public in 2018 if it wasn't what the market seemed to demand every cannabis company do. In August 2018, Ascent was valued at $60 million and had 120 employees. They grew recreational marijuana on one side of their building, which wasn't yet licensed, and medicinal marijuana on the other side, which was.

Marijuana for medical or for recreational use is the same stuff. There aren't particular strains that do one thing that others don't do, and there aren't different ways to medically or recreationally grow weed. It's all personal choice, and the plant affects people differently. However, for licensing reasons, the two halves of the company — medical and recreational — needed to be separated. Before they received their recreational licence, Poelzer says, the company had Health Canada approval to arrange their facility as they did. Again, he stresses that his record-keeping was so good because he wanted to use the data gleaned from their medical brand to help them gain insight into the recreational market.

In August 2018, Ascent sent out a press release: they were expanding their production facility from fifty thousand to seven hundred thousand square feet. "We weren't picked on by bikers. We were picked on by bankers," Poelzer says. "All we wanted to do was be legit."

Poelzer says both Aurora and Canopy looked into acquiring his company, but he and Philip Campbell held out. They were in Las Vegas at the MJ Biz conference in 2017 when staff back home informed the two friends that they had received a letter from Health Canada. Expecting it was their recreational licence at last, they received a notice of inspection instead. They were having their medical licence reviewed. "They came in obviously looking for something," Poelzer says.

Poelzer describes the Health Canada visit almost as if it were a raid: a team of uniformed agents asked the Ascent group to exit the building and proceeded to inspect every plant, seed, and document pertaining to both their medical and budding recreational business. Health Canada later determined that Ascent was performing "unauthorized activities," based on the very documents Poelzer insisted on keeping for the regulators. "They didn't go through security footage. There was no interview process. They just flatly turned our recreational licence down and revoked our licence to sell medicinal weed to our patients," says Poelzer, still sounding dumbstruck by what occurred. He thinks his small company disconnected from Ottawa was made an example of to illustrate the Health Canada commitment to law and order. Terry Booth says Ascent "got royally fucked." In knee-capping his company, insists Poelzer, the agency missed who the real law breakers were: connected billion-dollar Canadian companies like Canopy, Aphria, and CannTrust that played by their own sets of rules.

"Phil had never been a CEO, never been in the public markets," Poelzer told me. "He's a weed guy. All of us are weed guys."

The weed guys, the short sellers, the executives parachuting in — everyone, Bill Blair, Anne McLellan, the one hundred pot agents at Health Canada, Tony Dean, Hilary Black, Terry Booth, Terry Parker, Alan Young, Brent Zettl, Lorne Gertner, and scores of retail investors around the world still bullish on Canadian weed stocks — held their nose and cupped their lighters against the negative tailwinds. Prohibition was ending. Legalization was just weeks away.

CHAPTER 10.17

"Downtown St. John's kinda smells like weed."

The CBC

On October 16, 2018, Bruce Linton flies through a storm in a Tweed-branded T-shirt to sell Canada's first legal gram of recreational weed. Travelling from Ottawa to St. John's, Newfoundland, on a private plane, Linton looks out the window and sees the rain thrashing down. As the wind blows his small aircraft through the sky, he thinks, *Typical marijuana — can't we ever simply have blue skies?*

After he lands in St. John's, alongside the media embedded in his entourage, he winds his way to the Tweed store on Water Street, where he is greeted by an adoring throng. Willy Wonka opening another chocolate factory for his stoned fans. This is intoxicating for Linton: fame. It energizes him and makes him feel powerful, almost self-righteous. Cult leader, god. It's freezing outside, but it doesn't matter. It's a carnival. There are three hundred people in the street, and Bruce is about to legally sell weed. The countdown is on: at the stroke of midnight, prohibition will end. Seen from the right vantage point, the drug war is over. The good guys have won, and this propels Linton forward, shaking hands, signing shirts. Selling pot, making money — Linton can't help, at the moment of legalization, feeling like the king of the world.

"I'm just the tip of the spear," says Linton, whose team has worked with the city council to allow him to open his shop at midnight, which in itself is remarkable. Even in June, the law was still hazy regarding packaging and distribution, limits, and how the cannabis would be sold in each province. Executives didn't even know what date legalization would take effect until the middle of summer. On October 17, 2018, Justin Trudeau doesn't visit any stores, and he doesn't take a victory lap for achieving his campaign promise. (Neither he nor his staff — even Gerry Butts, a friend of John Aird's — would speak to me for this book.) Still, Mike Farnworth, British Columbia's minister of public safety, tells the *New York Times* on October 17, "Legalization of cannabis is the largest public policy shift this country has experienced in the past five decades."

In Canada, it's the day's top news, and for a segment of the population, it's a dream come true. For the people in line in the cold who greet Linton like a hero, it's Mardi Gras. The jubilation spreads out across the country, from Halifax to Toronto, Montreal, and Edmonton — where Terry Booth has rented out a nightclub for his Aurora staff and collected $10,000 onstage after winning a bet from 2013 that, within ten years, this day would come. People wait in line outside stores in Saskatoon and Alberta, many sleeping overnight to buy the morning's first grams on "10.17" — October 17, 2018 — and the police aren't arresting people for smoking weed out in the open. The line snakes around the Tweed store in downtown St. John's, pot smoke floating in the air like the Newfoundland fog. For the people celebrating the end of prohibition, the problem hasn't been finding Canadian weed. The problem, or the solution that they're lighting up for, has been the laws, which are over — right now.

"To think that the first legal gram of pot sold in this country was grown in little Smiths Falls," says Linton, who autographs the first Tweed bags filled with containers of Canopy pot.

"We won!" shouts Ian Power, the giddy first Canadian to legally buy a gram of weed. Linton himself makes the sale before the cameras. Power is wearing a Tweed hat and buying a Tweed product in a Tweed store, declaring that he won't smoke history's first legal gram, but will preserve it on a commemorative plaque. For Linton, it's sentimental free publicity — gold.

John Fowler is smoking a joint on 10.17. He's at the Supreme Cannabis headquarters in Toronto, off Ossington Avenue, just south of Dundas Street, right by my home. Fowler, who started his company in 2013, has assembled a collection of investors and activist friends to get stoned. It's a cold evening, a Wednesday night, and there are more than one hundred people amassed outdoors, just blocks from where Fowler grew up (and sold and grew his first pot plants). Obviously, there's marijuana being consumed. The moment is euphoric, and the former Bay Street lawyer feels justified now that his country is one of two in the entire world where it will be legal to buy pot. He knows all is not hunky dory. Even though pot is about to become legal, there are no stores — at least legal ones — in Toronto where an adult can buy weed. After Doug Ford replaced Kathleen

Plant Man: John Fowler, founder of Supreme Cannabis Company, lawyer, entrepreneur, pothead. His company was valued at over $1 billion.

Wynne as Ontario's premier, he moved the retail business from public to private and set back the opening of provincial stores in Ontario for months. This lack of retail options in Canada's most populous province adds to the general confusion about the status of legal weed, further hamstrung by the Canadian Medical Association.

Two days before cannabis legalization, the Canadian Medical Association released an editorial describing legalization as "a national, uncontrolled experiment in which the profits of cannabis producers and tax revenue are squarely pitched against the health of Canadians." This doesn't help Canada's 330,000 medical marijuana patients in their quest to remove the excise tax on their medicine. Cannabis can be prescribed as medicine, yet without the Canadian Medical Association's endorsement, it remains taxed like booze.

For a weed smoker, says Fowler, these are problems for another day. Because tonight the weed activist CEO can't stop smiling. He's proud of his company, his bud, his industry, his country, and his prime minister. Fowler's grandmother is his moral compass, and she isn't always happy about her grandson's choices. Active in her church, she doesn't share Fowler's enthusiasm for the plant, but she's slowly come around. She has invested in Aurora.

"For someone who smoked cannabis all his life, and made a pretty heavy bet on a life in the business, investing everything I have into the industry and my company, today is a dream come true," says Fowler, who first campaigned in Ottawa for legalization in 2010, at 4:20 p.m. on April 20, and has remained close to every facet of his industry: the growers, the investors, but also activists like Alan Young and Kelly Coulter.

Outside on the Supreme patio, the group counts down to midnight.

Unlike Linton, Fowler can't hold his festivities at a store he owns, because the city isn't licensed yet to open brick-and-mortar shops, and Ontario and Alberta, unlike Newfoundland, have rules against vertical integration (a licensed producer owning a store and selling their own product). As a block, at 12:01, the group takes out their cellphones, illuminating the night, to log on to the Ontario Cannabis Store (OCS) website to buy legal weed.

Except not a soul can get through. Not a person can shop. Not a gram of Supreme Cannabis, soon valued at over $1 billion, is sold.

"Fucking weed," Fowler says as the guests continue smoking their own bud and then drift away with mixed emotions. He goes back inside the Supreme building and turns on the 10.17 coverage of Bruce Linton on the CBC. "Downtown St. John's," says the reporter, "kinda smells like weed."

———•

By 10.17, Trevor Fencott and Michael Haines have sold Mettrum to Linton and now own five Fire & Flower cannabis retail locations in western Canada and Saskatoon. They are mining their data as legalization unfolds. Demand exceeds supply, as Fowler and his friends have discovered, but Fencott knows that won't last. Funded capacity suggests that there will be five times more weed in Canada than needed within the next few years. Trevor is calling that now. And while the product on his shelves can be inconsistent in terms of quality and it's hard to consistently stock cannabis with THC over 22 percent, everything he has is sold.

"The black market can thrive even in the legal industry because the [legal] retailers are product strapped," he says, estimating that his average price ranges from eleven dollars per gram to forty-five dollars for 3.5 grams, what are commonly known as dime and quarter bags. Fencott has his team conduct interviews with his customers. On 10.17, he learns something important. "Less than 1 percent of our customers have awareness of the brands," he says. This means that cannabis consumers may have heard of Canopy and Aurora, Aphria and Supreme, but when they buy Jack Haze, Grandaddy Purple, or Pink Kush containers, they have no clue who produces the actual weed. At the onset of legalization, there's no Kellogg's of cannabis, no Prada, no Chevrolet. Weed is weed is weed. In general, the people who line up at Fencott's stores — men and women, white- and blue-collar workers, all races and ages — want weed with high THC and low prices. Since you can't see or smell or sample the legal product, customers say they want the cheapest, strongest thing Trevor Fencott has.

———•

Alison Gordon is up at midnight on 10.17 and logging on to her computer. She is the CEO of the weed company 48North, and the only female CEO of a publicly traded weed brand. Her cannabis journey began with her mother-in-law's breast cancer, which led her to discover her country's legal medical marijuana regime. Gordon, a cannabis smoker with fabulous fashion, big hats, and furs, has one of her own 48North joints burning in her hand as she logs on to the OCS website and it ruins her high.

Her company is valued at $40 million. And she knows her stuff. She opened the dispensary in Los Angeles that eventually became the first MedMen location. MedMen, on 10.17, is valued at over $1 billion and is the first American cannabis company to reach that valuation on the Canadian exchange. On the OCS website, she drops her jaw. There are dozens of companies no one has heard of — ones even she doesn't know — all selling the same thing at the same prices. Her dream is to launch multiple lines but, seeing what's on the OCS website, with the same packaging and labels, it's clear what the legal market doesn't need: more versions of the same stuff. It's 10.17, and Gordon, blowing out smoke, says, "I have to rethink — everything."

On 10.16, the day before legalization, Hilary Black is in Ottawa giving the speech of her life. It's a buzzy Walrus Talks event at the National Gallery of Canada, and she holds nothing back. She's seen the opioid epidemic first-hand, and although she hears what the Canadian Medical Association is saying, she feels passionately that the group is behind the times, and absurd. If legalization is about stock prices to some, it's not about that to her, and never has been. "I have spent pretty much every day of my life since I was eighteen working to break down barriers for patients to access cannabis and working to free cannabis from the chains that bind her," she tells the audience. "Tomorrow that all changes."

She works at Canopy as the director of patient education and advocacy because she wants to harness Bruce Linton's power, and she says, to his credit, that her boss empowers her to speak her mind. Black has assembled a robust social responsibility team for the expungement of cannabis arrest records and elimination of the excise tax. She believes, and has convinced the cannabis task force, that even with the legalization of recreational marijuana, the medicinal program must remain intact. The same product can be used for different things.

She tells the Walrus Talks audience how she began: in the late 1990s, with HIV a continuing health crisis, she delivered weed on her bike to patients suffering side effects from their medications. They beeped her Motorola pager. She was nineteen years old and received support from gay men, who told her, "If they try to arrest you, we are going to chain ourselves to you and we're going to hunger strike."

From her early activism into adulthood, Black has seen the health epidemic change; today, the health crisis is opioids. Taking a deep breath, Black tells the story of Gemma Leroux Higgins, her best friend's daughter. In 2017, at eighteen, Gemma succumbed to a fentanyl overdose. After taking time off to support her friend's family, Black returned to Canopy to launch a $2.5 million Canopy-funded endowment at the University of British Columbia for a professorship of cannabis science. The BC government, in support of the initiative focused on the role of cannabis as a solution to the opioid epidemic, added $500,000 to the endowment.

It's an emotional time and she's exhausted. If Linton is the business face of marijuana, Hilary is the heart. However, she doesn't like feeling used. On the day of her talk, a story comes out about insiders at Canopy Growth who sold their shares prior to legalization. Every insider on the list, including Murray Goldman (Marc Wayne's stepdad, who helped launch Bedrocan), Mark Zekulin, and Linton himself, is a white man. The total profit, from selling over two million shares, is more than $135 million. Black, who has options, doesn't sell, and has a hard time reckoning with all the white men getting rich while activists still haven't had their cannabis records expunged. The activists' records can still bar those individuals from the legal industry they helped build. Black knows she's luckier than most, and yet, while advocating for patients, she also knows there's an alternate world of money from which she's excluded — despite being onstage. And in that world, white men cash out behind closed doors while she stumps for the cause.

Black doesn't mention this in her talk, but she carries the story around in her wallet as she tries to balance her nerves, frustrations, joy, and exhaustion.

"What I get excited about right now, and where I feel a tremendous amount of responsibility, is the global impact of repealing prohibition," she says, concluding her talk. "This is a war on drugs. And this is a war on people, and a war on families. And tomorrow is not just the beginning of a new legal industry. Tomorrow," she says, "is the beginning of the end of that war." The crowd gives her a standing ovation. Black flies from Ottawa to Vancouver and lands just in time — on 10.17 — to meet her activist friends. The group, in her words, "party their faces off," and when she wakes up the next morning, exhausted after years on the cannabis front lines, she won't leave her house for three days.

———⌐

Lorne Gertner has his own 10.17 story. Manitoba is the first province to have a real Tokyo Smoke, a Tokyo Smoke where you can actually buy weed. Manitoba, shockingly, has become a province close to his heart. Since the days of visiting Brent Zettl in Flin Flon, Lorne has been returning to the province and inspecting his store in a strip mall, beside Reitmans and Moores. On 10.17, these stores are closed and quiet. Tokyo Smoke is pumping and jammed. There is a line to get in. People are smoking weed.

"My God, this is fucking Winnipeg," says Gertner. "How high can this go?"

Gertner is ecstatic. From the moment he got into the business with Moses Znaimer back in 2000, he's been an advocate, mentor, and angel investor to the industry. Both John Fowler and Alison Gordon cite him as a help in getting their companies started. Bruce Linton spent nearly $300 million to acquire Hiku, Gertner's parent company behind Tokyo Smoke. (Between the time the deal was announced and its closing, Canopy's stock doubled, making the windfall for Lorne closer to $600 million.) When everyone was selling coffee, Gertner sold the coffee stores. And it worked — in terms of garnering press, setting the trend, and making him and his son business rockstars. Gertner has created the Apple store of weed and is rich. Well, rich again. Richer. And, having left Google to launch a new family business, so is his son. And now, after so many years, marijuana will be legal at the stroke of midnight.

Puffing on a Tokyo Smoke prototype vape, he says, "All of these people had broken the law for most of their lives, but not anymore and I was with them."

Gertner, like Linton, wakes up early the next day to rush back to Toronto, where people are still openly consuming cannabis on the streets. Legalization has started and the world was watching and there were no overdoses. No riots. Cars and markets didn't crash and the schools stayed open. 7-Eleven didn't run out of chips.

"Canada," says Gertner, "is the cannabis capital of the world."

PART III

REVENGE

CHAPTER 11

God Bud

"I look out the window and I see these fucking aliens. I'm the CEO of a cannabis company — and I'm going to die today for sure."

Terry Booth

The cannabis capital of the world attracted American money. Nelson Peltz is an American investor; he became Terry Booth's strategic advisor at Aurora on March 13, 2019. Recreational legalization was five months old and Peltz was seventy-nine. *Forbes* put Nelson Peltz's worth at over $1 billion. When Booth imitates Nelson's voice, he makes him sound like the Penguin.

Upon entering Canadian cannabis, Peltz had the option to purchase 20 million Aurora shares. When this fact was announced, the Aurora stock shot up 13.94 per cent. "I believe that Canadian licensed producers, and Aurora in particular, are well positioned to lead in the development of the international cannabis industry as regulations evolve, with a strong, globally replicable operating model," Peltz said in the Aurora release touting his involvement in the Canadian licensed producer.

Peltz got rich in the 1980s off, in part, Michael Milken's junk bonds. He is an activist investor, someone who invests in a company but isn't content to let his money ride. He insists on becoming a partner in the businesses he takes on. Peltz gets involved. He and his company, Trian Partners, are like when your mom remarries an army colonel, and now your new step-dad comes into your house and it's no longer okay for you to eat cheese strings in front of the TV. Trian takes stakes in companies it believes are undervalued and pushes management to make changes to boost the stock. Aurora's market valuation in the spring of 2019 was $6.85 billion. In 2018, it did about $55 million in sales. It was second, in terms of market cap, only to Bruce Linton's Canopy Growth, but Terry Booth was not content to be number two.

"Aurora? I remember that company vaguely," says Linton, "but they're so far behind us I sometimes forget what they are."

Nelson Peltz is a veteran of consumer packaged goods, or CPG, which is what the pot business was becoming: grams weren't sold in a park beside bushes, they were packaged, distributed, and replicated like thumbtacks, at scale. With billions invested in Procter & Gamble and Nabisco, companies that the Canadian weed brands were now trying to become, Peltz brought along serious know-how, but also a reputation for scuffling. He had waged a nasty two-year public battle with his partners at Pepsi. That fight, which ended in 2016, saw Peltz exiting the company after his $269 million invest-ment increased in worth to $1.83 billion. After seeing Pepsi's stock drop after Peltz's exit, a reporter for *Forbes* said, to paraphrase, that no CEOs want to see their stocks drop but, in ridding themselves of the truculent Nelson Peltz, it might be worth the cost.

Peltz, following his exit from Pepsi, was sitting with one of his partners and Terry Booth at a restaurant in Lower Manhattan. "Can you believe it? These Canadians are worth more than MGM," Peltz said to his partner, while Booth, clutching his Ketel One, smiled.

"We have better product," said Terry. "They make movies. We sell weed."

In September, just before legalization and at arm's length from the Ascent Industries fiasco, the cannabis industry was on a hot streak. Aurora, in par-ticular, was shooting flames. Before legalization, Bloomberg reported that Aurora was in talks with Coca-Cola to make CBD drinks. The next month, Booth listed Aurora on the New York Stock Exchange. By January, the

Rainbow Connection: Terry Booth, who started a cannabis company with his high school friends in Edmonton, graduated from stealing his father's weed to building a greenhouse in Edmonton so large that pilots would complain about the glare from its rooftop when landing their planes.

company had moved past Apple on Robinhood as the hottest, most liquid, or traded, stock on the exchange. Liquidity, Booth says, is what you want in a pot stock because it means investors are buying and selling your shares. This makes your company hot in a market where you can't advertise and creates fervour, leading to hasty choices. Fear of missing out drives movement in shares. If your stock is liquid, continues Booth, you're not reaching out to investors with your dick in your hand; they're coming to you. Aurora was trading hotter than Apple with some of the least sophisticated investors in the world. Many people investing in Terry were stoned.

Terry was, too.

In November 2018, at the MJ Biz conference in Las Vegas, Booth, onstage, says "Ontario and British Columbia shat the bed" when describing the province's approach to weed stores. That he'd had many drinks before he said it didn't make it untrue. Booth actively engaged in cannabis functions and with cannabis people. He wasn't in marijuana only to make a buck. He lived his brand. This might even have endeared him to Nelson Peltz, as long as his stock stayed hot.

In Las Vegas, he told Bruce and me the story of attending a 4.20 party in Vancouver. He was walking around enjoying himself when he met someone, and he was happy to engage. "This little dude steps out of the bushes. 'Buy some edibles?' Okay. So I buy two big-ass cookies from this guy and wolf one down." Booth made his way through the party, shaking hands with vendors and handing out T-shirts and hats. A typical CEO meeting the public. Except the public was smoking weed and selling edibles and this was Terry Booth. "I had a rip on a bong and the rip on the bong made me hungry, so I ate the other cookie," Booth says.

At this point, he was stoned. Bad stoned. Everything slowed down. He was paranoid. Hallucinating, even. He thought people were looking at him and they were — he was a marijuana celebrity who two minutes ago was handing out hats. He wanted to escape and his mind jolted from one idea to the next: *How am I doing? Am I cool? What about our stock price? Nelson Peltz looks like Danny DeVito. And where the fuck is this hotel?* Booth was decked out in his company clothes, which put a target on his back as he tried to disappear. It was a marijuana nightmare and one of the reasons Health Canada eventually put caps on the amount of THC in edibles: too much THC and you might as well have taken acid. Booth felt that way now, but somehow, praise the lord, he made his way back to his hotel room. He closed the door and turned off the lights. "I lay down on my bed and called my wife. I look out the window and see these fucking aliens. I'm the CEO of a cannabis company — and I'm going to die today for sure."

Aurora, Nelson Peltz would soon discover, wasn't Pepsi or MGM.

Constellation Brands wasn't Pepsi or MGM, either. Bruce Linton says Constellation may have given Canopy more money than their billion-dollar investment in the sector. The disruptive money was the original sum, says Linton, the $190 million investment the Corona-maker paid in 2017 for

10 percent of Canopy, at a time when cannabis manufacturing was still considered, by some, especially in the U.S., to be dealing drugs. After that, the next infusion — the $5 billion Canadian in August 2018, right before legalization — only made sense: they were building a moat around their investment with more investment. Constellation was prescient about the short term. On December 20, 2018, the Farm Bill in the United States was passed, signed by President Donald Trump. It allowed American producers to deliver CBD across state lines and created a federal system for cultivating, processing, and marketing hemp — which is weed without THC.

CBD comes from hemp and is legal. THC, the psychoactive compound also found in hemp, is not. After the Farm Bill passed, CBD became valuable and this, and CNN's Sanjay Gupta's viral endorsement of the molecule, created the CBD craze. Gwyneth Paltrow touted the product and soon it would be available on Amazon and at Whole Foods. CBD is the non-scary component of weed, and this reduced stigma and opened up a huge market for Canadian marijuana producers: marijuana for people who don't want to smoke weed.

Canadians were now leading hemp technology. They could isolate CBD molecules from THC in their cannabis plants. All that money spent on research and development and hiring scientists was now applicable in the U.S., a market ten times larger than Canada's.

The U.S. market for hemp-fuelled products like CBD was estimated to grow, after the Farm Bill, from $2 billion in 2018 to $20 billion in 2021. Linton, with Constellation money, was licking his chops. America, with its loose laws behind advertising and its huge population, was coming around on weed. On January 1, 2020, Illinois became the eleventh U.S. state to legalize recreational marijuana, a month after Michigan. You could now buy a joint in Chicago and Detroit.

And the American marijuana momentum kept rolling: at the start of 2019, cannabis nearly got promoted at the Super Bowl. Acreage Holdings was an American medical marijuana company and, for the big game on February 3, they wanted to place a sixty-second television ad. The opportunity would cost between US$5 million and $10 million. The money was no problem for Acreage, which had a market cap of over US$250 million.

CBS, the network broadcasting Tom Brady's New England Patriots versus the Los Angeles Rams, publicly mulled it over before ultimately rejecting the clip — a poignant plea from veterans and mothers to allow their countrymen to enjoy the relief they were currently experiencing thanks to medical weed. It was a sign of the times. After Oklahoma passed a bill in the summer of 2018, medical marijuana was legal in thirty American states.

Cronos, the company that Chip, the independent investment banker, once had to raise $100 million for on a Friday afternoon, traded on Nasdaq. Americans could also buy shares of CannTrust and Aurora on the New York Stock Exchange. Trevor Fencott says new bought deals were being offered to Canadian cannabis companies every day. It was all about expansion, press releases, and growth. CannTrust opened facilities in Denmark and Australia and told the press that Australian greenhouses would one day supply weed to Asia. If Asia legalized marijuana — and why wouldn't they? Argentina, Malta, Brazil, and New Zealand all had legal medical programs — how much money would the Canadian licensed producer be worth? Nelson Peltz said the Canadians had first-mover advantage in these markets. Bruce wanted to own them all.

The Acreage Super Bowl ad may have been shitcanned by CBS censors, but it nevertheless went viral. It caught Bruce Linton's eye. He saw American consciousness shifting: it was as if he were a minor league ballplayer getting called up to the Show. He appeared with Jim Cramer on *Mad Money* and talked to the pundits on CNBC; he said he liked the Acreage commercial. It touched him.

And two months later, Acreage Holdings was purchased by Canopy Growth for $3.4 billion. The two men — Bruce Linton and Kevin Murphy, the Acreage CEO — met in Davos, Switzerland, in January 2019, at the Cannabis House, a party house hosted by Lorne Gertner and the Canadian Securities Exchange.

———•

Still, there were problems. Because weed was still not federally legal in the U.S., American weed companies couldn't open chequing accounts.

Dispensaries in Chicago and Los Angeles weren't able to accept credit cards. An American investment bank couldn't help take an American weed brand public. Banking laws, not weed laws, were what brought the money back to Canada.

This was what made Lorne Gertner so happy after 10.17. You wanted to invest in mining, you looked to Africa. Energy, talk to the U.S. And if you were looking to seek financing for your weed brands, you had to venture to Bay Street in Toronto, the epicentre of Canada's big five banks, all able to support, invest in, and nurture publicly listed marijuana companies. After Linton brought BMO into the cannabis fold in January 2018 — the first big bank to publicly get involved with weed — the other banks followed, which sent the little guys scrambling. Now, most independent financiers like Chip devoted all of their time to American cannabis companies. McSalty, Linton's financier, couldn't compete with RBC and didn't want to; the independents made their money in the margins. At the start of something, in the grey zone, not at its crest. Meanwhile, unlike in the U.S., the banks in Canada would lend money to Canadian cannabis companies and even allowed such simple necessities for running a business as a line of credit and banking online. So as the Canadian pot stocks rose in valuations by the Super Bowl kickoff in 2019, more eyes turned to the Canadian cannabis market. If you were looking for weed — whether to short a company or start your own — Canada, over anywhere else in the world, was the place to be.

That was paying off for Bruce Linton and Mark Zekulin at Canopy Growth. At Christmas 2018, Linton's market cap was $8.9 billion. It was $16.6 billion on January 25, 2019. It was a start-up rivalling the market cap of U.S. Steel. God Bud, a strain named after a potent mix of Hawaiian crossed with Purple Skunk, had an effect like being submerged in a vat of Greek yoghurt set adrift in the Dead Sea. Linton says being him at this time felt something like that. He could feel no pain.

McSalty describes Linton's confidence after the Acreage deal like "King Kong on coke." Linton was walking on air. If you were an American entrepreneur or a multinational consumer packaged goods brand; if you made skincare or whisky, potato chips or soap; if you puffed a bong hit in college or danced at a bat mitzvah to Snoop Dogg; or if you were John Fowler's

Pride of Smiths Falls: Linton at the Pride Parade in Toronto, 2019.

church-going grandmother, you were likely to be thinking about or investing in weed. And the Canadian pot companies had so many businesses you could buy. The power that came along with a $16.6 billion market cap blew hinges off doors.

"It's rocket fuel," says Linton, who, like Terry Booth, tells me that he has attention deficit disorder, a condition that both men describe as a professional advantage. In cannabis, you needed to be doing everything everywhere all at once — there were other people for looking after the details. Linton says he took in the universe around him in early 2019, the Americans showing up at his door for deals and advice, and felt validated. After the risk came the reward: confidence. Entrepreneurs from all over crowded around him to make deals. I saw Bruce speak at a cannabis convention, and when he left the stage, it seemed like half of the conference followed him outside.

Linton tells me that he doesn't like quiet, doesn't read books, can't stand "sad emotions" or a non-ringing phone. It's like there's an Instagram feed constantly on in his brain and he's always in need of more likes, the next move. Linton made no bones about hopping a plane to Germany for a meeting, making it back in time to greet Ted Chung in Los Angeles, and then heading out to Smiths Falls, all without deep reflection. Lorne Gertner says nobody worked as hard as Bruce, and the movement was the point. It was always about the next thing, the next announcement, and he was able to compartmentalize and move on. The only people he was in contact with were the ones he was working with on current deals. And the more he ate, the hungrier he became. At the Raptors game when Kawhi Leonard played for Toronto to beat his former team, the San Antonio Spurs, Linton was in attendance. He wore a Tweed shirt. He shit talked with Toronto mayor John Tory. Life was thrilling. He was eating too much. Travelling all the time. Drinking every night in a new city for a meeting. And hustling. Always hustling. He had assets in Europe, the U.S., the Netherlands, and bought up the companies he wanted from his peers. Linton tells me he didn't get jet lag. He didn't check the market. Didn't keep track of the value of his shares. Didn't worry about Constellation. It was the happiest time of his life.

"What should I do?" he wondered. He smiles. "Everything."

———•

The Acreage deal after the Constellation investment was contingent upon federal legalization in the United States. It was the first deal of its kind and added to the Canopy war chest. Among the board of Acreage Holdings was John Boehner, the former Speaker of the United States, who now answered, to some small degree, to Bruce. If Bill Blair was divisive, John Boehner — in a cannabis activist's eyes — was the Moby Dick of assholes. He was "unalterably opposed" to marijuana while in office and voted against legalizing medical weed in Washington, DC. However, if the Acreage deal passed, Boehner stood to pocket $20 million. In an interview he said, "There's more interest in this than I would have guessed." It made Alan Young cringe, and disgusted Rosie Rowbotham.

"The United States," said Linton in his press release announcing the Acreage deal, "is the next stop on Canopy Growth's desired path."

With the U.S. having ten times the population of Canada, Linton thought, turning over his double-digit multibillion-dollar market cap, what could the value of Canopy be if it achieved equal scale there? Certainly that's what Constellation Brands, the maker of Corona beer, considered. Canopy was a start-up. But marijuana was working. One hundred and fifty-one thousand Canadians now drew legal paycheques from weed. Those were net new jobs in the marketplace. In Smiths Falls, Canopy was the largest employer, providing over twelve hundred people with work. There were sixteen Canadian cannabis weed brands worth more than $1 billion each, none of which existed before 2013. Marijuana executives were becoming celebrities. John Fowler drove a Jaguar and smoked out of an engraved vaporizer that read "$100 million," a gift from his partner at BMO. *Toronto Life* listed Alison Gordon on the city's fifty most influential people for 2019, ahead of David Thomson, who owns the *Globe and Mail* and has the most extensive private art collection in the country. Terry Booth had gone from stealing his father's weed and selling it to his buddies to growing so much marijuana in Edmonton that he changed the smell of his hometown. Cannabis had brought, according to Deloitte, $43.5 billion to Canada's GDP. The business hadn't even begun.

"Cannabis has been one of the greatest entrepreneur stories this country has had, if not ever, then certainly in the last few decades," says John Fowler, whose Supreme Cannabis Company had over four hundred employees at the start of 2019. Fowler remembers the first time he tried weed and how much it agreed with his constitution. He grew pot in his closet and remembers doing a bad job at selling dime bags from his backpack at his local high school. There were marches in Ottawa in support of legalization in the 1990s, and there were the blunts he smoked in law school, including during the bar exam. Fowler finished third in his class. I say to him, "You know, if you didn't smoke weed, you could've finished first." "That's backwards," he replies. "Without weed, I would've dropped out of school."

Thanks to legalization, pot was being reclaimed and reframed. The joke on *The Simpsons* that Alan Young liked back in the 1990s was an oblique reference to Otto having a funny smell on his jacket. In 2020, there was an entire episode dedicated to medical weed.

Deals in the sector blossomed from the $61 million that Linton paid in 2015 for Bedrocan to the $3.4 billion he had just agreed to in 2019 for Acreage Holdings. The scale was much different, and the mainstream, following Constellation Brands, was now looking for partners in weed. Molson partnered with Hexo, and Altria, the parent company of Philip Morris USA, with a market cap of US$163 billion, one of the hundred most valuable companies in the world, invested in Cronos. James Poelzer, at Ascent Industries, credits Linton and Booth with forcing the industry to think big. "The public markets and international expansion was never part of our original business plan, but right after legalization it felt like it was irresponsible not to pursue your biggest bet," Poelzer says. Between Linton and Booth, it was a race to grow. Non-cannabis properties like BioSteel, a popular hydration product used by the NHL, became legitimate potential partners for cannabis brands. The juggernaut that is the Ultimate Fighting Championship struck a deal with Aurora. Kristen Bell from *Veronica Mars* launched a CBD line. Bruce Linton was pursuing a British company that made lotion and soap. "It's not about grams," he tells me. "It's about milligrams. The trick is taking our shit and putting it into everything else."

St-Louis at Hexo had the same idea as Linton. Any fizzy water, shampoo, or pet food could increase its cost per unit by adding CBD. In turn, that was where cannabis companies could find the best margins. Even though the licensed producers were having trouble growing quality cannabis at scale, they were already looking past their internal problems toward future horizons. In the hub-and-spoke model — Sébastien's idea, in which a cannabis company is the hub and any number of different companies in different markets provide the spokes —you take anything with a distribution network and a brand name, and partner up with a weed company. A Pepsi cost a dollar. Put some weed in it, and you could sell it for ten. Cannabis made existing products more valuable. "A company that's a good partner for a cannabis brand is anybody with a platform, but no CBD," says Linton. "And what you buy leads to the migration of where you're going. The point is to do it faster than anyone else."

Not everyone, however, was convinced that Canadian companies could, or even should, take over the world. "Everybody wants to build these big mega-corporations, and it's like we're not only trying to become American, but 1952 America," says Trevor Fencott, who became a Canopy employee after Linton purchased his company Mettrum. Fencott wasn't sure about his new boss's approach.

Uncontrolled growth isn't necessarily good, Fencott tells me. "It's like somehow having offices in ten countries around the world offers legitimacy, but uncontrolled growth isn't the definition of success. In fact, it's the definition of cancer."

Fencott was going through a life change while working at Canopy. He liked Linton, but with his father battling cancer at the end of 2017, Fencott felt it was time for a change. Medical marijuana was relentless, and then, four days before he left Canopy, his dad passed away. He had worked hard at Mettrum, and it had begun quickly after he and Michael Haines started and sold their tech company. After selling Mettrum, Fencott and Haines both felt like they might leave marijuana altogether. Even though Fencott had fallen for the plant, the financials rang false to him, and he was beginning to worry about how the boom might end. Fencott spent time at Canopy and had stock options; still, he was concerned.

"We see grotesque corporate excesses happening and these crazy deals, and it looks like the high-water mark," he says. "But what you really see is something more like Wile E. Coyote at the edge of the cliff: he's running real fast, but all he stands on is air."

Before he could leave marijuana, however, Fencott's teenager brought home a pamphlet from school about the evils of pot. It wasn't written by the 1920s *Black Candle* scribe Emily Murphy — not exactly. But the dog whistle of *Reefer Madness* rang in his home. "It was garbage, not the truth, as if the way we're educating our children hadn't changed since before Le Dain," says Fencott, who sensed that the cannabis retailers were where a new generation of Canadians would actually learn about weed.

For the next generation of teenagers, weed could become more popular than beer. Still, Fencott hemmed and hawed until his wife Dana, a Big Pharma veteran (and cannabis consumer), encouraged him to remain involved. If pamphlets like the one his son brought home were how the kids were learning about cannabis, he owed it to the plant to tell the story properly. This time, however, says Fencott, he and Haines were going to work differently. Haines had Hoshi, an international medicinal licensed producer based in Portugal, and Fencott became obsessed with cannabis retail. An idea was born for Fire & Flower, which would use data to track every cannabis sale. Fencott met with Mark Zekulin at Canopy and Vic Neufeld at Aphria to discuss his nascent retail idea, an upscale, non-licensed-producer-affiliated retail-store chain that, above all else, could be a source for marijuana education. Says Fencott, "Against all these lofty valuations, I thought there could still be a space for truth."

———•

Ted Chung, Snoop Dogg's business partner, remained committed to Canada, and to Canopy.

In 2017 and 2018, Chung came monthly from Los Angeles to Toronto — and quarterly out to Smiths Falls. Chung says he saw the human element that Trevor Fencott had pitched all those years back in how a cannabis company could contribute to the re-emergence of a small town. Since 2008, the Hershey factory in Smiths Falls had been abandoned, a cottage for squirrels and raccoons. In 2013, Linton invested his own money into 1 Hershey Drive and, though they almost missed paying contractors and it cost Chuck Rifici his job, the team did get the factory converted into a forty-two-acre cannabis grow op with thirty-nine growing rooms, making it the largest indoor cannabis facility in the world. Both the mayor and Ted Chung were proud.

Chung witnessed the growth of the city up close and illustrates the impact with the story of a small restaurant. Chuckles Jack was a little chicken shop owned by a Sri Lankan chef in Smiths Falls where Chung would dine whenever he was in town. A bon vivant, Chung liked eating out, especially exotic food, or at least a step up from roadside-restaurant chains. He befriended the young Sri Lankan and marvelled at how, over the years, Chuckles Jack grew from five tables and a waitress into a three-story joint with a patio and a happening bar. If marijuana was an incubator for job creation, Smiths Falls became ground zero for growth. They were creating jobs.

"Bruce and Mark made sure they connected with the people of Smiths Falls, and I saw their commitment to the town," says Chung, who was the right guy to impress; as the creator and producer of the hit show *Martha & Snoop's Potluck Dinner Party*, he began talking to Martha Stewart about cannabis. Stewart, a billionaire, had questions. She was curious about California and Colorado.

Ted Chung had a different idea. He knew who she should meet. "I was impressed by the guys, and knew that she would be, too," says Chung.

"What do you know about Canada?" Chung asked Stewart when she asked him how she might get involved in marijuana. "Canada," he said, "is the best place to try."

In Smiths Falls, Martha Stewart would bond with Hilary Black over their love of animals. While Stewart wanted to produce a line of CBD dog treats and ready-to-bake products, Black wanted Canopy to transform the country like it had Smiths Falls. She wanted Stewart to work with her on using cannabis to help fight the crisis with opioids. Black was still trying, with Mark Ware and Marc Wayne, the team that had been together at Bedrocan, to conduct research with medicinal weed. They did this work through Spectrum Therapeutics — the research arm of Canopy Growth that was looking to further the data on and comprehension of the plant. Despite the growth of these companies, quantitative data on what cannabis did to the mind and body was still hard to find. There were anecdotes all over. But in terms of science, it was still 2016-era evidence. The Acreage Super Bowl ad was poignant. But it fell short on proof. There was no doubt, however, that millions of people were using medical marijuana. And despite the increase in usage, to this day there hasn't been an overdose death from weed.

That's why Hilary Black wanted to harness the power of Canopy, the power of Martha Stewart, and the power of Snoop Dogg and Ted Chung to lobby the Canadian Senate and change the way that cannabis as medicine was taxed. She was supported by all of them in her work. Black had pitched Zekulin on a new job title — C-suite — and put together a team whose mission wasn't only patient advocacy, but also global legalization — not from a legal perspective, but from a human rights one, echoing back to the original case with Terry Parker. True, Black was still pissed about Zekulin and Linton selling their shares before legalization, but she learned from that episode, advocated for herself, and was rewarded. Both her team and her compensation grew.

"With wind in our sails in every facet of the company, it was time to, you know, change the world," Black tells me, adding that she ran into Martha Stewart in the Canopy headquarters and galvanized her, as she did everybody, with her personal story.

Chung had brought Snoop to Canopy for the partiers. But that was only half the business story. Next Bruce Linton wanted to offer Martha Stewart for the moms.

———•

Just three months after legalization, Linton had assets in Europe, Africa, and South America. He had health drinks and hair care, not to mention the most funded capacity in Canada and a line of weed drinks and edibles ready to hit the stores, which he owned thanks to Tokyo Smoke. Retail was coming to Ontario, and now Linton also had Snoop Dogg and Acreage. Linton and Zekulin flew to New York to pitch Martha Stewart; Chung says Linton's ready-to-bake concepts blew the entrepreneur away. "Bruce and Martha hit it off and the deal was consummated," says Chung. In February 2019, Canopy Growth officially partnered with Martha.

"The bigger the place got, the easier it was to run," says Linton. "I have more levers, more triggers, better currency, a better team — we need to always be moving." Linton didn't offer workers a shoulder to cry on or understand burn-out or fatigue. "I'm a bad motivational speaker," he says. "I told the team, if this feels stressful and you're bitching on your way to work, talk to HR. Stress should be when you have nothing to do because you're going to get laid off. If you're twenty-seven, this is the most interesting work experience you'll ever have in your life. When do all of these things synchronize in the world — let alone Canada?"

CHAPTER 12

Dark Clouds

"The industry's fucked."

Stephen Arbib

Dollars behind the Constellation investment into Canopy were negotiable, Bruce Linton says. The billions. What wasn't negotiable was the number of seats that Constellation would have on the Canopy board. Linton could have his money, but he'd lose his autonomy — and that condition wasn't going to change. Conversations between the two brands began in 2016, and Linton knew he needed a flush American partner to extend his product range and distribution network. He had gotten close to inking a deal with Diageo, the British distributor of Guinness, Johnnie Walker, and Captain Morgan rum. But it was still difficult to get mainstream buy-in from non-cannabis brands, despite major industries witnessing the valuations of the Canadian weed companies. Alcohol, as a vice industry, was the category analysts expected to be most negatively impacted by cannabis sales. All the new pot smokers might not need as much booze.

Looking at the Constellation deal, Linton had a choice. Did he want to grow and move beyond Canada, and, if he didn't, could he risk losing his pole position to Terry Booth or someone else? It was a Faustian bargain. Should he amass a bigger war chest than all of his rivals — combined — or pause, maintain full autonomy, and cede ground at Canopy Growth? Just like that WEED ticker, Linton knew: if he didn't take the Constellation money, someone else would.

"It's difficult to find another scenario where a five-and-a-half-year-old company got $5 billion for seventeen percent of the company — cash," Linton says. He knew there was a risk involved, not necessarily to his company, but to him. Bruce faced the wind. "If you're worried about your own skin more than you're worried about your company, you should be taken out and killed — immediately."

Like Terry Booth getting in bed with Nelson Peltz, these were considered risks. Giving up power for money. Both men wanted their companies to be the world's biggest marijuana companies. And growth was oxygen. What Trevor Fencott warned against, being too big too soon, Bruce and Terry pursued, like addicts. And so now, after the Constellation deal — the big one, the C$5 billion announced August 15, 2018 — Linton's Monday morning board meetings were different. Painful. The kind of guy who took the small office so he could escape meetings was now trapped in them, all the time. Before the Constellation deal, Bruce's board — his close friends, including real estate wizard Murray Goldman — rubber-stamped his plans. Budgets and projects were approved quickly, without too much navel gazing. Cannabis was not the industry for beard-stroking and philosophy. Linton's favourite philosopher was Elon Musk.

"Every Monday morning since acquiring Bedrocan, we had a nine-fifteen with the board," Linton says. "It's way easier to have frequent board meetings where I tell them what we're going to buy and sell. That allowed us to move faster than anyone else." He says Canopy was built for speed. After the Constellation billions, however, Bruce was ordered to go slow. "I don't understand when they say 'Sit, roll over,' all these fucking commands," Linton says, adding that in January 2019, four months into Constellation Brands' investment and just around the time he was announcing his deal with Ascent, he was talking to a banker friend and came to a realization: "I don't speak corporate lingo."

The time for corporate lingo was upon him: presenting the numbers the board needed to see, a path to profitability, and detailed forecasts of EBITDA (earnings before interest, taxes, depreciation, and amortization) — the true revenue number and the metric by which cannabis companies would suddenly become judged. But the founder wouldn't budge.

He thought his new board's request for a five-year plan illustrated how little Constellation Brands knew about weed. Linton explained how quickly things changed in cannabis. The board wanted forecasting, but Linton believed that was impossible in marijuana. When he started Tweed, there was no way of knowing that Trudeau would be elected promising to legalize pot, to sell it not like a medicine, but like a beer. How could the end of prohibition sit in an Excel cell? And other laws were still being written.

There was a whole slew of new products — edibles, vapes, and weed drinks, stuff that Linton and his cronies themselves could consume — that were legal in California and Colorado but Linton still wasn't allowed to sell in Canada. He owned a Hershey chocolate factory! How much would it earn when he could sell cannabis chocolates? John Aird had raised millions of dollars for an edibles company in Canada called Olli. Originally, Aird was going to make edibles for Vic Neufeld at Aphria, but when that partnership faltered, he used his licensing know-how to work with new partners and open a Cannabis 2.0 business for himself. When would he be able to sell gummies, brownies, and sugar-free mints, and what would that be worth? What could happen to cannabis revenues when the soccer moms came to Tokyo Smoke? Or when Canopy products were sold at No Frills? No one knew. Not Health Canada's Eric Costen. Not Anne McLellan with the cannabis task force. Not Alan Young, the lifelong cannabis lawyer. And certainly not me. Though it was fun to attend cannabis parties and try and find out.

In March of 2019, however, there still weren't any cannabis stores open in Ontario. Despite the dreams of Trevor Fencott and Lorne Gertner, their fancy pot shops in Toronto sat empty on expensive real estate lots, like Ferraris that just sat in the garage. "Ontario shat the bed," says Terry Booth — and you didn't have to be drunk to know that.

Even in provinces where there were retail shops, provinces with small populations like Manitoba and Newfoundland, the industry was hampered with problems. According to retailers in Alberta, where there were stores, a shop would purchase their week's allotment of legal cannabis on a Thursday. On that same Thursday, the weed was all gone. It sold out in a day, and the retailer had to wait another week to restock. So much potential revenue was being pissed away exactly at the time when cannabis companies were being challenged to show profits.

In early 2019, legal pot shops, like the five owned by Alcanna in Alberta, cleared $1 million each week in the first five days after receiving their cannabis shipments. However, the other two days were spent with employees sitting in a shop with no inventory. "You can't sell what you can't sell," Linton says, meaning that if your product isn't on the shelves because you don't have any, and there's nowhere to sell it anyway, it's hard to forecast your EBITDA. Linton tried to explain this to the Constellation Brands board.

Meanwhile, all over the country, legal cannabis growers — just like during the medical days — were desperately trying to speed up harvests, which couldn't be done. Marijuana isn't produced on an assembly line. And growing identical bud at scale isn't the same as bottling Coronas. Whether it was Aphria's outdoor crops in Leamington or Aurora's million-square-foot greenhouse weed in Alberta, no one was getting their pot to the retailers fast enough. Despite spending billions of dollars, none of the licensed producers were growing enough cannabis. Or making their cannabis good enough. And this played into the hands of the black market, which was terrible for Justin Trudeau and the Liberal government because defeating that black market would determine if the Cannabis Act was a success and, to some extent, if the Canadian model — legalized weed — should be replicated all over the world.

"This is the thing," says Alan Young, echoing Woody Allen. "The pot was terrible in 2019, and there wasn't enough of it."

Linton was expanding, explaining himself, and pivoting, all at the same time, while retailers told me they received packaging without product inside their childproof bottles. Complaints ricocheted across the internet that the legal weed was crumbly, dry, mildewy, expensive, and— worst of all — weak. At one point, the only cannabis available on the market was milled marijuana, ground up from the bottom of the plant, à la Prairie Plant Systems 2.0. A year into legalization, it was embarrassing that billion-dollar

Green Giant: Alison Gordon, founder of 48North, standing before bags of her weed. She was named one of fifty most influential people for 2019 by *Toronto Life*.

companies with global ambitions still couldn't do the one job they had: grow weed. You're bigger than Air Canada and you can't grow bud better than someone's cousin?

Of course, weed smokers have been complaining about their purchases since John Fowler sold dime bags, but now the grumblings affected the New York Stock Exchange. Plus, a byzantine distribution network created bottlenecks, so even if the pot was good, which it wasn't, it certainly wouldn't be helped by sitting in a warehouse for weeks, or even months, before it made its way into smokers' lungs.

"We did a terrible job, a brutal job — all the LPs [licensed producers] — and I was losing my shit," says Terry Booth, who produced eleven thousand pounds of weed in 2018, and, together with Linton, controlled 50 percent of domestic recreational sales. Canopy had the global funded capacity of 4 million square feet. Aphria was licensed across more than 1 million square feet just in Canada. In March 2019, Sébastien St-Louis at Hexo — he had renamed his company Hexo from Hydropothecary, influenced by Hennessy X.O — purchased Jay Wilgar's Newstrike Brands for $260 million and increased his funded capacity by 470,000 square feet. And yet, even without Ontario opening a single store, there still wasn't enough weed to go around.

Hard to make money with that kind of overhead and nothing to sell.

Rob Sands is an unlikely person to have changed Canadian weed. Constellation Brands was a legacy play for the Sands family, who'd begun their family business in 1945 and grown their company into America's leading wine distributor and third largest beer maker. Sands, the Constellation CEO, made an offhand comment in a beverage industry trade rag suggesting he was open to the marijuana market, and Linton had hunted him down. There were a few false starts before Bruce's underlings began side-channelling up the Constellation ladder on LinkedIn. Eventually, Linton and Sands connected, and they consummated their first deal in October 2017. Then Constellation Brands made its big investment into Canopy in the summer of 2018, right before legalization. Canopy would take Constellation Brands from the past, alcohol, to the future, weed.

On the day pot was legalized, however, October 17, 2018, it was announced Linton would lose his biggest booster. In March 2019, Sands would retire. His replacement, Bill Newlands, former Constellation Brands chief growth officer, took to his CEO job with garden shears — cuts, not growth, were on the horizon. In his first earnings report, Newlands's initial public comment on Canopy was this: "We're not pleased."

Linton didn't understand. He was doing exactly what he said he'd do: grow. Newlands, however, wanted to see Canopy make, not spend, money. Linton said he just needed time. Production was streamlining — every cannabis CEO swore the same thing — and, on June 14, 2019, Health Canada finally announced a release date for Cannabis 2.0: as of October 17, 2019, edibles, vapes, and cannabis beverages could legally be sold. These were new revenue streams, pot products not for stoners, but for everyone else.

"Canada was in the pole position. We had the best public policy, best access to capital, and there were no Americans on the playing field," says Linton. "The last time Canada had a lead like this was Alexander Graham Bell. BlackBerry didn't come close."

Canopy was leading in market share, earned media, market cap. It was a behemoth. Let us grow, Linton told Newlands. Plus, when Europe opens up, when the States do, the profit will come.

Newlands, a Wharton graduate and a Harvard Business School MBA, wasn't sold. Many tables were set — science, Europe, soap, energy drinks, Martha Stewart — but they weren't producing enough money. Canopy couldn't be Uber: scale as a strategy to wipe out the competition, without profit. The Canadian cannabis model, Newlands told Linton, was through.

Linton blames the communication gap for the friction. "Because I didn't focus on their explanation to their shareholders and their shareholders didn't love the deal, that put pressure on Bill," Linton says. He explains that the Constellation shareholders only saw Canopy's millions in losses, and Linton couldn't reassure his new board that an uptick for Constellation Brands, on the back of Canopy, would occur over time. Not speaking corporate lingo drove a wedge in the partnership from day one.

"I should've made sure I understood how they were going to explain to their shareholders that while their earnings per share may have diminished in the short run, that by giving us money, they had a robust future, and their stock, eventually, would become three hundred dollars per share and not one hundred and eighty-two dollars." It's not regret Linton feels exactly. Not anger. Certainly not shame. It's missed opportunity: a Hall of Fame pitcher taken out in the third inning after working his whole life for the decisive World Series game. "Had I just explained it to them in their own language, they would have said, 'Mr. Linton, you're a genius. What would you like to do?'"

———•

Vic Neufeld, the president of Aphria, citing health problems and a need to spend more time with his family, stepped down on January 11, 2019. He didn't mention short reports or the allegations that Gabriel Grego had made about personally profiting from paying too much for international properties. Looking for the quiet life after leaving Jamieson Laboratories, Neufeld discovered instead that cannabis was as chaotic as his beloved Detroit Lions' Thanksgiving Day football games. Marijuana, however, gets into your bones and Neufeld is still active in cannabis, advising many cannabis companies, including John Aird's Olli. "It was one hell of a journey," Neufeld tells me between cigarette breaks over breakfast one morning in a Marriott Hotel near Pearson Airport in Toronto. "I created a behemoth in Canada."

Neufeld says he fondly remembers competing with MedReleaf to sign up veteran patients for his medical weed, and the time Bruce Linton tried to hire him away from Aphria. Neufeld is proud to say that he went through his Rolodex, not consultants, to build the Aphria infrastructure and his financial team. He says that, even though both Bruce Linton and Terry Booth badmouthed him on Bay Street, saying sunlit greenhouses wouldn't work for growing cannabis, he liked all the people he competed with.

"I wasn't a user," he says. "This was all new to me."

As for the short report, the acquisitions, the accusations, the Scythian deal, Gabriel Grego, and what happened in Jamaica and Colombia, Neufeld is obviously in no mood to confess. "We always, *always* played within the rules of the game," he says, and talks wistfully about Aphria being down to its last $100,000 while awaiting its medical licence in 2014. He talks about how much he loved Cole Cacciavillani, his childhood friend from Windsor, and John Cervini — "my boys" — the farming entrepreneurs who first brought him the idea of working in weed. "I had my boat already, my Florida home, but I still had a little gas left in the engine," he says of the time just before he joined Aphria in June 2014. "It ended up getting personal. I don't like failure and I never felt fear. If you feel fear, you will fail. I had the right fortitude to accept risks. It all worked out in the end, oh my."

The Aphria experience, culminating at the start of 2019 with Neufeld's exit, did nothing to enhance the industry's image to a sobering financial audience, from Constellation executives to regulators at the Nasdaq exchange. Marijuana executives always struggled to achieve respectability. All along, they were telling the world, the business community, investors, and also activists, consumers, and colleagues, from Martha Stewart to Bill Newlands, that they were sober professionals, serious people. However, bad behaviour in the sector made them look like amateurs, or worse, criminals, as critics had always warned. The huge market caps didn't entirely wipe the stigma away.

"If you don't take us, our product, or our industry seriously, why give us money?" John Fowler would think, after taking the investment bank's money. Almost as if to double down on his cannabis principles, to draw a line in the sand and define himself as a "weed guy," not a suit, Fowler quit drinking on the Halloween after legalization and made a point of excusing himself during investor dinners to step outside for a joint while the bankers got sauced. Lorne Gertner also quit drinking. So did Alison Gordon. So did Marc Wayne and John Aird. As Vic Neufeld says, by 2019, pot was personal and often made strange bedfellows.

Weed guys and investors, the two camps working together, but not quite seeing eye to eye. Pot always had an us-against-them mentality, and sometimes, be it the growers versus the executives, or the cannabis executives versus the legacy market, or the independent investment bankers versus the big five Canadian banks, or, just as often, the companies against one another, the animosity made cannabis a divisive, even dangerous industry.

"You mean you're coming into our sector, but make fun of it, or you're willing to profit from it while actively against it, against us, and what we do?" asks Fowler, who has trouble understanding how a white CEO of a cannabis mega-company could profit off marijuana while believing people who sell weed outside the legal system are criminals who belong in jail. "Anyone who thinks you should be in jail for pot while selling pot is an asshole," Fowler says.

Stephen Arbib agrees with Fowler. He also thinks the reason the companies struggle mightily to grow — the reason why funded capacity doesn't equal actual weed — is because most cannabis companies didn't start as his company, MedReleaf did, well capitalized and with a black market grower like Tom Flow. Cannabis, as the legal market learned after the Deloitte valuations, isn't tomatoes. Expanding your greenhouses before perfecting your growing methods squandered millions of dollars. "We knew that these companies could barely grow in ten thousand square feet. They could never grow in a million," says Arbib. "That's a reason why I was like, 'This industry is going to have a massive correction. None of this makes sense.' I can buy a piece of land and my company goes up one hundred times in value, but I've never demonstrated that I know how to grow."

Arbib says, "That's why there's cannabis shortage — that's why the industry's fucked."

———•

Alan Young, the lawyer who fought to establish the Canadian medical marijuana program in the 1990s, feels like the industry in 2019 wasn't fucked, just fucked up. He doesn't like seeing business schmucks getting rich all around him. Especially since those same schmucks paraded through his office in the early 2000s looking for an assist with their medical licences. "Always the same types of people — a money guy and a grubby grower — and they'd come in and bring me samples and they were never great. I'd always say the same thing: if you guys are in for the long haul, this is a good investment, and I believe recreational is in the air," recalls Young, who met with Canopy, Aurora, and Cronos in the early years and has a hard time rationalizing the fortune he let walk away. He didn't have money to invest, and the companies weren't looking to make him a VP.

While he was taking on pro bono possession cases and staying close with Health Canada in order to be involved with regulations, he didn't have the capital of Lorne Gertner and never became a pot millionaire. Young loves weed, but he's not a martyr. All around him, pot millionaires who didn't consume the product celebrated their IPOs and American partnerships while the Canadian system forgot about him, Terry Parker, Rosie, and Aaron Harnett. Young, mirroring the counterculture, viewed the police and politicians, the money guys, lawyers, and bankers as enemies, phonies. Legal pot made people rich. Other people viewed the counterculture as us against them. Pot smokers, as Brent Zettl discovered — "They think it's their God-given right to grow cannabis," he tells me — distrusted the government system. Part of the reason the black market still exists today is consumers actively opting out of the legal system. At the start of 2019, more than half of Canada's cannabis consumers, even after legalization, bought weed from the black market. Not because they had to. Because they were making a choice. What the legal market discovered was that pot smokers, not soccer moms — despite pot shops that look like Tiffany's — consume the greatest amount of weed, and the heaviest consumers buy their weed illegally. Sales in the first year of legalization of cannabis reached nearly $1 billion. Sales in the illicit market ranged from $5 billion to $7 billion.

"These bank people just assumed all these revenue projections. Are you fucking kidding me?" says Young. "Cannabis users that I know are not coming to you. They actively hate you."

Terry Parker never buys legal weed. Rosie Rowbotham said he can't stand the stuff, though he never even took a puff. He hated it on principle. He used to fight against the police, he told me, not buy weed from them. Alan Young says he isn't hateful of the industry after legalization, though he wishes Bruce Linton could have offered him a better job than a decorated tour guide at 1 Hershey Drive. But what rankles him, what enrages Alan Young — what he feels contempt for — isn't the executives or the bankers. It's the law-officer cannabis profiteers. It's not only John Boehner, who became partners with Bruce Linton from his perch at Acreage Holdings, but Julian Fantino and his Aleafia co-founder Raf Souccar, both former Toronto cops.

"You're not entitled to make money from an activity that you ruined people's lives for doing. It's morally reprehensible," says Young. None of those original people — Terry, Rosie — made a dollar from legalization. "As much as the system barred growers and compassion centre people, they should've barred cops and vice squad officers. It's just wrong. How do you sleep at night?"

Nick Lalonde at CannTrust was having his own trouble sleeping. On January 14, 2019, three days after Vic Neufeld at Aphria resigned, Lalonde was still trying to get someone at his company to take ownership of erecting the false walls around the unlicensed grow rooms.

He got an uneasy feeling when his company signed a deal to sell fifteen thousand kilograms of Aleafia bud. Aleafia, which listed on the Toronto Stock Exchange on March 19, 2019, was co-founded by Fantino, the former Ontario Provincial Police commissioner, and Souccar, former RCMP deputy commissioner, and was hated, even more than most government weed brands, by the legacy market. Back in 2004, Fantino shared his thoughts on cannabis legalization with the *Toronto Sun*. "I guess we can legalize murder too." Lalonde felt sick to his stomach. "A company breaking the law," he says, "shouldn't be selling weed from the police."

———●

In September 2019, a month before vapes would become legal in Canada, the Centers for Disease Control and Prevention (CDC) told Americans to stop vaping.

People were getting sick from vaping, to the degree that the president of the United States warned Americans on Twitter about their harm, even though the vapes they were using were illegal. Vape pens from China sold at drugstores around North America contained a vitamin E acetate that was making people ill and, in at least forty-two documented cases, causing death. The vapes that were killing people were illegal. They weren't sold at licensed stores or made by licensed companies. However, there was very little differentiation between the legal products and the illegal knockoffs; customers tended to think that if it was being sold at their corner shop, how could it be against the law?

But vaping has always been part of medical marijuana, and Cannabis 2.0 was seen as a giant new revenue stream. John Fowler believed vapes would be bigger than edibles. The reason why vaping has always been the preferred method of medical marijuana consumption is because people with cancer, with asthma, with heart conditions — really, anybody — shouldn't inhale combusted materials. In the legal cannabis industry, vapes started popping up even before they became legal. Their discreet, odourless method of delivery makes them perfect for micro-dosing inside a club, investor dinner, or bar. The first pot from Flin Flon was ground up for vape pens. When Tony

Dean was trying to change the weed laws in the Senate and tried pot to counter his side effects from chemo, he vaped. Linton paid $220 million for Storz & Bickel, a German vape company, in December 2018. Lorne Gertner had been working on vapes with Moses Znaimer since the very start of Cannasat, way back in 2005. Now, vapes were finally about to become legal, and the president of the United States was saying not to vape.

At the start of 2019, vapes were passed around high schools, mostly thanks to a company called Juul — which made candy-flavoured faux-cigarette products — but the CDC wasn't targeting the legal tobacco vape market. Bubble gum nicotine flavours may be a deplorable business ploy, but Juul did well enough to attract $12.8 billion in December 2018 from Altria for 35 percent of the company. Altria, in the heavily regulated tobacco industry, was used to pivots. And would make more. On December 7, Altria invested $1.8 billion to own 45 percent of Mike Gorenstein's Cronos Group — a deal further marrying Big Tobacco, like Big Alcohol, with Big Weed.

But the September announcement couldn't have come at a worse time. The industry was pinning at least some of its hopes on vapes. In terms of the legal cannabis market, the big bet on vapes — which were expensive to produce — took a publicity hit before the first legal vape pen could be sold in October. Who could have forecast something like that?

"We loved vapes and were ready to bet big," says James Poelzer, the former CFO of Ascent Industries, whose regulatory nightmares continued after recreational legalization and through the new year. As his dreams were tied up in edibles and vapes and recreational flower, he had both his medical and recreational licences suspended by Health Canada. To this day, Poelzer is bitter. He says Health Canada found a box of his documents regarding his grey market medical sales.

"We should've just shredded that shit," Poelzer tells me, then drops the most notorious name in weed. "Like CannTrust."

Poelzer resigned from Ascent at the end of November 2018, when his company's licence was suspended. Ascent then announced Blair Jordan, former

CFO, as their interim CEO. In a press release in April 2019, Jordan talked about appointing a crime expert as an independent director and, as the executive of a licensed weed brand, stamping out his industry's connection with organized crime. To Poelzer's dismay, Jordan said in an interview that his company had ties to the Hells Angels. He still says that today. "A huge amount of money, especially in BC, that found its way into the industry is from organized crime," Jordan told me, speaking on an encrypted line. Jordan said he couldn't even sit by a window in the Ascent office for fear of a Hells Angels drive-by. "My head was spinning," said Jordan, who added that he walked with a bodyguard around his company's headquarters in Maple Ridge. "They don't come at you with guns and say, 'Do this for us or we'll kill you.' Instead, they sit with you over coffee. They're professional, but the threat is implied."

Alison Gordon of 48North is friends with James Poelzer and has visited his facility in Maple Ridge many times. She says she never needed anything resembling bodyguards and didn't catch any dangerous vibes. Whatever the truth is, a public cannabis company breaking the law and tied to criminals, and more BC underground growers operating lawlessly, attracts the same kind of negative headwind as the vape crisis, the police, and political profiteers. Despite the Altria money — because of it? Or maybe the money just made bad things look worse? — the industry was in crisis. In November 2018, a thirty-one-year-old Indigenous man in Winnipeg was arrested for possession of eighty-five grams; in April 2019, he was sentenced to ten months in prison. No one at Ascent Industries ever served time, and Blair Jordan ended up taking a job with a uranium corporation.

In January 2019, Malcolm Gladwell wrote a story in the *New Yorker* titled "Unwatched Pot," with the subhead "Is Marijuana as Safe as We Think?" It was a tough time for Bruce Linton to offer Bill Newlands reassurance, but maybe there would be a silver lining.

CannTrust, on February 25, 2019, listed on the Nasdaq.

CHAPTER 13

All of the Lights

"It's a no-brainer. You just keep buying shit."

Terry Booth

On March 31, 2019, a Brink's armoured truck carrying $900,000 worth of marijuana arrived at Hunny Gawri's pot shop on Queen Street West. The shop didn't have a loading dock, so Gawri's team of twelve formed a daisy chain to pass the odd-shaped boxes of marijuana from the truck, through the back of the store, and directly into the secured upstairs safe room, to be locked inside the $350,000 vault. A new word has been created to describe the people who sell weed like bartenders; they're called "budtenders." These guys — and they're mostly guys and mostly kids — are giddy, ecstatic: modern-day hippies buying into the legalization dream of some sort of liberation. Legal weed being sold like bed sheets or paper towels from an actual legal store in Toronto was a thrilling sensation, and it felt like getting away with something. But it was perfectly legal and there was jubilation in the air. The people on the ground with Hunny were mostly hardcore smokers. Being a minimum-wage-earning budtender isn't a dream job unless you love the product and share a sense of pride in being front-line pioneers. There were pot shops already in the rest of the country, but the cannabis experiment would be judged, in part, based on how Hunny Gawri, opening Ontario's first pot shop on April 1, 2019, sold his weed. Forty percent of Canadians lived in Ontario; if you wanted to beat back the black market, if you wanted to earn market share, you needed to sell the pot that Gawri and his young team was unloading there.

Gawri had never smoked marijuana. He'd never seen it before. "I just feel like, as an entrepreneur, I missed out on the chance to grow weed and become a licensed producer, but I wasn't going to miss this," says Gawri, then thirty-three, a fast-talking real estate agent, and father of five. He became synonymous with the Ontario brick-and-mortar pot shop moment when his store, Hunny Pot, sold the first legal gram from an actual store — not online — in Toronto. "I feel excited, nervous, and, if I'm being honest, a little scared."

Gawri says that when his team formed their first daisy chain to unload the pot from the armoured truck, there was no smell of weed in the air. The pot, an even mix of product from Aurora, Hexo, Aphria, and, of course, Canopy, was sealed in childproof packaging, and inside the packaging was another box, so there was no way to sample, smell, or even see the product he'd just spent almost $1 million to purchase. But he was used to operating on faith. Gawri says that he struggled to get loans because of his business. Landlords, even in the fall of 2018, were reluctant to rent to cannabis businesses. "As soon as cannabis got mentioned," Gawri says, "ridiculous red flags went up."

Gawri, however, like all the cannabis frontier explorers, was plucky. What he had was belief. He called on family and friends for seed money, called every real estate contact in his Rolodex, and finally secured the dream location on Queen Street West, across the street from the old MuchMusic headquarters. At Christmas, Gawri learned he'd won a conditional marijuana retail licence. "At first I thought it was a joke," he says.

He took four months to build his store, a job that, he says, normally might have taken a year. It wasn't until the middle of March that Gawri received his actual licence, two weeks before he expected his first shipment of weed. But Gawri wasn't stunned. He'd been working full out since Christmas, living in an Airbnb near his store. Gawri says he counted marijuana trees in his dreams. By the time the armoured truck arrived, he'd invested everything he had into his store. It was not easy, he says, inventing the wheel.

The Hunny Pot was designed for customers like Hunny Gawri. When he toured California and Colorado on a legal-pot expedition, he found himself baffled by the choices. Wasn't pot *pot*? His shop would be different. Less like Costco, more like Uber Premier. It was an expansion of the Tokyo Smoke concept: Starbucks meets Vera Wang. Personal attention was the key. Each customer would have a one-on-one shopping experience. Since there was no advertising, and by law his windows were covered, customers didn't come into the store knowing what it looked like or what they wanted, and they didn't know which licensed producer made which gram of weed.

Alison Gordon of the licensed producer 48North had known this would be a problem since 10.17, when legalization began. It was difficult for consumers to choose their cannabis. We used to buy weed and take whatever we could find. Now there were different brand-name products in the same packaging at similar prices — and no one knew what the brands were. A budtender at the Hunny Pot, however, armed with an iPad, produced glamour-shot photos of the different strains, matched with descriptors of the marijuana.

It was a pot store for people like Hunny Gawri: people who had never tried pot before.

The first legal weed store in Ontario was three storeys high, with a cash register on the first and third floors. After Hunny's team unpacked his stash, it was artfully arranged in clear glass snifters; you couldn't touch the pot, but you could smell it. There were staff picks, like at a bookstore, in a glass case by the front door, and there were specific instructions outlining what the budtenders were and weren't allowed to say — no medical suggestions, no promises for what the results might be. You couldn't tell people how they'd feel or what the weed actually did. "Low and slow" was the mantra of the legal industry for beginners: take a low dose, consume slowly. No one wanted legal customers, who would ideally become repeat customers, taking too much pot their first time — or their first time since college — and calling their mothers because they were scared.

When the Hunny Pot opened on April 1, like when the first Tweed opened on 10.17, there was a line down the street of hundreds of people waiting to shop. The budtenders were personable, young, enthusiastic, and forbidden to take to the sales floor high. (You couldn't sell wine drunk either.) For many cannabis customers, and all of the cannabis brands, the budtenders were the most important part of the process. What was legal pot like in Toronto? The budtenders set the tone. No Ontarian had ever shopped in a store for legal weed before, and the night before opening, again, as in St. John's and Manitoba, people slept outside the store for a spot in line. History was being made.

Alison Gordon had her office directly across the street from the Hunny Pot, and on April 1, she passed out 48North lighters and rolling papers to the people in line. Inside the store, customers took selfies, and on Bay Street, analysts predicted cannabis revenue in Ontario would shoot up from $7.6 million to $19.6 million just from the opening of brick-and-mortar stores.

It had been a convoluted path to get here. Kathleen Wynne was the premier of Ontario when Justin Trudeau tabled the Cannabis Act; her plan for cannabis retail was similar to that in Quebec, in that cannabis stores would be owned and operated by the government, the same way the province sold booze. However, in June 2018, Doug Ford beat Wynne's Liberals, and he wanted to privatize the system, similar to the models in Alberta, Manitoba, and BC. Wynne foresaw opening 150 stores within the first two years of legalization, which was far too few. For Ontario's 14 million people, there were 666 government-owned and -operated liquor stores. With supply issues dominating the legalization rollout, stores in Quebec had to close a few days a week and Alberta had to shut down licensing between November and May. Despite the companies being so large, there still wasn't enough weed.

Premier Ford, re-examining the scene in December 2018, announced that Ontario could open twenty-five stores, based on a lottery system. For Trevor Fencott and Michael Haines, the Mettrum cannabis partners who sold their cannabis company to Bruce Linton and Canopy before getting into retail and who already had seven Fire & Flowers up and running in Saskatchewan and Alberta, the system was a mess.

"Half of my time as CEO of Fire & Flower was spent arguing with the government," says Fencott, adding that Ontario's minister of finance, Rod Phillips, seemed to actively hate the sector. "He made no bones about wanting to take us down. And the lottery winners? They'd ask for $10 million for their licence, and for people who'd taken out a second mortgage to open their legal cannabis dream, they stood no chance to succeed."

Fencott's main beef is the Ontario Cannabis Store, a government-owned cannabis retailer that would also act as a wholesaler for the legal stores. A licensed producer like Canopy would sell their pot to the OCS, and then Fire & Flower would order pot from the OCS. (In Saskatchewan, the retailers could buy directly from the licensed producer.) Meanwhile, the government also sold directly to consumers online. The OCS had had an operating website since 10.17, and could, in essence, get its pot to consumers faster and fresher than any retail location, which had to take another step in the process — buying weed from the government they were also competing with. "It was the bastard offspring of two terrible things," Fencott says. "Small business and private enterprise can't thrive with a government monopoly competing directly with you. They want mom-and-pop stores living on scraps."

The Ontario government signed agreements to buy weed from the biggest licensed producers like Aurora, Aphria, and Canopy, which didn't have enough product, while Fencott, acting as a private businessman, had no problem securing more weed from other legal sources. He was an entrepreneur. He knew how to get things. But the government, he says, created a prohibitive system. He was legally unable to buy the legal weed his customers wanted. This, while all eyes were on marijuana. This, during a cannabis drought. Fencott says he once met with the team at the Indigenous-owned licensed producer Redecan and saw rooms of legal marijuana sitting in a vault awaiting distribution. But it was locked up until the OCS made the wholesale purchase and then sold the product to the stores.

"All of the bigs like Aphria and Canopy always overpromised and underdelivered," says Fencott, mentioning that he had history from the medical rollout of working with, and selling cannabis for, the other licensed producers. "We all came from that medical universe and bought and sold to each other when we ran out of stuff: Terry Booth, Bruce Linton, Vic, and I. We'd constantly discuss who's going to supply who — we had to when we needed product."

Ontario's supply problem, says Fencott, was really the OCS's problem with distribution. The OCS, says Fencott, was hated by licensed producers and retailers alike. "Redecan hated the Ontario Cannabis Store!" he says. "They had a huge warehouse full of product, but the Ontario Cannabis Store rejected it. I would've bought it, but the OCS was a regulator and they had unlimited power — a monopoly."

Two weeks after the Hunny Pot opened, April 14, 2019, another pot store called Nova opened its first location in Toronto. It was a simpler, one-storey affair, in an old Urban Outfitters that had been repurposed. The staff, like at Gawri's store, looked like groovy summer-camp counsellors. I spent a day in the store checking it out for the *Globe and Mail*.

"No one asks me how I am," a customer said to a young Nova budtender on that late spring afternoon.

"I got you," the budtender replied, and the customer gave him a hug.

The budtender had dreadlocks and fancy sneakers and recommended an oil with CBD. "This will help you sleep," he said, "and it's odourless, so you don't have to worry about detection from the kids." His advice would probably be outside the lines with Health Canada. But it was a beautiful exchange to witness, and everything seemed to be working fine.

Hilary Black, the long-time cannabis activist still, at the time, making hay at Canopy, confirmed this with her own metrics. "In 2014, two hundred and fifty thousand people were arrested in Canada for marijuana, and we know that number is at least eight times higher amongst people of colour," Black said. "How's legalization working? By 2018, that number dropped down to five hundred souls."

At Nova Cannabis, on Queen Street West, in the spring of 2019, Aurora, Canopy, and Aphria products commanded the most shelf space. The customers reflected the neighbourhood's dynamic: a mix of groups of girls wearing Lululemon, a gaggle of talking-on-their-cellphone young men, some businesspeople, a few legacy hippies.

"What's the highest strain of THC?" was the most popular question. Also, "What's the cheapest pre-roll you've got?"

Customers wanted cheap, customers wanted strong, and customers felt like they were making history. "You can't minimize what this means to a lot of us who spent our lives outside the law," says Alison Gordon. "It's not that you need the government to condone your actions to feel good about yourself, but think about that — everything you do, every day, you put yourself at risk and then, suddenly, the persecution stops."

While stores opened in Ontario, spring was a land grab for Aurora's Terry Booth. "It's a no-brainer. You just keep buying shit," says Terry, who adds that when your market cap is $14 billion and Nelson Peltz is looking for growth, if something costs $10 million, you buy it, whatever it is. "You're trading super fucking hot and it's like, I don't need due diligence — it's done."

Like all the Canadian executives, Booth was spending his time in the U.S. and dreaming of owning their CBD market. On April 18, 2019, the Horizons Marijuana Index began trading in the States — an ETF, or exchange-traded fund, a basket of cannabis stocks mirroring the markets — and it started with a billion-dollar valuation. Terry Booth believed in the valuations and tells me he was working joyfully around the clock. He cut a deal to be the UFC's official provider of CBD products. He wasn't nervous, reflective, or slowing down. Up all night, firing off emails — driving his executive vice-president, Cam Battley, crazy — having a ball. "Risk-takers having the time of our life" is how one cannabis executive described it. (That executive was Matei Olaru, then twenty-eight, who was the CEO of Lift & Co., a public company that hosted those first cannabis Oscars way back when in 2014. Lift filed for bankruptcy in 2020, and are now an American brand.)

Like at Canopy, however, Aurora's new partners didn't see the world through Terry's eyes. Booth had been getting pushback from his board. Nelson Peltz, the activist investor, didn't want the company sending out press releases or investor guidance. He thought it was wise to pipe down. But Booth wasn't having it. "If you don't have liquidity, you don't have value," he says, referring to volatility, and the press releases stoked movement: you had to have a story to get investors to pay attention to you, to make your stock move. Since the story at Aurora wasn't going to be profitability, the story Booth sold in the spring of 2019 was growth.

Of the race to acquire new brands, Booth says, "Buying something, we can get a definitive agreement and exchange ratio [the number of shares stockholders of an acquired company will receive after the deal], and it's just, show me your financials and I'll have an auditor look at it. But we don't need an audit. We just want it done."

What got done in the cannabis industry is often described as an arms race. The Canadian cannabis producers were trying to keep the market's attention and expand their revenue streams, through acquisition and partnerships — diluting their shares — with meagre revenue relative to expenditures. With pot companies unable to advertise or make medical claims, having a high-profile partnership, like the one Booth courted from the Professional Bull Riders or the UFC, an international brand, could keep a cannabis stock liquid. But it was expensive. "Of course you want to be first and do the next thing," Booth says. "If you don't do it, you know Linton will."

Meanwhile, Sébastien St-Louis was trying to keep Hexo part of the conversation. He wanted to spend in tandem with Terry and Bruce. "It's a steel cage match," he says. St-Louis says the idea is to use your market cap to keep growing. "There's tons of opportunity, so the job is to leverage that and go faster," he tells me. "To go faster, you need to start acquiring — start consuming — other companies." St-Louis had targets. All of the companies did. Brands you could purchase for market share, for funded capacity, and for the press release. St-Louis says that he nearly purchased three different medium-sized cannabis companies but, even after having definitive agreements drawn up, the deals fell through.

The deal he landed was for Newstrike, Jay Wilgar's company that partnered with the Tragically Hip. Wilgar had seen the CanniMed deal fall apart because of Terry Booth, back when he was almost partnered with Brent Zettl, and begun to grow sick and tired of weed. He liked hanging with the Tragically Hip, but Gord Downie had died in 2017, and toward the end of 2018, Wilgar was looking for an exit. "Even with $110 million, the fact was that Canopy was partnered up with Constellation. How do you compete against that? And Hexo [was working] with Molson Coors. Unless you want to be an ultra-niche brand — and I don't see that working — I don't know how you compete," he says.

The valuations made cannabis a smoke-and-mirrors industry that attracted a certain type: tech bros. And even the people who didn't smoke weed had a certain personality type. Wilgar says he loved his time in marijuana, but even though he was CEO of a weed brand worth nearly $400 million, he was naive about the product. One night in Kingston, Wilgar was with the Tragically Hip at a restaurant they liked, where they had a private room with a door onto the roof. The guys smoked "hashers," little hash joints, and usually Wilgar refrained. However, after some drinks, Jay lit up.

"I take a few hauls at about ten p.m., and everything's spinning so I go out on the roof," Wilgar said. He tried to regain his composure. To be less stoned. But that's impossible once the train's left the station. "I take my suit jacket and put it between the air conditioners and lie down." But Wilgar got too comfortable. He began to snooze. "I wake up at one a.m. and the door's locked. I'm on the roof of this restaurant, and I can't get back in."

Nobody realized that the Newstrike CEO had gone missing or knew Wilgar was stuck on the roof. "I end up shimmying down the drain pipe between this place and a Vietnamese restaurant and jumping onto the recycling bin."

It was a strange time in a new, rich industry, bleeding cash. For St-Louis, who began consuming cannabis more frequently in the middle of 2018, pot was also a substance different from alcohol for him to consume. He was hosting an end-of-the-year work event with 350 Hexo employees at the Canadian War Museum in Ottawa when his vice-president of business development wanted to show him a new product. He had a prototype of a vape. "It was a work event, but I work in weed and it was a party, so I said, 'Okay, I'll try it.'"

Cannabis isn't Chardonnay. It's different for everyone, but it rarely makes people aggressive. A high person is more likely to become introspective or self-conscious — energized, maybe. It stimulates the endocannabinoid system and sends the mind on a different track. A stoned person might take twenty tries to find the keys that are in their pocket. "I was high on my way to the event, and I don't really consume. But then a speaker cancelled. I was told 'We need you to address everybody!'"

St-Louis says that this was his come-to-Jesus moment with weed. He knew people liked it. His co-founder was Adam Miron; it was Adam's dad who bought the first gram of Hydropothecary medicinal product. He used it as a pain relief while he struggled with chemotherapy to fight his cancer. But the way Sébastien felt wasn't quite bliss. He wasn't using it as medicine, but it also wasn't booze. He felt lucid, creative, and free. "I get up onstage and give a beautiful speech. I wasn't self-conscious. I told everyone I appreciated them and wanted them to really, *truly* have a great time. I meant it," St-Louis says. "Not something you'd do if you were drunk off your ass."

St-Louis had distribution where he was based in Quebec, and his company was valued at $1.6 billion. Wilgar had distribution everywhere but in Quebec and had the Tragically Hip to promote his recreational marijuana brand. The deal to buy Newstrike was for $260 million in an all-stock transaction. Jay Wilgar was out of weed, but says he's never going to forget those memories (at least the ones he can remember).

The hub-and-spoke model that Sébastien St-Louis dreamt up and Bruce Linton pioneered was being used throughout the country. The cannabis executives felt like they needed to expand: new territories, new products. Bruce Linton says he felt the breath of the other companies on his neck. He says he hadn't been thinking about expansion in Canada since the summer of 2017. He didn't want another recreational marijuana brand. And he knew the pot surplus we have today was coming. In April 2019, to address the lack of product, Health Canada approved the first outdoor grow on Salt Spring Island, British Columbia. The outdoor grows had bigger yields and required less capital. To deal with the supply issue, Health Canada tweaked its policy and made production more cost effective, lowering the barrier of entry and, the plan was, stocking the shelves of weed stores and eliminating the black market.

But Linton, with Constellation Brands behind him, had already moved on from funded capacity. He says cannabis had bad margins in flower, which became the shorthand for actual weed, as opposed to pre-rolls or CBD products. But if you took the flower and added it to other products, everything became worth more money. It's not grams; it's milligrams. And milligrams could be added to anything. Linton liked to stay at the Marriott when he travelled. "I started looking at Europe for some of these things and I'm staying at the Marriott and every day I use This Works soap," Linton says. An idea came to him in the shower. "A sleep company and a cosmetic company? Perfect for CBD," says Linton. He was interested in the distribution model. This Works was distributed in the Marriott Hotel chain. There were Marriott Hotels all over the world. "Their product had zero value, but when you put CBD into it, you get the premium of our shit — the margins go up."

The Canopy board was used to quickly putting Linton's shower thoughts into action. "I kept them up to date anytime I was going to use cash or equity every Monday morning at my nine-fifteen," Bruce recalls. One Sunday, Mother's Day, he made two deals and spent $523 million. "You know what? It was fifteen minutes," he says of the approval process. Things were different after the Constellation investment. Even in November 2018, Bill Newlands, CEO of Constellation, was making his presence felt. "They told me I had to do five things. 'Guys, this is your first board meeting. You've been here for about two seconds and three of those things would cause us to lose our fucking licence. Let me tell you what we're doing — relax.'"

On March 21, 2019, after being told to slow down, Bruce Linton hit the gas. Canopy acquired AgriNextUSA, a hemp company built to take advantage of the U.S. Farm Bill, which would now allow hemp and hemp-derived CBD products to be transported across state lines. Sizing up the Canadian landscape, the founders were looking for inroads to the States while fighting a price war for shelf space in the Canadian stores. Market share was important for the brands to make claims in their news releases and it was not uncommon for the founders of the cannabis companies to call one another and forcefully ask for help.

For example, one night after legalization, Terry Booth called Alison Gordon at 8:00 p.m. She says he was screaming at her to sell him some weed. Aurora wanted 48North pot in Aurora packaging on the shelves of the Hunny Pot. At the legal licensed cannabis stores, the margins on a gram were brutal. Gordon says she could make six dollars per gram if she sold her weed to the OCS, but ten dollars if she sold it to Aurora and Terry Booth. For Aurora, it was worth losing money to be number one in sales for the press release. And the owners all knew one another. They didn't exactly like each other, but they were all part of a strange, stoned Canadian business subculture.

Alison tells me she had to disappoint Terry Booth about her marijuana. She couldn't sell Aurora her weed, she told him, and he was pissed. Booth didn't work very hard to hide his emotions.

Bruce Linton and Terry Booth never broke bread before our steaks in Las Vegas, but Terry took pains to let Bruce know who he was. At a cannabis conference in Vancouver, Booth took the stage, with Linton in the crowd.

"Knock, knock, Bruce," Booth said.

"Who's there?" replied Linton from the audience, always game.

"Aurora, and we're knocking down your door."

But it was hard for Terry to keep pace with Bruce Linton. Alison couldn't sell Terry her weed — it had already been purchased by Canopy.

CHAPTER 14

50 Shades of Grey

"My supervisor had a gun to his face, but he said,
'Not my money.' It was fucking jokes."

Jackson Flynn

Legalization had changed Canada, but one thing had not changed: in the spring of 2019 in Toronto, the most popular cannabis dispensary was called CAFE, and it didn't have a licence to exist.

"We thought we'd be able to effectively deal with these places, but we never anticipated such brazenness as the operators of CAFE," says Mark Sraga, the city's director of municipal licensing and standards, who'd been tasked with shutting down the illegal cannabis dispensaries. "We knew they were making a shitload of money."

CAFE still is a bustling, trendy, illegal retailer of cannabis that sells products without a licence from companies that don't have licences — some which they also own. It still runs a bustling operation two kilometres from my house, where they sell edibles with one thousand milligrams of THC, one hundred times the legal limit. Founded by Wes Weber and Jon Galvano in 2016, CAFE — "coffee and fine edibles" — sells lattes and macchiatos,

On the Rocks: CAFE, an illegal weed store in Toronto. The city erected large concrete blocks in front of the store to block entry. There are five illegal CAFE shops operating in Toronto today.

infused or not, which is illegal, alongside their marijuana strains, which aren't available on the legal market. To the average consumer, all pot is the same. But to the heavy smokers, the folks who buy 80 percent of the product, strains matter. The heaviest consumers, like the lawyer Alan Young always says, like buying pot outside of the government system. They shop on the black market because the pot costs less. They buy the marijuana because it's stronger. And they buy it, Young says, to say "Fuck you" to Bruce Linton, Lorne Gertner, and everyone else making money on and gentrifying cannabis culture.

Jodie Giesz-Ramsay, who was the face of cannabis activism, calls Canopy Growth "a rotten cartel corporation," and tweeted, "Temporary foreign workers are slaving away in Canada's factory farms, like Canopy Growth, where profits are more important than people." Pot came from the counterculture. Serious consumers don't want to buy Julian Fantino's weed. The counterculture couldn't care less about Terry's stock price — or else actively wants him to fail. Weber and Galvano, the owners of CAFE, two white marijuana profiteers, are, according to the Toronto police, criminals.

"It is without question that the Ontario Cannabis Store system and its subsequent rollout of cannabis retail in Ontario is flawed," the company said in an unsigned July 2019 statement to the *Toronto Star*. "We are here to provide reasonable dignified access to the many Canadians who have come to rely on us." So who were these cannabis consumers relying on?

The CBC produced an in-depth report on the founders in July 2019. Wes Weber is one of Canada's most notorious counterfeiters, who reportedly started his first ring of illegal money at thirteen. It's been reported that Weber, forty-nine in 2025, made so many counterfeit one-hundred-dollar bills that Canada briefly took the currency out of circulation. But Weber is bookish and shy, a computer nerd who loves cryptocurrency. He has always loved marijuana, too: he was arrested in 1999 and again in 2010 for growing pot and has served jail time for forging cheques. He grew up with his business partner, Galvano, who was a gym rat with bulky muscles and social media fame. Before he took down his Instagram account, Galvano would flaunt his lifestyle of Lamborghinis and racehorses, named Indica and Sativa, and shooting ranges in Colombia. During the Raptors playoff run, Weber and Galvano posed showing off their matching Rolex watches. Both men reportedly kept a penthouse above the CAFE shop on Fort York Boulevard in Toronto. A CAFE staff member says that Galvano travelled with bodyguards. Galvano posted on Facebook about opening his first CAFE location on July 23, 2016, two months after Toronto police conducted their Project Claudia raids. That summer, Toronto police estimated that the city had more than one hundred illegal pot shops. (New York is estimated to have over 2,900 illegal pot shops today.)

"There was no one single illegal player that really stood out other than Marc and Jodie Emery. It was more of the Wild West with no organized structure," Mark Sraga, the city licenser, says. "I've heard the source [for the unlicensed shops] — and still the source today — is federally licensed medical grows growing far in excess of what they are legally entitled to and converting it to the black market."

In 2016, cannabis was still against the law, but, as Bruce, Sébastien, and Terry presided over companies worth more than several *billion* dollars and Prime Minister Justin Trudeau announced legalization was coming, police were no longer focusing on illegal marijuana. The opioid epidemic was raging.

After Project Claudia, there were fewer illegal pot retailers in operation; however, the surviving illegal shops shut down and reopened as if playing a game of whack-a-mole with the cops. As soon as they were closed, they reopened again, sometimes in different locations, sometimes with a different name, sometimes not. The profits were enough for the illegal operators to treat closures as an inconvenience. CAFE, however, operated on a different scale. After legalization, they *expanded*, from two shops to four. And that's not because the police didn't try to stop them. At the Fort York CAFE location, the city enforcement team installed a steel door over their entrance. They were physically barring CAFE from breaking the law. It didn't work. "Someone just cut through the door," explains Sraga, dismayed. "They just crawled back in to defeat the locking system and were operating again the very next day."

Sraga was disgusted, outraged. Trevor Fencott at Fire & Flower couldn't open his legal shop in Oakville, but in Toronto, CAFE did whatever it chose and sold whatever it wanted. Sraga decided to put his foot down. "Fuck this. Let's go to the next level," he told his team, including his manager of cannabis enforcement. His next move will go down in the annals of cannabis history. Mark Sraga instructed his people to erect massive, heavy, imposing, concrete blocks before the entrances of the CAFE stores. The owners were blocked out of their stores — by boulders. Sraga told me, "These blocks were four feet long, almost two feet high, and two feet deep, very substantial. Nobody was going to get around them." To erect the blocks, they had to use a flatbed truck and a crane.

Goomba is the alias of a friend who used to work at CAFE and was onsite for seven raids, arrested at one. He has a long beard and long hair and looks like a cannabis Jesus, which makes sense because he was raised in the church. CAFE, to him, was a family business: his sister worked in CAFE's law department — they have a law department. He was a cook before he went over to CAFE in Fort York Boulevard in CityPlace. He'd work stoned. During Toronto's huge annual Afro-Caribbean festival called Caribana, the busiest time of the year, he could bring home $300 in tips. The store was huge with cannabis connoisseurs and Americans staying locally in Airbnbs. Weber, the CAFE co-owner, is married to Michelle Kam, a top real estate agent in Toronto. CityPlace is Toronto's largest residential development of all time, and Goomba says the CAFE team owned multiple units and had a visible, intimidating presence in the building.

In the summer of 2019, Goomba sold edibles, vapes, and drinks, months before they were approved on the legal market, and though their price on flower was roughly equivalent to that on the legal market — about $12 per gram — the vibe in the place was different from what you could find at Fire & Flower: customers could buy weed and consume drinks and edibles, and they could sit on the CAFE patio after making their purchase and listen to tunes. Fencott — in the legal market — couldn't even sell coffee. Wes Weber was selling coffee infused — creating his own little Amsterdam.

"Tell you the truth, we never even gave a fuck," Goomba tells me one afternoon outside Tokyo Smoke, where he worked at the time of our interview, near his home on the east side of Toronto. When the concrete blocks in front of CAFE went up, Goomba says, it only *increased* his sales.

"We thought that shit was funny," he tells me, and describes how the company pivoted its business when they couldn't open their doors. When the concrete blocks were erected before the four Toronto CAFE locations in July of 2019, Goomba helped raise a canopy in front of the shop and set up a table and chairs. He took orders from his lawn chair, and when news crews came out to film the action, the police left him alone.

It was a stain on the entire legalization experiment, according to Mark Sraga. "At the Harbord Street location, CAFE even arranged an SUV limousine service to take their customers to other stores." He points out that once the CAFE proprietors began selling weed in an open-air drug market on the street, the crime was no longer part of his jurisdiction.

No charges were laid against Galvano or Weber. The city removed the blocks from the front doors by the end of July. Sraga retired in August. Galvano died from unexplained causes in Mexico in 2021. Someone on

Reddit said it was a brain tumour. CAFE is still selling weed today from its five locations in Toronto.

Sraga doesn't not look back at that wistfully. He says, "It would appear CAFE has deeper resources than the police."

———•

At Fire & Flower, Michael Haines and Trevor Fencott were now competing against CAFE with the help of Couche-Tard. They, too, had deeper pockets than the police.

On July 24, 2019, a few days before Mark Sraga retired, Couche-Tard, the retail and real estate champions, invested $26 million into Fire & Flower; which meant that now a company even bigger than Constellation Brands had put real money behind the premise that pot was moving away from its stigma, pot companies could be profitable, and real companies with massive global footprints wanted to sell weed as part of their portfolio. Fencott says the deal with Couche-Tard was designed to take advantage of the U.S. market. Retail cannabis was going to eventually come down to a game of American real estate locations, and the pot company that could dot the United States like so many franchises of Dunkin' Donuts would be the one that could last and win. It was Sébastien St-Louis who connected Fencott with Alain Bouchard, the founder of Couche-Tard. The Quebec connection was bestowed on Fencott because St-Louis, over at Hexo, didn't want Bruce Linton to corner the market on retail.

However, even with Couche-Tard's war chest and retail learnings, and even after the Hunny Pot drew lineups to its doors in Toronto on April 1, 2019, the legal system was plagued by kinks and the black market. The illegal market had edibles, a cannabis product for potential new cannabis consumers. Olli's John Aird, meanwhile, a master of licensing regulations in Ontario and business development with a small army of lawyers behind him, hadn't sold a single product while the illegal stuff at CAFE flew from the shelf. The illegal market also didn't charge tax.

Supply issues continued to be a problem, as was the slow adoption of the Cannabis Act. Trevor Fencott lives in Oakville, Ontario, a township, like Mississauga, Ontario, that initially declined to opt into Canada's legal system. The Cannabis Act was supposed to kill the black market. But legal consumers, like Bruce has said, couldn't buy what they couldn't buy.

"Twenty-five to forty percent of Oakville's constituents, my neighbours, are consuming cannabis, and that number is almost certainly underreported. And politicians don't want a store that looks like a Lululemon in our own backyard?" Fencott says. "The treatment we received as pioneers in a nascent business that was supposed to be a priority for the government was absurd."

Fencott and Haines at Fire & Flower — publicly traded national cannabis retailers with deep-pocketed backers — were trying to meet legal customer demand, but even with outdoor grows now legal across the country, the turnaround time to plant and sell marijuana was upwards of four months. Customers hadn't, by and large, developed a taste for specific legal brands, so you could basically put any marijuana strain behind the legally mandated generic packaging. There was no advertising, and even the legal stores needed to have blacked-out front windows (which, of course, CAFE didn't have, except when the city covered them with giant cement boulders). Consumers weren't going to Fire & Flower to shop for a product they couldn't get from an illegal store. Customers didn't even have any way of knowing which stores were illegal. The illegal shops looked better than the legal ones. There was no Gucci (or, for that matter, Gap) of legal marijuana flower, not yet. And people might know Aurora or Canopy and even own shares in the companies, but a smoke test wouldn't likely produce brand recognition, and no single product in the industry had any real buzz.

But the industry continued to be buzzy, and the mainstream struggled to cash in. At this point, I was not only writing about weed for subscription-based cannabis newsletters at the *Globe and Mail* and the *National Post*, but also helping to launch, with Josh Nagel, *KIND* magazine, which would eventually be distributed in the licensed retail stores and host events and award shows, much like Lift. In 1999, I had stories all over New York about Lenny Kravitz. Twenty years later, I had stories all over Canada about weed. I don't have any particular marijuana expertise. I can't identify terpenes based on smoking, but I fit the oddball work hard/play hard cannabis profile, love the people, and, if I'm honest, the product. I don't smoke much but do find that weed boosts not only my creativity but also my empathy — a much better form of existence when there are two kids kicking around the house.

I remember being in Ottawa in the fall of 2019 and talking to the marketing manager at Hexo. It was the first time I heard about the cannabis tax. This is the idea that if something costs a regular company $5,000, it will cost a cannabis company $50,000, because there's an understanding that weed companies are not only flush, but desperate to spend their money. Only, by the summer of 2019, the pendulum was beginning to turn. The Hexo guy told me he was tired of paying a premium and that profits were becoming important to shareholders. I feel almost like the mainstream press that I was part of mirrored the retail investors. We were all trying to cash in at the exact same time that the smart money already had left. The underground didn't have this problem.

The underground — illegally — continued to bloom.

Jackson Flynn is a friend who smokes weed and worked at the Nova store on Queen Street in Toronto on 10.17 and at Tokyo Smoke at Yonge and Dundas before joining a licensed producer. Before he worked in the legal industry, he worked at an illegal dispensary. This, in his words, is what that was like in 2018:

> I was supervising: fill the jars of weed in the morning, do cash drops, take the money out. It was ridiculous to sit there on some Friday nights and hit refresh [on the cash machine] — thousands of dollars per minute. I would go by with the cash drop, with the cash envelope, and take all the money out of the tills. I literally had to shove it down my pants and walk back to the office.
>
> It was like ten, fifteen grand in the envelope in cash. Some guy would come near the store in the morning with a big duffle bag with ten pounds of weed. I'd walk two blocks with it. It was the same size as me, and at the end of the night, someone would come shove forty grand in cash down their pants and leave for the night. It didn't even feel like a job.

We were doing production all day — twenty, thirty pounds of weed — production all day long in a basement in Kensington Market. Scaling up like fucking 1,000 one grams, 500 half quarters. Other people were making pre-rolls, doing concentrates. It was crazy. We couldn't do it enough. We could've stayed there twelve hours a day and we wouldn't be able to bag it all.

It was a movie, man.

From the basement, I moved up to budtending. There were pounds behind us and the storefront above us, and we had a little cut-out in the floor, and we'd pass up weed through the cut-out. It was like a dumb waiter from the basement to the manager's office. We cut a square in the wall and we'd pull up the weed like that all day long. We were allowed to smoke pre-rolls. You have to be stoned to be able to sit there and fucking, "one gram," "three point five," all day long. It was my first job in Toronto. We got paid like eighteen dollars an hour to do it. I was nineteen. It was love.

We couldn't keep up with the demand. All the shit we could ski up [package] would be gone within the first half of the week, but then that store got raided and shut down for a week, so I moved over to Yonge and Eglinton. Same owners. That's where I saw big numbers. That store ruined me. Fill a jar with weed and it would sell out and that was four grand. It was dope.

Dope — but a shitshow with the fucking robberies. Two different employees let their boy in through the back door. He came running up with an actual gun and said, "Everyone down!" He cleared the place out. My supervisor had a gun to his face, but he said, "Not my money." It was fucking jokes.

Another time we got lifted. We were doing the Square thing, the credit card reader? We were doing that for credit and debit for two months, but for three weeks some dude hooked it up to his own account before we fucking realized. Oh yeah, that guy took in quite a lot of money, 70K? After that, we never took debit or credit cards again.

Our goal was to hit 100K in one day. And finally, on the last Friday, summer 2017, we hit 101. A lot of the weed came from BC, but later we'd get bricks of hash that were stamped like some Quebec biker stuff. When I was at Yonge and Eglinton, we got hit like five times, but wouldn't ever close. One time the police came in and shut off our power so the landlord brought in generators, put them in the back, and we were up and running the next day. He'd just go to Best Buy with a checklist for thousands of dollars — new laptops, TVs, all this shit.

We had seven stores in the city, probably each making forty grand each day, 300K they're making, and the overhead was nothing — especially if it was their product. Growers from BC shipping it to stores they own here in Toronto. But it was sketchy as shit and you never know what can happen. Just like that, you get popped and you get shut down.

After we made all that money — we finally hit 101 — the Friday after, we were hoping to do that again, but around twelve in the afternoon I'm standing in the office, doing my thing, and all I hear is loud noises and banging. Then there's a bunch of uniforms, like SWAT team black uniforms, they had all the gear on, their guns are out, full body suits. I look at the camera and there's fifteen fully dressed uniforms coming in with their weapons drawn like, "Everyone against the wall!" The music was playing. Customers were against the wall, too! They thought we'd be armed, but we had no guns, no other drugs — nothing in the store except weed and money.

Some of the stores (not ours) had cocaine. They were sticking twenty-year-old kids in the store to take the risk and they were the ones walking around with 40K in cash.

At the point of my first arrest, I'm not high. It was about mid-day. They're coming in. I opened the door and a bunch of them just rushed me, I'm just like ... "Fuck."

The cops held the customers for about two hours. The staff for about six. They smashed the ATM to get the money, smashed our vault in. But what was heartbreaking was they had this big bag and dumped all the weed in a fifteen-pound sack. That's some shit.

Soon as they left the store, one of our security guys was waiting to meet us. We went around the corner, he took our papers and sent it off to the lawyer they hired for us. That was it.

Two days later I got a phone call. "We're opening up another store," I'm like, "Here we go again."

They were like, "Twenty-five dollars an hour — cash — and you'll get overtime." Yup.

I went back to Kensington, then I was in Park Lawn and Lakeshore. I was working eight hours at twenty-five dollars, then another four hours at forty dollars, overtime. I'm making three hundred, four hundred dollars a day in cash and I sit in an office, spin money through a counter, and fill up jars of weed. But it never lasts.

My last bust was crazy. I didn't even know what it was. A few guys came in and they're like, "We're here to raid you."

"Guys," I said, "Don't joke. It happens all the time."

They came in and opened the door, took a long look. I mean, this store would get hit every week by 5-0. Thankfully, I just happened to be off all those days and it was wack — I was supposed to be off this day, but I had switched shifts with someone and now this. They came in wearing regular clothes. "We're raiding you," and as soon as he said that, from the back door, people came in — from the front door, they came in and kicked in the office door.

We probably had five grand and a couple pounds on us, so it wasn't a big deal. But this is the one I went down for — this is the time I spent the night in jail.

We all got taken in separate cop cars and I sat in a holding cell for about two hours and they strip searched us and we had to call our lawyer, Jack Lloyd, a fucking pioneer in this industry, man.

"It's Jackson Flynn. I'm calling from Canna. We got raided again."

I stayed in a shitty little cell with my boy I was working with. He was in the cell beside me, then they brought in some fucking kid who got arrested for the first time who cried all night and kept us awake. I was scared, but whatever, man.

You're in this situation, you can't do anything about it. Accept it.

Still, the next day got intense. They chained our ankles and hands, threw us into the paddy wagon, like the court services armoured truck. There it was a little more intimidating.

You're in the basement with all the other criminals who did the same shit. Thankfully I was with the people with drug charges, not murderers or rapists or some shit, but listening to these people talk — "oh yeah, take the six-month deal" — it was foreign to me. Finally, after four hours, I saw a paralegal across the glass thing, and she said I'll be out on bail in two hours and that's how it happened. Jack got me out, but I still lived with my pop and I wasn't sure about weed. I was twenty years old, and I had a goal that I'd pay off my credit card and have ten grand in the bank, but for me it was ten grand in cash in my suit pocket in my closet. I was buying any shit I wanted, and me and my boys were playing Cee-lo after work for hundreds of dollars. We didn't care.

Playing $800 dice games, why not?

———•

There were 260 companies operating in the cannabis industry in Canada in the summer of 2019, most in agriculture and retail, but also some in manufacturing, according to Statistics Canada. The cannabis industry was responsible for $6.7 billion in gross domestic product. From January to March 2019, 2.5 million consumers purchased cannabis from a legal vendor. In the first three months of the year, 18 percent of Canadians older than fifteen used cannabis, up from 14 percent before legalization. And the industry was still growing.

To combat the lack of stores and to help defuse the illicit market, Ontario premier Doug Ford announced a second lottery for forty-two cannabis retail locations on July 3, 2019. You couldn't just open a cannabis shop, not a legal one. You had to win a licence through a lottery because there was more demand from would-be shop owners than the government was willing to license to sell weed. That July, 4,864 applications were submitted. To participate in the lottery, cannabis shop owners had to submit a background check, present their bank balance, and have already secured a lease for their location; this was supposed to eliminate shop owners who weren't set up to succeed at such a seriously expensive, regulated job.

On August 20, 2019, the government announced the winners of the lottery. That would make sixty-eight pot shops for 14.57 million Ontarians. Alberta, during the summer of 2019, had 277 shops for its population of 4.3 million. So there still wouldn't be a lot of stores in Ontario, but it was slowly getting better in terms of access to weed for Canada's most populous city.

The licensing announcement on August 20 was mostly subdued, except for one thing: CAFE, the most notorious illegal operator in the country, scored a licence at their 104 Harbord Street location. How could that be?

It was always rumoured in cannabis circles that the CAFE team had ties to the Doug Ford government. The *Globe and Mail* reported that in the 1980s, Doug Ford had sold hash. So had Ford's siblings, Randy and Kathy, and of course Rob Ford, the former Toronto mayor, had his own underground connections. Could there be ties between Ford and CAFE's Jon Galvano and Wes Weber? Nothing's been proven, and the name on the retail licence application was Rob Heydon, a Toronto-area film producer and director. The application didn't mention the name CAFE, but there it was: the location at which they had been operating had been granted a licence. Twelve of the winners had been disqualified for not submitting their paperwork in a timely fashion. Heydon, at the CAFE address, was not disqualified. Of course, once the media heard about the CAFE team winning the lottery — after remaining open before, during, and after the episode of the concrete blocks — we had a field day.

What more could you possibly do to be disqualified from selling weed?

"It's the craziest thing you could've possibly seen," says Lorne Gertner, whose Tokyo Smoke, now owned by Canopy, won a licence in the first round of Ontario's lottery and opened a shop at Yonge and Dundas, in a three-storey former HMV location. "They did everything wrong in the face of the regulators and picked up a licence which they had no chance of winning — to even apply takes tremendous balls."

In the end, following the brouhaha, CAFE had its licence rescinded and Rob Heydon moved on, opening 420Love in Hamilton. But after all the new legal stores opened, the CAFE shop at 104 Harbord Street continued selling illegal weed and inviting its guests, without a licence, to drink infused lemonade and iced tea on the patio, which was still against the law. There were forty-two new licensed weed stores in Ontario by the fall of 2019 — and the most popular retailer in the country remained the biggest, most notorious illegal store, still out in the open selling illegal weed.

Lift & Co. was Matei Olaru's company. It began as a small Canadian cannabis review site and grew into a cannabis expo and award-show business, listing on the TSX Venture Exchange in September 2018. In addition to its other businesses, Lift created a training program for budtenders, in partnership with Mothers Against Drunk Driving Canada. The program,

CannSell, provided certification for budtenders before they worked behind a cannabis store till. It was against the law to sell marijuana without a CannSell certification.

Lift filed for bankruptcy in 2020, and in the proceedings, CannSell was left to open tender. Who ended up buying the government program?

A company at least in part owned by Wes Weber and Jon Galvano — owners of CAFE.

CHAPTER 15

Licensed to Kill

"We raised twenty million with two phone calls."

Trevor Fencott

The back of Drake's sweatshirt read "Kawhi Me a River." The rap superstar went over to Bruce Linton, sitting courtside at game six of the 2019 Eastern Conference Finals between the Toronto Raptors and the Milwaukee Bucks. Linton, at the game with Lorne Gertner and decked out in his Tweed uniform — hat, button, and shirt — was never a basketball fan, but the Raptors had become, alongside Drake and cannabis, the hottest ticket in town. Basketball audiences spilled out from the Scotiabank Arena into Jurassic Park, outside the stadium, where an ESPN producer was picked up on a hot mic warning his reporter: "Just FYI, there's a lot of weed going on out there."

Weed had become like maple syrup and free health care, shorthand for Canadian. With that came swagger, money, fame. The Raptors had been a fledgling Canadian NBA franchise where NBA superstars, arbiters of style, didn't want to play. The team had some runs — Vince Carter, Chris Bosh, and DeMar DeRozan were loved by Canadian basketball fans — but the admiration was local, and many NBA stars, though they enjoyed our strip clubs, didn't want to live in Canada. Too cold, too small, and also, Canada? Too uncool.

Then, in 2017, Donald Trump became the U.S. president, and *Rolling Stone* put Justin Trudeau on its cover. "Why can't he be our president?" read the headline. And then things in Toronto just got better: the Raptors got Kawhi.

Kawhi Leonard, the mercurial forward formerly of the San Antonio Spurs, who sullenly sat out their 2018 season — maybe from an injury, maybe not — wore his petulance like a crown of thorns. Until he arrived in Toronto. Then the Raptors, like Drake, began to bloom. At the end of the school year in 2019, my daughter was walking to the bus for a field trip. She cheered and chanted "Let's go Raptors" as she crossed the road with her grade 4 classmates. That season, Kawhi Leonard was the best player in the NBA, and Canada, behind the Raptors, had begun to puff out its chest.

There was no apologizing in Drake's sweatshirt or Terry Booth's public appearances, or when Booth negotiated with Heineken, Nelson Peltz, or Coca-Cola. The world was re-evaluating the country, and marijuana, slowly, cautiously, was attracting the mainstream: alcohol companies, tobacco, shampoo, supermarket chains. Businesses were curious about marijuana, and to get in, brands had to come to Canada.

Bruce Linton hugging Drake in a Kawhi sweatshirt at the Raptors game suggested that the value proposition had changed: We don't need you, America. We're doing fine on our own.

Acreage Holdings had ten times Canopy's revenue, but Canopy still had a market cap that was one hundred times bigger than Acreage, because the U.S. hadn't caught up yet with Canadian financings and public markets. Alison Gordon says that in late spring and early summer 2019, Canada had all of the world's marijuana prestige.

For instance, MedMen was an American chain of California dispensaries who hired Spike Jonze to direct its commercial. Its executives flew in private jets and had a marriage counsellor on staff. But founder Adam Bierman needed to fly to Toronto when looking for a reverse merger on the Canadian Securities Exchange and $30 million in investment capital. MedMen had retail locations on Fifth Avenue, off the Strip in Las Vegas, and on Abbot Kinney in Venice Beach, but it was Captor Capital — a

Canadian firm — that first valued the chain of retailers to be worth over $1 billion. (It's a penny stock now, but those were the days.)

The Americans, because of banking restrictions due to federal laws, *still* couldn't raise money for their pot companies. Bruce Linton, on the other hand, could sit back, and investment bankers would bring money to him. And he spent it. Money circulated around him because he had to deploy this war chest, this capital, to get his next cash infusion. Companies in Florida and Los Angeles were outside of this flow of cash. The cash was in Smiths Falls.

Early summer 2019, if you wanted a hit single, you called Drake, who was in Toronto; if you wanted to list your cannabis company, you raised money on Bay Street, in Toronto; if you had an idea for a CBD-infused dog food or, if you were Steph Curry or Kevin Durant of the Golden State Warriors on your quest for a consecutive title, you had to come through Toronto, where Drake sat courtside with Bruce Linton, smiling from ear to ear. Outside, in Jurassic Park, as the ESPN producer told his reporter, the people got stoned.

Seven billion dollars, according to Deloitte, is the tally Canadians would spend on legal and illegal weed in 2019. Marijuana created a population of new-money Canadian millionaires. Canada had hardly invented marijuana. But we repackaged it with legalization — repopularized it — and created the federal template for a marijuana industry, which meant huge tax dollars and jobs. Watching the final seconds of the Raptors semifinal game against Philadelphia, when Kawhi Leonard's shot hit every corner of the rim before it bounced in, it was a good time to be in weed.

In three years, Canopy had skyrocketed from a $300 million to a $20 billion company. It was a start-up. At the end of April 2019, Canopy was trading at $69.90 and Linton had 2.5 million shares. He didn't get a new car, a new house — didn't buy anything. He thought night and day about work. When Drake came over to Bruce to exchange hugs, Linton played it cool. He already worked with Martha Stewart and Snoop. Beverages, vapes, and edibles were going to be legal in a few months, and Canopy had been built in that abandoned Hershey factory in anticipation of that very day. "I want effect and duration in a format nobody has," Linton says. He didn't smoke weed. But he would take an edible or pop a weed lemon iced tea. He built his company for people like him and he was good at making people believe.

Once, he gave his entire board marijuana drink samples. He smiles when he tells me that story. These were serious business people. But they were also in the business of getting fucked up, and Linton says the board took the drinks, got giggly, then got weird. By the time he put them into limos to take them back to their hotels, he says, some of them couldn't even stand. Working in weed wasn't like working in widgets. Taking mushrooms, for Terry Booth, was just part of the job. And in a moment of perfect-bliss synchronicity, on June 14, the day the Raptors beat the Golden State Warriors to win their first championship in franchise history, Health Canada announced edibles, drinks, and vapes would be legal marijuana products for sale starting October 17, 2019, one year after legalization — Cannabis 2.0.

"Cannabis was a dirty, smelly business, and it was filled with criminals, and then, after Trudeau, people were interested in being in the business. Until then, I couldn't find anybody who wanted to go down this rabbit hole," Lorne Gertner says. "All of a sudden, cannabis goes through the roof. I had weed stocks trading at a dollar, then five dollars, then ten dollars — then fifteen, then twenty, then thirty dollars — *seventy bucks*? Everyone was like, 'What the fuck? This is amazing.' But it's what I've been telling you people for years: weed is the best thing on earth."

Deloitte estimated that the newly legalized Cannabis 2.0 products could be worth $2.7 billion, on top of the $16 billion already estimated from legalized cannabis sales. And while the 2.0 products were difficult and expensive to produce, they offered better margins than flower. But, despite the rosy appearances, there was also serious trouble afoot.

In June 2019, Linton was saying it was business as usual, but his figures for that quarter revealed $323 million in losses. This was a staggering amount, almost four times analyst expectations, and a bitter pill for Constellation Brands CEO Bill Newlands to swallow. Linton assured the market and his board that the losses were intentional. He was following his business plan: buying things now when they were available in order to make huge payouts later, as the laws around the world changed. This is why, he

Happy Customer: Lorne Gertner, restocking at his Tokyo Smoke in Toronto.

proclaimed, Constellation gave him the money in the first place. He was thinking long-term to sew up the entire cannabis market, and the 2.0 products would bring non-cannabis consumers into weed. "Edibles is what we've been built for," Linton told the *Globe* after announcing his losses on a June 22, 2019, analyst call. "It's the whole point of this exercise."

Linton says that in the summer of 2019, there was a widening disconnect between the Constellation executives headquartered outside Rochester, New York, and his world before popping flashbulbs, courtside, hugging Drake. The vocabulary was different. The cultures. The timelines and cool. Once, in a conversation with American reporters, a Constellation executive said that marijuana had come a long way since "buying bud from a Rasta in an alley." Linton says he was furious; you're not even supposed to use the phrase "black market," let alone refer to a racial stereotype. The American team seemed clueless. Linton thought, I'm supposed to take instructions from that?

The answer was yes, he was. When Bill Newlands spoke to analysts after presenting his own quarterly report, Linton's boss said he wasn't happy with Canopy's fourth quarter results. Constellation Brands went from being a profitable company to losing $484 million on their investment in Canopy. Linton was projected to earn revenues of over $700 million in 2019 and $1.35 billion in 2020. "Let us do our thing," Linton said. He was embarrassed, if not stunned, by Newlands's comments. "We were following our plans to the letter," he tells me, a plan Newlands knew: spend now to earn later. That was always the Bruce Linton Canopy plan. "The reason your margin goes down is you increase your capacity. So you have 56 percent gross margin increase, but you increase your capacity eight fold," Linton says. "You have 18 percent gross margins, and if you start using your capital, it goes back up to 56 percent margin — that was the plan! So how can your script say you're disappointed? Are you disappointed about the fact that your birthday's on Tuesday when it's been your fucking birthday forever? It's a fact."

——————

The Cannabis 2.0 products infused hope throughout the entire sector. For Fencott and Haines at Fire & Flower, it meant new products with better margins were coming. Their new stores were opening where rich people would want to buy 2.0 products, such as on Bloor Street, beside Hermes. The business of cannabis changed again that summer. What began as a race to get medical cannabis producer licences and then became a race to grow funded capacity, evolved, that summer of 2019, into a race to open retail locations. For Fencott and Haines, backstopped by Couche-Tard and their fifteen thousand stores all over the world and seven thousand Circle Ks in the U.S., it was high time to expand.

Couche-Tard was teaching Haines and Fencott about shelf space and customer service. The convenience store company, one of the largest shop operators in the world, excels at using customer data to arrange their stores in order to maximize profit from each customer visit. They know about ordering and human relations — they have 150,000 employees. And they know about "quick convenience," providing customers an efficient way to shop. Weed shops might not need to be Apple stores. The Hunny Pot model had lots of overhead. Wouldn't they make more money if they were organized like Circle Ks? Plus, Couche-Tard wasn't squeamish, not like Constellation Brands. The company already sold products that had unsavoury associations — gasoline and cigarettes — and saw both of those businesses as losing favour and market share. Couche-Tard wanted a new revenue stream from Fire & Flower; they were experts in distribution, location, and data; and they knew all about scale.

Fencott fell, like all of the founders, for weed. He told me he wasn't a weed person when he started working in cannabis. Growing up in Scarborough, he was engineered to be an engineer, or doctor, or lawyer. He had graduated with a law degree from Western. But he didn't want to stick with the plan. He found that he was an entrepreneur, and, like a lot of cannabis guys, he made his early money in tech. After Canopy bought Mettrum, Fencott worked at the company, but the death of his father prompted a change of heart. He decided to go out on his own. For Fencott, marijuana began as an unlikely economic opportunity and morphed into something deeper. He never got high in university and didn't smoke weed at law school. He says his wife, Dana, was the cannabis consumer in his household. He never tried the product until Mettrum made a mistake.

His company had created a cannabis distillate and it failed, producing only enough for three patients. Since they wouldn't be able to sell the concentrated marijuana, each of the founders took some home themselves. Fencott had written the warning labels on the Mettrum packaging: start slow and go low. At home, however, with his own product, with his wife and kids away, he didn't follow his own advice. He loosened his necktie. Fencott, who favours pocket squares and called paperwork his super power, who voted for Doug Ford and looks like a *Wall Street*–era Charlie Sheen, took a dropper full of the high-THC Mettrum oil. Nothing happened. So he took another. His limbs got loose and his mind started to wander. Suddenly, he had thousands of ideas. He then climbed into his bed and flicked on *Law & Order* and felt like he was on a waterbed. He felt as comfortable as he'd ever been, free and easy — like he was rafting — and casually optimistic. He drank one of his kids' juice boxes and was astonished by how delicious it was. He chased it with a Rice Krispies square and took another dropperful of the concentrate. He tells me he marvelled at the complexity of *Law & Order*. *No wonder this series is so successful*, he thought, sipping another juice box and digging into another treat. *Smart people solving such complex crimes* was his final thought before he drifted off into a deep, peaceful sleep.

Marijuana, maybe there's something to this stuff after all.

In the morning, he woke up to find he'd drunk all of his kids' juice boxes and eaten all of their Rice Krispies snacks. But he didn't have a hangover and hadn't done anything except disconnect from his conscious mind. For Fencott, endlessly analytical — in a word, uptight — it was a vacation from the tight leash he held on his surroundings. That day he had a meeting with Michael Haines to discuss production expansion, but he felt, twelve hours later, that he was still too high to drive. Sober Fencott is cautious. Still, marijuana made an impression. He finally saw for himself what the fuss was about. And Trevor began using cannabis. By the time he left Canopy and sat at his father's bedside, he was smoking weed, like Sébastien St-Louis, three times a week. He says he wasn't surprised to find backers when he wanted to start his retail company. Since he respected and had respect from what he calls "the Bizarre Camelot Roundtable of Marijuana" — Terry Booth, Vic Neufeld, Bruce Linton, and Sébastien St-Louis — it wasn't hard for him to find investors. "Between Aphria and Hexo, we literally raised twenty million in two phone calls," Fencott says.

Terry Booth at Aurora was, of course, excited about Cannabis 2.0, and when the products finally did come out, it seemed like the Aurora Drift gummies were all you could find. That quarter, September 2019, Aurora sold the most cannabis of any licensed producer, and momentum was at an all-time high. They did $98.9 million in sales, up from $19.1 million the previous year. Booth had a $150 million growing facility nearing completion beside the airport in Edmonton. Called Aurora Sky, it would automate the growing process. And he already had the three-hundred-thousand-square-foot Aurora Polaris under construction, for making edibles, among other things. In Denmark, Aurora had one million square feet of production greenhouses and was leading in the medical marijuana sales. Thanks to its purchase of MedReleaf, Aurora had over ninety thousand medical Canadian patients, who still spent a premium on their weed (no race to the bottom with price structure there, with insurance companies paying for veterans). Aurora had the most patients who spent the most money on weed. And Terry Booth tells me he would taste-test his gummies and feel the possibilities of his universe expand. But what he didn't expect was that selling the most marijuana in the history of the legal market wouldn't be enough. Like Bruce Linton, Terry Booth was learning the new rules of the game.

Aurora had promised investors they'd reach between $100 million and $107 million in revenue that quarter. The company was no different from the young budtender Jackson Flynn, playing dice games. Aurora had promised $100 million in sales. They didn't hit their number. In the fourth quarter of 2019, Aurora was so bullish that they issued a "reiterated guidance" to investors with revenue projections between $100 million and $107 million. This was two weeks before their earnings report in September 2019. Booth says he wasn't consulted on the reiterated guidance announcement, but he knew Aurora was flush. If you issue "reiterated guidance," Booth explains, you have to hit your number; you're *reiterating* to investors who cover your company what your projections will be.

Aurora reiterated, and was wrong.

"The single biggest fuck-up in Aurora history" Booth calls it. The hopped-up founder was irate. They had sold $98.9 million in legal marijuana, but failure was all anyone could see. The stock dropped almost 10 percent in a day. After all that accounting, Booth says, wasn't there $1 million, somewhere, that could be added to the books? All of those people he paid? In the past, if Booth needed cash, he could tell his chain of medical retailers to pump the Aurora product. Now he was too disconnected from the inner workings of his company to directly affect sales, or accounting, or both.

In Booth's telling, his lieutenant, Cam Battley, was orchestrating investor relations and publicly disclosing financial reports. The board, headed by

Michael Singer, who was the CFO of Bedrocan before it was sold to Canopy Growth, called Booth and told him Aurora had missed its guidance in its earnings report.

"What do you mean we missed?" Booth asked.

"You know how much we missed by?" replied Singer. "A million bucks."

"Tell those auditors to give me a million bucks back," screamed Booth. "We shouldn't miss by a fucking dime!"

But they did. Booth couldn't find the last million, and he'd discovered the problem too late.

It didn't bode well for the sector that you could sell nearly $100 million of legal marijuana and your stock would drop ten percent.

Kawhi Leonard would only stay with the Raptors for that one season. The team hasn't come close to winning a championship since.

CHAPTER 16
Edible

"Constellation put a bullet in this dude."

Bruce Linton

Watching his son's university graduation, Bruce Linton was ignoring his phone.

It was June 30, 2019, and Bruce was buoyant. He was with his wife at his son's outdoor graduation and he let a few phone calls from Constellation Brands go to voice mail. When he was a kid, he'd loved university so much that he enjoyed it for six years. Something about the exploratory nature of school. He hadn't felt pressure. He'd had options.

He watched his boy earn his diploma while other parents asked him investing advice, then called back his boss. He was told that he needed to come to Toronto on July 2, the day after Canada Day, for an emergency board meeting. Linton knew there was no emergency at his company — losing more than $300 million didn't count as an emergency. That, in his mind, was his company running according to plan. So he figured it out, chalked it up. The emergency must be him. *Fine, fine, I'll listen to them moan.*

His stock had dipped from its astronomical highs. His industry felt contentious. The dreamers who built the legal weed companies were being run by their boards, and his board had publicly disclosed being angry with him. But Linton was feeling a bit dissociated from work. Maybe it was a survival mechanism. Maybe it was denial. Maybe it was supreme self-belief after growing so big, so fast. How many Canadians, in history, built a $19 billion company? With Cannabis 2.0 coming, he was hardly panicking. He let more than one call from head office go to voice mail before calling back.

He was at a dynamic juncture. After the graduation, Linton was heading to Berlin for a tech conference and it just so happened that he'd be flying with his other son, Max, who was about to start a semester abroad. Both of his kids were thriving and his company, despite Constellation's worries, was still on top of the world. He was giving the keynote address in a country on the cusp of cannabis legalization, and he was poised to run Germany like he was about to run the U.S. He was not feeling reflective — he almost never was — and he was not preparing excuses for his stock price, down 25 percent. Instead, he was beaming. The Constellation board members were coming to Toronto to see him. He wasn't beckoned to New York. They needed to listen to Canopy's founder.

He had so many deals on the go in so many countries across so many sectors that it wasn't far-fetched, Linton sometimes publicly mused, to think that one day he'd be running his parent company. Bill Newlands, Constellation Brands' CEO, was no Rob Sands (and since he was Constellation's first CEO outside the Sands family, his appointment attracted scrutiny).

Linton didn't kowtow to Newlands, even after being publicly chastised. When Linton appeared on BNN on June 21 to discuss his 2019 Q4 earnings — doubling of sales to $225 million, doubling of losses to $323 million, both twice as high as Aurora, his nearest competitor — he was asked point-blank if he felt pressure to rein in expenses. Linton, decked out in his trademark Tweed T-shirt beneath a grey blazer, talking quickly, as always, and looking not unlike the cannabis twin of Boris Johnson in a rumpled, off-kilter way, stared directly at the camera, smiled, and said, "No."

This answer, coming directly after Linton's Constellation Brands CEO told investors he was disappointed with his Canopy Growth CEO — well, disappointed with his company's earnings, but the company's performance and Linton's, like that of all great salesman chief executives, went hand in hand — was clueless, defiant, or true. Linton was probably all three.

"I get it, $5 billion Canadian gives you authority, but I think my current depth of knowledge is never achievable for a board," Linton tells me. It would make sense for him to find his new board distasteful. Literally what he had done — start from scratch a company with a value now over $1 billion — was create what's called a "unicorn." Of course he felt special. Canopy might be down from its $22 billion peak, but Linton had created an international company in a field where the smart money wouldn't go. He had first-mover global advantage and was the face of the coolest industry in the world.

The current quarter's losses were steep; Linton knew this, but he maintained he was just following his game plan. You have to be super small or super huge to win in cannabis, Linton believed. Spend now, as opposed to spending later, and the initial pain would make the long-term value twice as good.

At this point, he also had more money than any of his competitors. A deeper reservoir of cash. He didn't need to turn a profit. He could sustain losses. He could afford — and this is the trick up his sleeve — to bleed the market dry. "Drop the fuck out of the price because we have five billion in the bank. Let's napalm the fuck out of the market." Cannabis companies were having trouble selling weed with three-dollar margins, but Linton could afford one-dollar margins because of his war chest. By dropping his price, he could sell the most weed, starve out the competition when no one bought their product, and be the last one standing. Bruce knew what he wanted to tell the bean-counters at their emergency meeting. "Disrupt the market. Kill everybody. Then come back with real pricing."

It took an hour to fly to Toronto from Ottawa and Linton was still thinking about his sons. He had a smile on his face and he liked his idea for the napalm. With the Canadian launch of Cannabis 2.0 products the cannabis industry was going to expand. The new products had higher margins, plus were more difficult than flower to produce, which meant larger, more technologically advanced companies, like Canopy Growth, had an advantage over their peers. And the government was going to help cannabis companies like his. If the goal of legalization was to eradicate the black market, which, in June 2019, still accounted for at least 50 percent of all cannabis sales, the presence of 2.0 products in the legal market — just the tip of the iceberg of what companies like Linton's could do with weed — would help that succeed.

There were more stores opening in Ontario, more Fire & Flower shops across the country, and more Canopy products poised to hit shelves, including a line of Canopy beverages in collaboration with the comedian Seth Rogen, sold under his Houseplant brand. Canopy was growing. First in Canada. Then the U.S. Then Europe. South America. Mexico. Jamaica. India. New Zealand. Everything, Linton believed as he travelled to his emergency meeting, was going according to plan. Bumpy, sure. But the company was soaring. It was a rocket ship burning jet fuel. Newlands was just flexing for his shareholders. He must have known that Linton was following the plan.

"We saw the script for what they were going to read for their quarter, which occurred just after our quarter," Linton tells me. "And in the script there was some mention of 'disappointment with Canopy's results,' which, in our opinion, the results were, give or take one percent, exactly the plan — exactly the plan."

His stock, though, was at $53.28, down 98 cents a share since that Raptors game, although Linton still didn't watch the market closely. The stock was at $75 before legalization. He had made well over $200 million from his Canopy shares. And he was surfing a legal wave that had never washed ashore before in Canada or, outside of Uruguay, anywhere else in the world. Constellation wanted Bruce to give guidance. Linton thought his track record earned him their respect. "I hope you guys realize," he had just told them, "my fourth quarter of the last three years has been greater than the prior quarters since. You realize that, right?"

The board demanded he be specific. Where was he going to trim expenses? When would he be profitable? How much revenue would he earn? What would he cut? "I'll say whatever the fuck you come up with, because I don't know the answer," Linton told them in response.

After Constellation made their multibillion-dollar investment, they asked Linton for a five-year business plan. Linton laughed. "I can't give you five weeks," he said.

———

Bruce obviously was used to spinning fanciful narratives to bankers. "This is how much money we could make," he'd say, and he believed it in his very core. He had already done so much; who knew how far this could go?

The bankers were always impressed with Linton's story, but after 2015, they had a follow-up question when it came to projecting cash: "Can you get bigger?"

"Sure" was the answer each time. And there was always a case he could make for rosy futures, blissful fantasies. Linton was certain that 2.0 products would increase the number of Canadians buying his weed. Smoking was out of fashion. And rolling a joint was hard. Drinking a sparkling Seth Rogen beverage? Anyone could do that. Constellation Brands knew that better than most. And when more legal stores opened, stores like CAFE would finally close, the vaunted soccer mom category would come into the sector, and they'd spend more money on their average receipts. The future of pot wasn't what's strongest and cheapest. It was what's healthiest. New product categories were the future, Linton believed. Which was awfully convenient, since the price of flower kept dropping.

In 2018, a gram cost, on average, $9.40. In the summer of 2019, that price was seven bucks. Adjust that for inflation and factor in all the new licensed producers who wanted to enter the market, growing pot inexpensively at their outdoor grows, and legalization had made weed as accessible and inexpensive as beer. It was cheaper now to buy weed than it was in 1961. And the pot was stronger, too. So the smart companies sold more than weed. Olli edibles, the bespoke products crafted by John Aird and team, were products designed for the shelves at Whole Foods. And the stigma around marijuana was dissipating. Canadians, in 2019, spent the same amount of money on pot as they did on wine: almost $2 billion. We were in the first inning of this cannabis thing. Eventually, Linton was preparing to tell his board, we'd all be ordering Canopy weed drinks at restaurants and bars.

Linton was flying into Toronto certain that he was going to export his intellectual capital into Europe and the United States. He felt momentum — but it was mixed with the frustration of having to explain himself to Americans who didn't understand. They had just arrived at his party. It used to take Linton fifteen minutes to get approval, on Mother's Day, from his Canopy board for $500 million in acquisitions. Those were serious people. Murray Goldman, real estate tycoon, wasn't a naïf. Linton didn't have the patience to explain himself to his new bosses, who now occupied four of seven board seats. And what was more, he didn't have the vocabulary. He once said he doesn't speak "corporate." He shouldn't have to. He's Bruce.

Throughout the weekend, Linton had paid the meeting no mind. How could Constellation be upset about earnings and expenses when the numbers were within his forecast? They'd seen his books prior to his reporting. They knew his script and he was following it. But when Newlands made that comment in the press, Linton knew he was being poked. The question was how hard?

Sure, the situation was urgent. Fuck them. It had been urgent since they'd launched.

On Tuesday morning, Linton flew into Toronto, once again wearing his Tweed shirt beneath his blazer. He found this part of the job annoying: the hand-holding the board now required took up as much as half of his operational time. It was the same thing that aggrieved Terry Booth at Aurora. Founders used to running on jet fuel and their ADHD, being obeyed, and not having to answer for losses were now under scrutiny. Founders were asked to become accountants. Totally different jobs. But okay, Linton would play ball. Canopy had 27 percent market share when Linton walked into the emergency meeting. He'd signed off on Drake's agreement, which would be announced in November, and brought in Snoop and Martha Stewart, along with Rogen and his Houseplant staff. He had the BioSteel deal cooking, which he thought would work great for Constellation, and he figured with BioSteel, he could leverage Constellation Brands to take on Gatorade. "Gatorade would need fucking Gatorade when I was done," Bruce says.

The CBD drinks that he was planning with BioSteel, made without THC, could be distributed legally on Amazon throughout the U.S. With everybody jockeying for difficult American penetration, Linton had it. The drinks, which were coming out as part of the 2.0 rollout and were an impetus behind Constellation getting involved with weed, hadn't yet been released. All Canopy needed to do, says Linton, was keep rolling. His R&D department was making strides in providing data suggesting that cannabis could be used as an effective medicine for cirrhosis and for sleep, which was something that cannabis researchers had been working on since the 1960s. And more than half of American states had a medical marijuana program.

In May, Linton had inked a deal in Germany with Cannabinoid Compound for $342 million. On the flight to Toronto, he had in his pocket a first-class plane ticket to Berlin, where he would tell a room full of investors, scientists, and technology experts how Canopy used technology in their agriculture, research, and development. Canopy was the largest pot company in the world and Linton was working hard at the time to get a special-occasion permit in Smiths Falls, so his drinks could be served to his neighbours at a licensed outdoor show. The government was still restrictive in its cannabis policies. But things were changing. Consumption was banned at festivals and concerts, but there was wiggle room being explored. In July 2019, the Festival of Beer in Toronto would open a cannabis-smoking section for the first time. Surely, if you allowed cannabis smoking, drinking a cannabis beverage couldn't be far behind.

The board meeting was an emergency, but Bruce was animated, prepared. He walked into the office to silence. The kind of quiet that said tons. He was not stunned — more like sobered up. He had tried not to think about the meeting, but meeting time had definitely arrived. "It's the kind of meeting where you don't bring your computer because they're going to ask for it back," says Bruce, who sat down solemnly to absorb the news.

The board was recommending his removal. He was asked to leave his company. In fact — something he should've already known — the company wasn't actually his; he gave it away when he took a $5 billion investment before legalization and acquiesced to Constellation Brands' demand for a controlling number of board seats.

Sitting there, he heard this from people he had sought out as investors, who hadn't been there when he'd bought the Hershey factory with his own money or fired Chuck Rifici; who had never spoken with Hilary Black or become involved with medical marijuana; and who couldn't possibly understand what it felt like to work with Michael Haines on the tarmac outside of Kelowna when he was boarded by the RCMP and they uncovered hockey bags stuffed with BC weed.

It wasn't their job to care about Bruce's legacy and he should've known that. Still it stung. "You have to be super fucking calm because if you aren't, you might find yourself reaching across a desk," Linton says. The board showed him a draft of their press release announcing his exit. The release said he was leaving to focus on his family. It was like how Aphria framed the exit of Vic Neufeld: a lion past his prime going out to graze in the jungle, making way for new blood.

Linton suggested, instead, that he should move to the States and run Acreage, the American weed brand that Canopy was poised to acquire once the U.S. approved federal cannabis legalization. He was reaching. He said he didn't want a job, though he was still sort of asking for one, and that he'd be happy to help finalize all the plans he had in the works. All those things he told the bankers he believed. But he was rebuffed at every suggestion.

He continued to try to find some oxygen for himself at the company he loved.

"Do you have my replacement yet?"

"Mark Zekulin will run the company for the time being," he was told.

So, no, Linton thought, *they have no fucking clue.*

"Well, have you hired an executive recruiting firm?" he asked.

"No," they said, and Bruce swallowed this. Clearly they'd made no decisions beyond their one big emergency decision: fire Bruce.

For Linton, the sticking point wasn't about his package. He maintains it was never about the money. What Linton negotiated was the press release. Leaving Canopy to spend time with his children? "Fuck you I am," he said.

The last thing he wanted it to look like was his retirement.

This is the message he wants people to know: "Constellation put a bullet in this dude. It's not like he decided to walk out to pasture."

Linton collected his things and walked out of the Tweed office without looking back. He met his son at Pearson Airport. He wouldn't be joining Max in Germany. There would be no first-class ticket, no tech conference, no keynote for Bruce. At the airport, he was still wearing his shirt, and he hadn't felt any particular emotion, other than simmering rage. He says when he's angry, he represses that emotion because it clouds his wits, and he didn't want his wits muddled during his termination process. "You have to compress a lot of urges," he says, "or you might choke someone."

Max asked him what he'd miss most about Canopy. Linton thought it over. He loved the microphones and the business cards. The travel, the restaurants, the ringing phones, and the public eye. He liked making work for other people, executing crazy ideas. Acquisitions, of course. And trying to build something new. He truly began believing in marijuana, and he liked being the face of an industry. But what he'd most miss, he told his son, were the tours of that Smiths Falls facility, showing people what he'd built and telling the story of the old, abandoned factory. About the time the mayor ran across the street to get a coffee for Mark Zekulin. How a closed-down Hershey plant with mice running around gave rise to a company that grew to be worth more than $20 billion in five years selling weed. It had been a wild ride and he could retrace it to all those tours at the old Hershey factory.

Bruce put his son on the plane and headed back to his house in Ottawa, wiping the first tears from his eyes.

PART IV

REDEMPTION

CHAPTER 17

Got 'Em

"I'm not going to let this go."

Nick Lalonde

Linton getting axed from Canopy should have been the summer's big weed news, though Trevor Fencott believed in his heart of hearts that Linton — weed's King Kong on cocaine — was actually glad to be relieved of the burden. He had to have seen the reckoning coming. "The problem with promoters is eventually you have to deliver, and it almost always amounts to less than their vision," says Fencott, who describes Bruce's behaviour around his Canopy board as "death by cop," daring them to take him out. "Eventually he was going out," Fencott says. "This way, when a plan that has no chance of working didn't work, he has someone to blame."

Still, industry fluctuations around the termination of Bruce Linton were stifled because something that had much greater impact on the entire legalization experiment came just days later. In early July 2019, while Canadian cannabis companies struggled for legitimacy against supply shortages, a lack of retail locations, and the backdrop of the CAFE saga — like Linton's firing, the concrete blocks in front of the stores were front-page news — another bombshell was exploding. This one began behind a plexi-glass wall in Pelham, Ontario.

For months, Nick Lalonde had been complaining to superiors that he felt uncomfortable about the task he'd performed that winter: erecting plexi-glass walls and hanging pictures in front of grow rooms at CannTrust that had not been licensed by Health Canada. Lalonde got into weed because he loved it. He smoked it, and he wanted to be part of the legal industry. He was a minimum-wage worker at a $470 million company (down from a billion) run by Peter Aceto, a former banking executive, and Eric Paul, CannTrust's founder, a pharmacist turned entrepreneur with forty years of experience in health care. CannTrust listed on the Nasdaq exchange and counted Merrill Lynch, Citigroup, and Credit Suisse as partners. While Hexo partnered with Molson Coors to make infused drinks, CannTrust partnered with pharma giant Apotex to make medicine.

CannTrust, with its leadership pedigree, was considered by investors to be Canada's best-run legal cannabis company. It was their differenti-ation. Hence their Nasdaq listing and American partners — a potential watershed moment for other Canadian cannabis companies looking to move away from independent Canadian investment banks to American com-panies like Merrill Lynch, companies that ran the world. There was more money, the industry hoped, flying into the sector behind the investments created by CannTrust. The industry moved as a block. When Linton netted Constellation Brands, Terry Booth met with Coca-Cola and Heineken, and Trevor Fencott secured Couche-Tard. Stigma would make it hard to break into the mainstream business world. Terry Booth says that even after Nelson Peltz signed on to the board at Aurora, Peltz saw the industry as askew.

"Peltz is sitting across from another monster fucking billionaire, eating and talking about Aurora, and he goes, 'This fucking thing is worth $12 billion,'" recalls Booth. "Here I am trying to justify the cannabis space and he's coming to work with me! I should've sold my shares that day."

Justifying the cannabis space was every weed executive's job. John Fowler, the founder of Canada's Supreme Cannabis Company, one of the sixteen Canadian cannabis brands to reach a billion-dollar valuation, says he never escaped his financier partner's weed jokes: about the Cheeto stains on the keyboards, the boardroom meetings held beneath clouds of smoke. The industry was started by unconventional outsiders. But by the summer of 2019, you couldn't still be investing serious sums in marijuana and laugh at the product, which made many of the original founders shift their beliefs. Trevor Fencott was no longer that far off, ethically, from Hilary Black. Terry Booth at Aurora financed Akwasi Owusu-Bempah at Cannabis Amnesty. And the companies prided themselves on obeying the laws. The licences still meant everything.

Cannabis companies were being judged by Merrill Lynch and audited by Ernst & Young. CannTrust couldn't be Ascent Industries or Bonify. Its licence to sell recreational and medicinal pot was the engine behind its entire valuation. Without its licence, it would go broke. The industry was competitive and it was always a race: to build facilities, grow weed, come out with a new product. But you couldn't screw with Health Canada, couldn't screw with the prime minister's Cannabis Act — so the Canadian companies adhered to the rules. The success or failure of legalization, a major Liberal election platform, would be measured on companies' not embarrassing regulators. And the people running the companies, they'd assure investors, didn't even use their product; at most of Canada's largest weed brands, it was everyone else at the companies who did.

Eric Paul and Peter Aceto at CannTrust could assure their backers that they didn't smoke weed. They were above it. Someone like Nick Lalonde, however, thought that pot was important; legalization mattered to him. Pot wasn't an iPhone. It was a community. Meanwhile, Paul and Aceto, so the market was led to believe, were valuable executives because they could keep potheads in line. Lalonde says he wanted nothing more than for the industry to succeed. "Legalization was a dream come true," he says. "I grew up in the city, and weed was a big part of my life — when you hung out, you smoked it — and so when I got over to CannTrust, oh wow, the best growers in the world were my colleagues. This was it for me. But I didn't want to commit a crime."

Crimes committed at CannTrust, emails later revealed, weren't only committed and covered up by Nick Lalonde. The *Globe and Mail* reported that on November 16, 2018, Graham Lee, the company's director of quality and compliance, emailed his bosses, including Paul and Aceto, after a Health Canada inspection. "We dodged some bullets," wrote Lee. Unlicensed rooms were filled with plants. And vast sums of cannabis were lost and not reported. Health Canada hadn't discovered these mistakes — this time. But eventually, concluded Lee, they would.

The company was steps ahead of the firing squad, and Graham Lee didn't know what to do. He turned to his professional bosses for help. "Although serious on their own, each of these [breaches] can be talked through," wrote Lee. "The concern is that together they will paint a picture with the regulator of a company not in control."

These emails did not mention Lalonde's concerns, and Health Canada never got the chance to prove Lee right about the multiple violations at CannTrust. Because, Lalonde says, he couldn't hold his tongue any longer.

No one at CannTrust would listen to Lalonde, so he quit his job in May. Before leaving, he told his bosses, "You're going to get caught. You're screwing over so many people. It's not the right thing to do. I'm not going to let this go."

Lalonde tried to let it go, he really did. But when he read the CannTrust press releases about their production volume, he knew the company was duplicitous. He understood the pressure his former company was under to produce volumes of weed. But he also knew the facility inside out and knew the company was exaggerating its numbers. There was no need to lie. They were (really) about to legally acquire two hundred acres of outdoor production in British Columbia, which could add three hundred thousand pounds of production in the new year. It wasn't fair. On June 14, 2019, two weeks after leaving CannTrust and taking a job in construction, Lalonde sent a letter to Health Canada, the *Globe and Mail*, and his local paper about the role he had been asked to perform at the company.

When Health Canada again inspected the CannTrust facilities, this time it knew what it was looking for and found it. On July 8, three weeks after the Health Canada inspection, nine days after Bruce Linton was fired, CannTrust announced that Health Canada had put a freeze on 5,200 kilograms of cannabis grown in five unlicensed rooms — the rooms that Lalonde had been instructed to disguise. CannTrust, in announcing a freeze on its product, also admitted it had provided inaccurate information to regulators. It was determined 12,700 kilograms of marijuana had been grown in unlicensed rooms from October 2018 to March 2019.

In two days, the company's share price dropped 33 percent.

Peter Aceto and Eric Paul were fired on July 25, but the biggest bombshell was yet to drop. It was one thing to be accused of growing weed in an unlicensed room that was exactly the same as your licensed rooms — because you needed to get weed onto shelves and you were growing faster than Health Canada's staff of inspectors. It was simply stupid. And there was a well-established legal workaround in the industry. "If they were one or two months away from their licence, and they're losing ground to guys like us, guys with product, then do something about it — buy cannabis!" says Aphria's former CEO Vic Neufeld. The weed companies often bought each other's stuff and still do that today. Cannabis companies had operated in grey zones since the medical days. Insider trading allegations, however, stank of old-fashioned corruption.

"CannTrust officials sold shares after email about unlicensed pot" was the *Globe and Mail* headline on July 30 after investigative reporters David Milstead and Mark Rendell discovered that Eric Paul and Mark Litwin, CannTrust's vice-chairman, sold their stock on the day they received Graham Lee's email. Paul and Litwin sold $1 million worth of their CannTrust shares that day, and then they sold $5 million worth of their shares over the next thirty days.

"We will not allow our company to be associated with the illegals, period," Eric Paul had written back in 2016, on an early email thread started by Hilary Black and Marc Wayne among the original medical cannabis companies about the need to end taxation of medical cannabis. The signatories on the associated press release would include grey market wellness dispensaries. Eric Paul said no way and Terry Booth of Aurora had a response: "The 'we don't want to be associated with illegals' bullshit is simply put, bullshit. Get off your pedestal. You wouldn't be here without the fight/risk that these dispensaries, compassion clubs and MMAR over-growers have taken to provide medicine for the safe, wonderful cannabis plant you are now hoping to profit from."

Trading by company executives and board members who have confidential information about the company that would affect their stock price is insider trading. The people buying cannabis stocks, by and large, are retail investors, many of whom feel a close connection to the plant. On July 8, CannTrust was trading at $6.46. After it revealed its Health Canada sanctions, it was trading at $2.86 and froze sales of all its recreational and medical products.

The industry had little sympathy for the company, especially because it seemed like the executives had parachuted in without paying dues. "[Just] because you wear a suit, you're not smarter than my cousin who fixes a tractor," says Sébastien St-Louis at Hexo.

St-Louis says he never felt CannTrust deserved to be put on its pedestal. While the market turned on cannabis companies, he thought the real problem lay somewhere else. "I don't blame cannabis — I blame the power structures," he says. "At CannTrust, it was up to the board of directors to sniff the bad behaviour out, but when they don't, and when it's rewarded, people get hurt and the results speak for themselves."

Lalonde says CannTrust was under tremendous pressure to produce more cannabis. But that same pressure was felt by all the leading cannabis brands, and CannTrust's revelations sent the industry into free-fall: Canopy's stock dropped by 7.99 percent. Aurora dropped by 5.98 percent.

"Just as CannTrust does a listing through the Bank of America and trades on Nasdaq across a whole U.S. group, it turns out they're not doing what they said they would do and they were very bad," says Bruce Linton, who did a press tour the day after his sacking, wearing a hometown Martello Technologies T-shirt on Bloomberg, which sent that company's stock up 89 percent.

On the day of his firing, Linton said something that would often be repeated: "Canada is through."

None of the major companies were profitable and there was a stench around the sector — a reckoning in the air — and hopes around Cannabis 2.0 felt deflated. In August 2019, Lorne Gertner had flashbacks to what it was like when he first started seeking financing back in 2013: the money dried up for weed brands. Citing "prevailing market conditions," Tom Flow, now the CEO of a company called Flowr, backed by Stephen Arbib, decided against his $125 million public offering.

Linton says, given the CannTrust situation, he was not surprised. "So what does the situation with CannTrust do? It makes all institutions say, 'I'm out of this shit until there's a sheriff in town.'"

Hilary Black, Akwasi Owusu-Bempah, Alan Young, Jodie Giesz-Ramsay, Rosie Rowbotham, and Terrance Parker all feel CannTrust confirmed their worst apprehensions of the legal industry. The wrong people were running the show. "It's painful that rich white businessmen getting into marijuana see it as an avenue to circumnavigate the rules and use it merely to focus their greed," says Black. Now that she was working as Canopy's chief advocacy officer, without Linton, Black was concentrating on removing the tax on medicinal marijuana. While her efforts were based on patients accessing cannabis, as they always had been, it was hard not to be dismayed by the corporate world she'd been defending. Bruce Linton was her buddy and he sold his stock before legalization without telling her. Everybody in the legal sector piled on CannTrust.

"I've seen more bad actors in the legal space than I ever did when I was buying illegal weed," says John Fowler.

Alison Gordon says everyone was losing money and confidence in the weed stocks. She says her massage therapist lost a significant amount of money after the CannTrust breach. The therapist said that everybody in cannabis broke the rules, right? "I was like *no*! Maybe I'm naive, but I can tell you one hundred percent that we don't!" Gordon reiterates that the entire value of a cannabis company is tied to its licence, and if you jeopardize that licence, you risk your entire business.

The cannabis companies, however, were plagued by mistrust, as if the stigma they were trying to alleviate was given licence to return, full thrust. And it wasn't just in Canada.

On August 15, 2019, the U.S. Federal Bureau of Investigation released a statement. "States require licenses to grow and sell [marijuana] — opening the possibility for public officials to become susceptible to bribes in exchange for those licenses," FBI public affairs specialist Mollie Halpern said on an episode of the *FBI This Week* podcast. "The corruption is more prevalent in western states where the licensing is decentralized — meaning the level of corruption can span from the highest to the lowest level of public officials."

Corrupt officials. Fake walls. Insider trading. No more Bruce Linton. And CAFE was selling unlicensed marijuana out in the open while budtenders on the front lines at the retail locations struggled to hold on to their marijuana dreams. The stocks were down and the investment capital was dry. Alison Gordon is dismayed. "Everything is compliance, that's why CannTrust is shocking — it's sad. Fake walls? What's going on?" she says. "Part of the problem with the markets is a lack of trust and that my friend would say, 'Everybody in weed's doing that.' No! How could you risk something so valuable?"

Nick Lalonde took a job in construction. He says he received death threats. He never wanted to be a sheriff of the industry, least of all at CannTrust, among people he viewed as mentors, as friends. He gave up booze, but not marijuana, and moved in with his girlfriend, helping raise her son. "Part of the problem with the pot industry is the people they had running it," he says. "There's this air of superiority, but it's like, 'No, you're not superior to stoners.' We're not idiots and you're not smart, and you can't do whatever you want because you went to a fancy college. Fuck you. Weed was here before you and we don't need you — we'll be here after you're gone."

CHAPTER 18

2.0

"We all get the bullet eventually."

Terry Booth

In the fall of 2019, Sébastien St-Louis stopped drinking alcohol and started smoking weed. The pounds had been accumulating and the hangovers had gotten worse, and with two children and nonstop work pressure, the rigours of cannabis life required intense concentration. Booze could not be sustained. St-Louis was a former weightlifter and athlete who saw the corporate world through anecdotes about sports. Alcohol, despite being part of the Hexo culture, had become a distraction. One of his favourite days was when, after announcing to the team their joint venture with Molson Coors — one of Canada's oldest companies, born and still based in Quebec — he had a fifty-three-foot trailer pull into their warehouse. He opened its rear doors and proceeded to hand out six-packs of Coors Light. "Look how far we've come," Sébastien couldn't help thinking. The idea that a trailer full of Coors Light represented the apex of success betrayed his youth. It was the suds of choice shared by Sébastien and his brother-in-law and founder-in-arms, Adam Miron. That had been a year before, drinking a Coors Light with his partner, with a billion-dollar valuation, on top of the world.

St-Louis was ready to double down that fall after CannTrust imploded and Bruce Linton was axed. In July, before the October release of the 2.0 products, Miron had decided he'd had enough marijuana and left the company he helped create. Miron's dad had been Hexo's first medical marijuana patient, and Adam and Sébastien had done everything together those first few years. But the times were changing, and the approach had to change as well.

"Adam had built a marketing organization that was stakeholder focused as opposed to consumer focused," St-Louis says. "You had to [be], at the time, competing with guys like Bruce, but we needed to make a reversal and we needed to cut expenses."

St-Louis says he never considered stopping. Instead he would pivot his company. The first problem to address was that, in the fourth quarter of 2019, his stock was sinking, losing 20 percent after missing their guidance projections, just as Aurora had done. St-Louis said he'd hit $26 million in revenue, but it was closer to $16 million, a shaky enough quarter to have the company rescind guidance for 2020, blaming, among other things, the slow pace of store openings in Ontario and regulatory uncertainties. "With the stock collapsing and the stock pressure, we needed a capital raise and we thought we had more runway. We needed to cut expenses, but all the while I knew the company was maturing," St-Louis says.

So, as CEO of a weed corporation, St-Louis began using his product. Just like Trevor Fencott. Terry Booth, on the other hand, had always smoked weed. There had been times in Sébastien's life when he drank too much — and this was not going to be one of those times. Without his brother-in-law, the success of the entire company sat on his shoulders. Despite everything, he was optimistic. "I saw the CannTrust failure as a positive. It created uncertainty in the market, but the market is short term," he says. "When CannTrust happened, I saw it as getting rid of a competitor that was using an unfair advantage and taking up a lot of airtime."

He had the same thought about Canopy's firing of Bruce Linton. "He's a wild card. He's able to create unexpected angles of attack. Without

Sky's the Limit: Sébastien St-Louis, the Canadian cannabis founder of Hexo, who would outlive most of his peers, at least for a time.

Bruce, I know Canopy isn't going to do anything bananas to blow me out of the water."

With two major players out of the industry in one wild week and a redirection of his own company, Sébastien St-Louis could focus his mission. He wanted Hexo to win market share in Canada. But that wasn't the whole plan. He didn't want to be the CFL. Sébastien St-Louis — shaved head, black Under Armour T-shirt, French — wanted to be BlackBerry, minus the crash. He saw the void in the market as his time to shine. Why couldn't he be the next Bruce Linton? "I'm always looking at the field of players," he tells me. "Keep eliminating, keep eliminating, keep eliminating."

Beginning October 17, 2019, 2.0 products were poised to infuse $2 billion into the industry at the exact time that Canadian brands needed the cash. On top of the CannTrust debacle — which chased away the American institutional money that had finally made its way into the sector — the negative headwinds included, as St-Louis discovered, the exposure of overvalued companies. Tilray had a market cap of US$10 billion in 2018 with US$43 million in sales. Before legalization, weed stocks were tall tales with fanciful price tags. But afterward, when you were no longer trading on speculation, it became like any other business. Hype was being replaced — even punished — by financials.

"Everybody wanted to be Diageo, InBev, or LVMH overnight," John Fowler says. Through the years, Fowler fought with his board about expansion. He wasn't Lorne Gertner, who wanted to see Tokyo Smoke in Tokyo. He wanted to sell premium weed in Canada. In January 2018, Supreme had a billion-dollar valuation; Fowler, when he won a *High Times* award, stayed at the Four Seasons Hotel in LA. Things were good, but his board wanted better. They wanted him to expand into Switzerland, Denmark, Jamaica, Lesotho. Fowler had started the company, but he couldn't get his board of directors, many of whom he'd hired, to focus on making a good product at home. "You see the valuation of other cannabis companies from two times to ten times, probably getting close to twenty times our valuation, and at some point, everyone gets impatient," Fowler says. "As much as I would tell everybody I didn't think those valuations made sense, nobody listened. I didn't think the global market would expand as quickly as everyone chose to believe."

In the summer of 2019, Fowler stepped down as CEO of Supreme to become the company's chief advocacy officer, a title he shared with Canopy's Hilary Black. Fowler had more in common with Alan Young than he did with Terry Booth. And he's proud of the hiring practices he pioneered, in defiance of conventional pot wisdom: first, hiring staff with cannabis convictions and then, after that initiative had been a success, hiring people with convictions of any manner. Of course, potential employees would all be carefully scrutinized but, he believed, the cannabis employment laws were misunderstood and unjustly applied, even racist. He wanted to position his company not as a global juggernaut, but as a Canadian example of how a cannabis company could be ethically run. Part of his ethics was making and smoking really good weed. "I do find it hilarious that ours was the only industry I've ever heard of where quality is viewed as unimportant," Fowler tells me one night over a joint. Business decisions in weed focused on everything but the product.

"How can an industry look past its consumers?"

Fowler says he shares an ethics principle with Larry Fink: equal hiring isn't just the right way to run a company — it makes good business sense. "Those people we employed who knew about cannabis and respected the plant, which became our company mantra — respect the plant — were often our most dedicated workers, especially ones who appreciated getting a second chance," says Fowler, who had a personal stake in the cannabis movement. He wasn't like Peter Aceto. He was a weed guy. He tried all of the products and could attest that the legal weed being grown by Aurora, Canopy, Aphria, Hexo, Tilray, and all the other major players was no good. At Supreme, the CEO used to compete with his employees at joint rolling contests. "It matters," he says.

Like Alison Gordon, Fowler became something of a cult cannabis executive. I wrote several stories on the two of them, including ones in the *Globe* where we got high and talked about their stock prices. It might have added to their allure that Fowler, who had dark skin and curly hair because his mother was South Asian, and Gordon, still one of the only cannabis female executives, struck a contrast to their white, non-cannabis-smoking, male peers.

But no one is untouchable. On Monday evening, October 28, 2019, Fowler was working late on a podcast with guest Akwasi Owusu-Bempah, from Cannabis Amnesty, when he received an email. He was asked to come in Tuesday morning at 8:00 a.m. to meet with CEO Navdeep Dhaliwal, along with the head of human resources. The head of HR had been with the company Fowler started for only one month.

Tuesday morning, he wore a tie-dyed Supreme T-shirt to his funeral. It was a throwback to how Bruce Linton had dressed for his own walk down the plank. Dhaliwal put an arm around Fowler and told the person who had brought him into the business that he would invest in whatever his old friend chose to start next. He just no longer had a job here. Fowler was handed two envelopes: a severance package and a media release, which was to be deployed in three hours, at 11:00 a.m. He was told "It's just business" and had his key card deactivated.

Fowler had celebrated 10.17 in the courtyard of his billion-dollar company. He had partnered with Wiz Khalifa on a Canadian strain. None of it mattered. Fowler was told to clean out his desk.

Under supervision, he walked out the front door and never returned.

With Fowler out — following Vic Neufeld, Bruce Linton, Eric Paul, and Adam Miron — Canadian founders were falling like so many consumer products off an assembly line while the warehouse workers took lunch. Cannabis 2.0 no longer seemed to mean just new products, but also a new face of the industry. Meanwhile, the American cannabis companies were beginning to mature and set up shop along Bay Street, where they were finding willing investors.

Curaleaf — a vertically integrated Massachusetts-based licensed producer — had an IPO target around ten dollars in the fall of 2018. When it listed on the Canadian Securities Exchange, it raised $400 million, giving it a valuation of $4 billion. While there were once no Americans on the playing field for international investors looking to get into weed stocks, now Chip, the Canadian investment banker, was the book runner on go-public deals with American cannabis companies with more revenue, and fewer $300 million losses, than their Canadian peers. While the Canadian market buckled, Chip earned his highest commissions to date helping American cannabis brands Harvest, Cresco, and Trulieve list on the Canadian exchange. In banking the patriotism is always to money. Trulieve, with its positive EBITDA, had a multibillion-dollar market cap and listed in Canada while selling medical marijuana and running a chain of dispensaries in Florida. Canadian money, to the chagrin of the surviving Canadian founders, was leaving the country and building American weed brands.

Terry Booth and Sébastien St-Louis both said at the time that they needed 2.0 products and they needed Ontario to increase its number of retail locations. But instead of celebrating the one-year anniversary of legalization with new products on the shelves on October 17, 2019, something else happened: the launch of the 2.0 products got delayed. "Of course I'm watching all the Americans and see what's happening and we have to navigate the asshole regulations and I'm trying to run this fucking company," Terry Booth says of the time. "That hold on the 2.0 launch on the seventeenth — come on, man! We are ready; 2.0 is ready. The fucking provinces won't give us a chance."

The stores in Ontario numbered just sixty-six at the end of 2019 — the Fire & Flower on Bloor Street still sat closed. Finally, in December, heeding the industry's call, the Alcohol and Gaming Commission of Ontario announced an end to their lottery system for cannabis retail. Beginning in April 2020, they'd roll out twenty new licences a month. The question was whether any of the original Canadian cannabis founders would still be in their jobs.

"It's about the win with me," Terry Booth says. "I want to win. When you know that, you have an advantage in your own head — I think I'm the bee's knees." This, despite the fact that his stock had suffered the same fate as Hexo's — down 18.9 percent. Meanwhile, Booth also had a ticking time bomb in his office: his company was funded largely with convertible debentures — an investment that has to be repaid at a certain date if the company's stock doesn't perform. For Booth, the date on his convertible debenture was March 2020, so he needed 2.0, something, anything — fast.

But his hands were tied. Even more than he knew. Booth tells me he wanted to fire his chief commercial officer, Darren Karasiuk, the original author of the Deloitte projections way back in 2016. He thought Aphria had a better sales force than Aurora, and Karasiuk concentrated only on San Rafael, his recreational strain of choice, his baby. Booth wanted Aurora to sell premium weed inexpensively. He'd spent billions of dollars on laboratories and production facilities and had millions of square feet to grow weed. He had scientists and experts, but the Aurora sales weren't moving fast enough. He was more than pissed. He was nuclear. Then things got weird, he says. He discovered something when he tried firing Darren: he couldn't.

"I knew my days were numbered when the board reversed my position. The CEO can't fire the chief commercial officer? I'm pounding the table. The sales force he assembled wasn't worth shit," Terry says.

He wanted Aurora to attain brand recognition with pot smokers and blamed Karasiuk for holding him back. "You can't sell my weed? Fuck you, you're fired," says Booth, who was working sixteen-hour days, seven days a week — not seeing his vision implemented. "Well, apparently not. Fun times."

October 17, 2019, the official starting line for 2.0 legalization, came and went with no legal 2.0 products on retailers' shelves. The black market, of course, had these things. At CAFE, you could get an illegal edible and consume it on the premises; the edible could have a dose as high as one thousand milligrams of THC. Since they weren't following any laws, they didn't follow the potency laws, either. The legal limit on edibles was ten milligrams, something the legal industry would buck against, saying they weren't strong enough for avid consumers, incidentally the people who most consumed these things.

Terry Booth felt like he was in a straitjacket, as if he was wearing restraints and a muzzle like Hannibal Lecter in *Silence of the Lambs*. At his local Nova Cannabis shop in Edmonton, which almost became an Aurora property until legislators nullified the deal — the same kind of vertical integration deal that was helping to enrich the American cannabis companies now listing on the Canadian Securities Exchange — there were no Aurora edibles for sale on October 17. To make matters worse, the San Raf Aurora pot they sold was derided by the industry. Meanwhile, Booth awaited the 2.0 product approval, which finally included vapes.

But the vape issue continued to cause alarm. In September 2019, one month before 2.0 legalization approval, fifteen years since Lorne Gertner wanted to come to market with this product, more than one hundred Americans got sick from illegal vapes. By January 2020, sixty deaths in the United States were linked to illegal vapes. "People are dying with vaping," Donald Trump told reporters on September 11, 2019. "A lot of people think vaping is wonderful.… It's really not wonderful."

Nobody liked to see people get sick, but it was a strong case for the legal cannabis market that the illegal market was getting folks killed. Regulators didn't think that way. The headlines forced Health Canada to paint all vapes with the same brush. And even though it was illegal vapes in the U.S. creating the crisis, in November Quebec outright banned the category. In response, Sébastien St-Louis — who had a billion-dollar contract with the SQDC, Quebec's recreational cannabis board — shut down his vape production.

St-Louis wasn't the only one needing more than marijuana to calm his nerves. "I'm psychopathic," Terry Booth says.

The official Cannabis 2.0 rollout commenced with testing by Health Canada on October 17, 2019, the anniversary of legalization, and there would be a sixty-day turnaround before approval could be granted for the products to be sold on the shelves. It was Hail Mary time for Sébastien St-Louis. He closed down the Newstrike facility in Niagara at the end of October and laid off two hundred people. He was operating lean and on his back foot, dealing with angry shareholders and a dispirited company as the stock settled below five dollars on October 25, after being over thirty dollars the previous May — back when the Raptors and the industry seemed to roll over everybody. Now, says St-Louis, those days felt long gone. But the wily founder of Hexo wasn't giving up. With his Molson Coors deal, he believed he was going to be the industry leader on cannabis drinks and, following Bruce Linton's path, he was trying to pivot his company into a global consumer packaged goods brand. He didn't want to sell flower. He wanted to stock grocery store shelves with CBD shampoo. His model was "Powered by Hexo," which positioned the company as providing cannabis for another, larger company's consumer packaged goods.

CBD, a cannabis molecule, can be infused into almost anything. Linton put CBD into Marriott soaps. And St-Louis dreamt of a joint venture with L'Oréal. He was looking at making more acquisitions; his premise was that Canadian cannabis would ultimately be run by three companies, so you eat or get eaten. He tells me the plan was to play offence. The current conditions didn't appear to put Hexo in an obvious striking position. Newstrike wasn't integrating well with head office and, despite its affiliation with the Tragically Hip, consumers hated Up, the Newstrike brand he now owned, and St-Louis had just closed their facility. These cannabis executives who'd started their companies were risk-takers and steel cage fighters, so it was within their twisted logic to expand even after the expansion they'd just completed had failed.

St-Louis even had a falling out with members of the Hip. (Jay Wilgar, the Newstrike executive who first landed the group, says this, more than anything, pains him the most when looking back on the deal, but the group's royalties led to unfavourable margins for Sébastien St-Louis.) So Sébastien was running flat out, minus his brother-in-law, and frustrated. Meanwhile, investment was moving down south into the U.S. or else around the world. Trevor Fencott and Michael Haines were pushing into Palm Springs with Fire & Flower, and Hoshi International continued building a licensed producer for all of Europe in Portugal. Michael Haines explains his decision-making like this: "Let's go somewhere and do it right. Let's not be better at something that's fucked."

Bruce Linton was helping open a group of dispensaries in Michigan. He was also investing heavily in psychedelics and distributing the cannabis brand Cookies in Canada through Gage Cannabis, which gave him a line to Berner, the American rapper who had done for weed what neither Drake nor Snoop could do: create Cookies, an actually coveted, vertically integrated, American billion-dollar weed brand.

Even without American federal cannabis legalization, the American companies had usurped Canadian cannabis brands as the powerhouses in marijuana. The brands just couldn't sustain the stream of falling dominoes in the summer of 2019. It was the Canadian cannabis executives' worst nightmare, losing their first-mover advantage. Meanwhile, Canadian companies were cash starved.

The year 2020 was grim. "We haven't raised more money and the stock started correcting," St-Louis says.

The 2.0 products didn't show up on quarterly reports until the first quarter of 2020, and though Trevor Fencott says that he wasn't surprised by the bureaucratic delay in the product launches, it forced the industry to hurry up and wait: hurry up in getting their products ready for deployment to customers, but wait for Health Canada to say they're legal to ship. And when Cannabis 2.0 was finally released to consumers, despite everything — the forecasting, concern, money spent, and joint ventures — vapes were the products that consumers most hungrily purchased. Not edibles. And definitely not drinks. Again, it was the seasoned cannabis consumer buying the lion's share of cannabis products. The soccer moms never materialized the way Deloitte and Bruce Linton predicted.

John Fowler thinks the gap between forecasts and actual sales receipts was so wide because the executives came from outside the culture. But that wouldn't be amended anytime soon. When Constellation Brands decided to replace Canopy Growth CEO Mark Zekulin with a permanent replacement, they choose David Klein — the Constellation Brands CFO, an American.

———

Terry Booth swore he'd go down swinging. He was fighting against the forces he felt were aligning against him, and it wasn't just the weed and the booze that were making him paranoid. He knew what everyone knew — the sector seemed to be outgrowing its founders — so he was spending his time calling each of his board members one by one to assess the number of days left in his corporate life. His stock was down — Aurora shares were trading at $2.50 — and the debentures were looming like a killer with a machete in the woods. Booth, who prided himself on being an operator and not a spinmeister — which is what he had Cam Battley for — was having to press the flesh, internally, just to know where he stood. He tells me that he was conducting his internal campaign with his board not to save his skin, but to save his vision: 2.0 products, European expansion, greenhouses constantly in various stages of completion. You can't just turn off the taps on expensive long-term projects.

And Terry Booth was just like Sébastien St-Louis and Bruce Linton: their projects were designed to outlast them, to be their legacies. This affected their business acumen. "Tell me what a man wants and I'll tell you who he is," goes a line in the Richard Price book *Lush Life*.

What these men wanted, desperately, was to win. It was impossible to divorce themselves from their egos, after standing for years before the firing line, and then being put up on a pedestal, made rich, made famous, proven to be brilliant. Booth believed with every fibre of his being in the bets he'd made. Why shouldn't he be confident? He'd outlasted Bruce Linton. He was the last man standing. He was the king.

Except, when his bluster faded, he realized the king wore no clothes.

The Darren Karasiuk situation left Booth exposed — he couldn't fire his CCO. And he truly couldn't stand Cam Battley, who he believed made a mistake without consulting him on Aurora's "reiterated guidance" investor call (assuring the market that Aurora would hit its $100 million in sales). That these men were still toiling beside him, having private conversations about him at his company, was disconcerting at best. Mutinous, if he allowed himself to indulge in his worst feelings, which he often did. So Booth was calling around to his board members and being reassured about the future of his tenure by each of them, one by one. He could carry on his mandate, he was told. Make cuts. Trim expenses. Slow down. The usual prescription for righting a company. Sure, Terry Booth said. Plus, we're going to kill the competition on 2.0 and our greenhouses are pumping out great margins on weed. Things were happening, and he was going to be okay. He was feeling somewhat confident — reassured — until he reached Ron Funk, who had spent time with MedReleaf.

Amid all the mergers and acquisitions in the cannabis industry, integration is always a problem. Trevor Fencott says Canopy was like a factory of broken toys. Mergers rarely work because cultures rarely blend. The MedReleaf team had a dartboard, Terry Booth tells me, and in the middle of it was a picture of Cam Battley's face. This was big money's worst fear: that these billion-dollar businesses in marijuana behaved in a juvenile fashion, and the acquisitions and mergers, bringing together bitter rivals, often created internal dilemmas. At Aurora, Booth believed that Funk carried a resentment hangover for his new corporate boss: Terry Booth, the man who enriched him, but also collapsed his big cannabis dream.

Booth understood. He says he loved buying MedReleaf and putting its loudmouthed CEO, Neil Closner, out of work. Closner, Booth says, was arrogant and short-sighted and looked down on Aurora as "an Alberta shit hill." Booth never got over their original email exchange about the illegal dispensaries, and sure, it made him happy when he bought Closner's company and cut off Neil's head. *Ah*, thought Booth, *those were the days.*

But now, there was a hangover from the MedReleaf folks on his board. Payback was a bitch. And Booth was listening to Ron Funk. "I looked around the room at the board, and not one of those individuals ever started their own business, not one — all corporate employees, four of them ex-CFOs. I hope one of them smoked a joint," Booth tells Bruce and me in Las Vegas.

He also tells me a story about Mike Singer, the former Bedrocan CFO, who told Terry that Aurora missed their reiterated guidance and who once smoked with him on Terry's private plane. "I got him a little stoned, and flying back, I couldn't get him to sit down. He runs into the bathroom and steals a bunch of shit. He's like, 'Look what I got.' He didn't realize it was my plane. I'm like, 'It's okay, man. It's my stuff.'"

Booth says of Singer, "He's a small-minded guy. He doesn't smoke weed."

Funk told Booth that he had no problem with Terry as chief executive officer. "It's not me, you understand, who wants you gone. It's Nelson Peltz," Funk said. Peltz joined the Aurora board in March 2019 to help the company enter the U.S., for which the billion-dollar activist investor was granted 19.9 million common shares at $10.34 per share over a seven-year period, vesting quarterly over four years. Booth was stunned at what Funk said, though he shouldn't have been. Booth had brought Nelson on to do the exact thing that needed to be done right now. That should have happened already. He considered Peltz a friend, even though he knew what Peltz thought of his company. He remembered that crack about MGM. Still, it was beyond his imagination to think that Peltz — though he was an "activist investor," who joined boards with the express purpose of not sitting still — would conspire against him. Why Peltz?

He just needed a little longer. *Why now?*

Nelson Peltz, however, was probably right on time. Aurora was bleeding cash, rife with conflict and backstabbing. With the ship going down, deckhands turned on each other and Booth no longer trusted his top two lieutenants: Karasiuk, who orchestrated the Nova deal (and now sat on Alcanna's board, Nova's parent company) and Cam Battley, the politician, who, after Bruce Linton, had become the face of the industry. It sickened Terry that neither man smoked weed. It sickened Darren and Cam that Terry did.

Booth got Peltz on the phone. "When the stock is tanking, you get rid of the CEO," Peltz told him, and reassured him that he wasn't just paranoid from the mushrooms and blow — insiders were talking about him. Peltz orchestrated Terry Booth's demise. "The best way to get rid of a CEO," Peltz told Terry, "is to mount a whisper campaign."

When the axe finally dropped on Terry Booth, it was February 2020. Aurora fired five hundred people. They wrote down $1 billion in assets. Singer — who stole Terry's soap! — was named interim CEO.

Terry told the press, "I'm the latest carnage." And into that carnage came Covid-19.

CHAPTER COVID-19

"The future of cannabis retail looks less like an Apple store and more like a Domino's Pizza."

Trevor Fencott

The pandemic made pot legal and haircuts against the law. In the spring of 2020, it was easier to score legal marijuana in Canada than it was to find a vaccine. Covid-19 was making hundreds of thousands of people sick, killing thousands. On March 14, 2020, Ontario schools were closed down, and on March 23, cannabis was declared an essential service. All businesses deemed non-essential were shuttered, and pot, seventeen months legal, had gone from contraband to essential. But the launch of 2.0 products arrived at a time when in-person shopping at stores was prohibited and curb-side pickup and delivery became essential, like oxygen.

"It's a mad scramble," says Trevor Fencott, trying to pivot his eighty Fire & Flower locations into delivery hubs and assuring his staff that their workplace was safe. Fencott had two children and five hundred employees and was, like everyone, making sense of the scene as it unfolded across the country and around the world. The first thing he did was suspend management's pay.

"Retail is a [cash flow] pyramid and we did the math — if you can't open a store, it feels like there's only a month or two of life left," Fencott says. Cannabis isn't like booze or toilet paper, other items that people hoarded at the outset of Covid-19; cannabis has a shelf life. The cannabis executives wanted their product to be a consumer packaged good, but it wasn't, not yet. The product weed customers bought the most of was good old-fashioned weed — grams (and sometimes ounces), not milligrams. This, however, remained a problem: If stores were closed or the supply chain was broken, the product would go bad. "It has to work. We have to deliver, and we move real quickly using the Circle K warehouse to divide up our radius [territories for drivers] and get cars on delivery in the streets," Fencott says. For him, the pandemic was an existential fight to keep consumers from returning to the black market. If the legal industry was going to keep its new clients, and their desperately needed dollars, then the government was going to have to lend them support.

On April 7, 2020, the government of Ontario once again declared cannabis sales an essential service and allowed the shops to stay open. The Fire & Flower chain continued to work. Sales shot up and people bought edibles, drinks, and vapes with their pre-rolls and grams. The pandemic was a good thing for weed. Fencott says, "In times of crisis, cannabis is better than a fifth of Scotch. It's better to have some gummies and go to sleep than drinking, arguing with your spouse, and kicking your dog."

In the first scary, claustrophobic year of the pandemic, cannabis sales increased countrywide. With no Bruce Linton, no Terry Booth, and no CannTrust, weed sales rose 25 percent. As new shops kept opening in Toronto through the summer, the number of available products increased in kind. Up against Covid, in that work-from-home, home-schooled springtime of our discontent, Canadian licensed producers made bank.

"My own cannabis consumption is way up," continues Fencott. "The pandemic is going to last a long time and I have to remain functional. I have cannabis after the kids go to bed and can sleep."

Epidemiologists aside, no one could have predicted Covid-19. But the Canadian cannabis executives found focus. Sébastien St-Louis says his supply chain wasn't the issue. He cut his distribution cycle — the time it took to go from cured and packaged in his factories to shelves across the country — down to thirty days. That August, he finally launched Truss, his joint venture with Molson Coors, and introduced six new drinks to the market. St-Louis was increasing his market share and liked his position against the raft of CFOs replacing Canadian weed founders; his new peers, he believed, lacked creativity. Of the new Canopy CEO, he says, "I know what Canopy is going to do under David Klein. It's predictable, which makes it easy for me to prepare."

What caused sleepless pandemic nights for St-Louis was the markets, which, he says, have always been short-sighted and easily spooked. If the markets crash, you can't raise money and it becomes a vicious cycle; your stock gets crushed. In the spring of 2020, pot sales subverted the pandemic economic crisis. Sales receipts at weed stores were countercyclical: with travel and restaurants closed, movies and schools shuttered — nowhere to go and nothing to do — taking an edible became its own vacation. The weed brands did very well for themselves.

Starting that spring, legal cannabis retailers offered 2.5-milligram, 5-milligram, and 10-milligram gummies, and chocolates and beverages from companies like Canopy and Truss. Heavy users complained that the doses were small, but the sales of these products matched, almost, the sales in Colorado and California. Except in those states, consumers could get edibles dosed with 100 milligrams of THC; in Canada, 10 milligrams was the maximum total dosage per package, which meant heavy users had to buy multiple packets, which was expensive and, with all that packaging, bad for the environment. But the products, like the vapes, were odourless and discreet. John Aird, who finally got Olli onto shelves in 2020 — two years after starting his company — says the 2.0 category came at just the right time.

"Would we have liked to advertise and make a splash and not have them come out during the plague? Absolutely, but we're still glad to get something of quality in a new category to market," says Aird, who had simultaneously been working with Fencott and Michael Haines to develop Hoshi, which would service the European medical cannabis market. With a manufacturing hub operating in Portugal, and Germany seeming to make monthly strides on their path toward medical legalization, momentum, amid the carnage of the Canadian industry, was starting to build again and the international adult-use recreational program was beginning to seem real.

Trevor Fencott says that Covid-19 helped open his marijuana eyes when pot was deemed an "essential service."

The miseducation of Trevor Fencott in cannabis had begun with pot as a product, and he'd never really considered it before as a social issue. He wasn't afraid of weed and didn't mind facing down the stigma, but he didn't care about it in any particular way. He had stood in a hockey rink in small-town Ontario and bathed in the locals' abuse, but he did that because he believed it was good for business.

But at that point, he'd really had no relationship with the flower; he was an entrepreneur discovering a niche. At Mettrum, over time, he began to form a cannabis relationship. It was medicine, he saw, and it worked. He was proud of what he did and of his business. Then, after Mettrum was sold to Canopy and Bruce Linton, the product became recreational in his eyes — like wine — as he opened locations of Fire & Flower and began using data from his Hyfire analytics to understand consumer tastes. Consumers had buying patterns. If they bought edible X, they might also buy a drink. He knew that vape users were interested in premium cannabis oils and that a certain kind of flower consumer only cared about the upper reaches of a strain's level of THC. Fencott became a data scientist, and his chain of retail stores harnessed information that the Canadian licensed producers could use. He knew how to stock his shelves. And he maximized turnaround time and shelf space, the same way Couche-Tard sold Snickers bars and gasoline.

However, with Covid, Fencott had his second marijuana aha moment. The first one had been when he realized the information his child was receiving was bad and it pissed him off. The second revelation centred around the actual product: pot could be used for medicine or recreation, but most consumers — especially during a global pandemic — probably used it as he did, as some delicate mix of the two.

The pandemic was stressful. His staff was scared. His children were home. His industry was laying off employees and closing facilities. His own government, via the Ontario Cannabis Store, was his competition. And Trevor liked booze. But like Sébastien at Hexo, he cut down on alcohol while increasing his usage of marijuana. For Fencott, and Fire & Flower, the pandemic brought an increase in sales, but it also brought about a change in the way he could do business. Before Covid-19, only the OCS was allowed to do delivery. When the pandemic started, cannabis retailers were granted permission to deliver marijuana themselves. During a pandemic, who wanted to wait in line with strangers in a crowded place to pick up their pot? But also, who wanted to get weed from an unknown source? Could black market dealers be trusted to get vaccinated and wash their hands?

Fire & Flower, with assistance from warehouse specialist Couche-Tard, created distribution centres and same-day delivery supply chains. This was a game changer because, before the pandemic, the OCS had been adamantly against weed shops being granted the Uber delivery model. The OCS was the traditional drug dealer, except instead of meeting your guy in the park, the government showed up at your door. With the pandemic, legal players could sell pot the same way: direct to consumer in sixty minutes or less.

"The future of cannabis retail," says Fencott, "looks less like an Apple store and more like a Domino's Pizza."

———

Arriving in time for the pandemic were kilos of legal Canadian weed. When all of the cannabis companies began to build scale, it took the better part of a year after legalization to optimize production. Following Cole Cacciavillani's Blessed 13 inexpensive Aphria model, using mostly greenhouse and outdoor grows, Sébastien St-Louis says it cost him on average forty cents to produce a cannabis gram. The licensed producers were finding efficiencies in their cannabis assembly lines (after doing this for many years, they were getting better at their job). There was plenty of pot — too much pot —in the legal market during Covid-19, which was good because it matched the uptick in consumer demand. Plus, the licensed producers were not only making more of it, by and large, but even Alan Young would now admit that the legal weed for sale was good. It was undoubtedly cheap. And there was variety. That was good because the black market, while still taking almost 50 percent of the cannabis market share in the spring of 2020, was receding — so an objective of the Cannabis Act was being achieved.

None of these improvements were quick enough for John Fowler, who started Blaise Ventures in January 2020 to invest in small-scale Canadian craft weed brands. Legalization wasn't perfect. But it's also important to remember how great it was, says John. In reference to the stimulus cheques received by many licensed retailers and licensed producers, Fowler wants us to imagine a drug dealer getting a check from the government to keep getting their pot in stores.

Legalization remained a Canadian success story, at least in terms of public health fallout. At retailers in Alberta or Vancouver, it wasn't hard to find a 50-percent-off sale. Imagine a drug dealer hosting Black Friday discounts. Pot had not become a societal problem. And during the pandemic, it became clear that the Le Dain Commission and Shafer were right.

Shopping for weed like shampoo became a perfectly normal thing to do and there was a party at Fire & Flower I remember loving. The people were caring and the food tasted great and the store looked amazing and then I remembered: everyone here is stoned.

In the U.S., however, the party could end much differently, especially if the attendees were Black. On the last Monday in May 2020, George Floyd was killed by police in Minneapolis for passing a counterfeit twenty-dollar bill. This murder of a Black man at the knee of a white police officer, recorded on cellphone and widely shared, would trigger the burning of Donald Trump's America during Black Lives Matter protests in Los Angeles, New York, and, especially, Minneapolis's city streets.

The repercussions travelled up north and Canada's marijuana industry was once again re-examined through the vantage of race. "I live in Canada for a reason," says Akwasi Owusu-Bempah of Cannabis Amnesty, which became a central point of attention in Canada as the world, and cannabis companies, responded to the George Floyd murder. "It's a good place to live, and we can take some comfort that our current and historical experiences are different from the United States. But we are not that different as we'd like to believe when it comes to the way in which we treat racialized populations." Owusu-Bempah, like Alan Young, holds his greatest level of contempt for the police officials running licensed cannabis companies while the very people they once targeted were left out of the industry. The hypocrisy reeks, Owusu-Bempah tells me, and exposes systemic abuse.

"You can't talk about cannabis without talking about injustice," he says, adding that the George Floyd murder also put the Canadian legal cannabis industry on blast. Where he felt strongest was in the failure of Bill C-93, which provided no-cost, expedited pardons for Canadians with simple cannabis possession offences. More often than not, these records for a product that was once illegal but was now an engine of big business — a product consumed by white and Black people at the same rates but that was six times more likely to result in the arrest of a Black or Indigenous person — had already wreaked havoc on the lives of the young people arrested. However, with cannabis legalization, Owusu-Bempah says, it's not too late for reparation. Weed is a billion-dollar industry, but while 10,000 to 250,000 people are eligible to have their records expunged, by the summer of 2024, only 845 people had actually been granted "pot pardons" (455 applications had been returned because they were "ineligible or incomplete"). To this day there's a system in place for reparation, but the system is broken, and that, beyond the moral implications, also leads to economic factors for the cannabis companies. "Canada had a great head start in legalized cannabis, but it's infuriating that people convicted for crimes that are no longer illegal have not all had their records uniformly expunged," says Owusu-Bempah.

Owusu-Bempah introduced me to a young Black man arrested for cannabis possession, and his thoughts mirrored that of many Black and Indigenous people toward the legal-pot world. "Why am I buying weed from you guys?" asked this man. "You've done very little to help the people in impoverished communities who have been jailed the most and now you want to play reggae at your store? You were arresting Black people for dimes."

The George Floyd murder reignited the race conversation in Canadian cannabis. The cannabis companies had no choice but to listen. Sébastien made a donation to Cannabis Amnesty and Aurora did the same. Fire & Flower put up a black box on their social media channels to show solidarity to the Black Lives Matter movement, and Hilary Black, still at Canopy Growth, intended to mobilize the company, even as it was now led by David Klein, Constellation Brands' long-time CFO.

"We're trying to create a meaningful, authentic plan for corporate social responsibility (CSR) and David [Klein], to his credit, has made this a priority — when our chips are down, we don't bail out on our commitments to the community," said Black, who had seen Canopy facilities close in cities like Edmonton and Bowmanville, and round after round of layoffs affect more than one thousand Canopy employees. As Sébastien St-Louis had predicted, the new boss at Canopy wanted to trim costs and edge toward profitability, so he closed much of what Bruce Linton built. Billions in acquisitions became empty warehouses on the side of the road.

The entire industry faced layoffs and closures, and the same thing happened at the second largest cannabis company, Aurora. Everything that was once deemed instant value became a liability. Funded capacity was now being shed with the urgency with which it had once been pursued. At Canopy, however, Hilary Black says the new guard from Constellation Brands didn't diminish her role and her CSR budget increased after Bruce Linton, which bucked against the "close everything" trend.

"It was slash, slash, slash — I get it. But David defended patient advocacy and sustainability and reiterated Canopy's commitment to reparation, and reconciliation," says Black. "Not just as a response to George Floyd, but because it's the right thing to do. David knew this: to run a successful company, you need a CSR team, just like a finance department."

———

By the summer of 2020, Sébastien St-Louis, a father of two, was going into work every day. He had played nose tackle in high school — the centre of the team's defence — and blunt French Canadian toughness is the attribute he believes wills him to win. During the pandemic, he made it a point of pride that his company didn't take any government stimulus checks. And also during the pandemic, St-Louis ascended up the hierarchy.

In March 2020, 48North announced the sudden departure of Alison Gordon from the company she had started. Like John Fowler, Gordon generated considerable press. She, too, was pictured (in a story by me) smoking a joint in the *Globe and Mail*, and while the details of what happened at 48North are locked in confidentiality agreements, she says she believes her time had come. "I think the role of the CEO of a licensed producer had changed considerably over the course of the seven years I was in weed," she says. "At this point, it's not a cannabis person who should be running these companies, but someone who's an expert in CPG [consumer packaged goods]."

With Gordon out, now joining Linton, Booth, Fowler, and Neufeld in the Marijuana Founders Unforced Retirement Club, Sébastien now saw himself — at thirty-six years old — as an elder statesman of weed. "I'm the longest running legal cannabis CEO in the whole world," he told me during the pandemic. "Eight years doing this — it says more about the industry than it does about me."

He made no bones about wanting Hexo to be the largest cannabis company in the world. Hexo, like every other cannabis company, saw sales increase during Covid-19 as a result of both weed hoarding and stores popping up around Ontario like teenage acne. Thanks to the beverage line Truss, he had robust Cannabis 2.0 offerings. He also launched Original Stash, a discount line to compete with the black market, on October 16, the day before legal weed's first birthday.

He was selling ounces for $125 — less than five bucks a gram.

"I know a lot of people in a lot of bad places, and Original Stash was the first time I heard from the black market, 'You're hurting us,'" Sébastien says with a grin. That's how, he says, you run a cannabis company — not by taking millions of dollars in pandemic subsidies.

Between bites of a hamburger in Ottawa in the spring of 2021, St-Louis was thumping his chest. "We're gaining market share and making money during this thing, and while our competitors are getting government handouts, we don't," he says. "It's ridiculous, companies with hundreds of millions on their balance sheets getting handouts. We play to a higher ethical standard." St-Louis still believes that the market in Canada will be led by three major companies, with everyone else falling off.

Like pot smoke, mergers, and acquisition, gossip was in the air. Since Hexo had the largest market share, always an expensive proposition — losing $12.8 million in the first quarter of 2019 and $62.4 million in the first quarter of fiscal 2020 —Sébastien was hell-bent, like Bruce and Terry before him, on spending his way to market penetration. He wasn't backing down and, channelling the memory of his father, felt like he was fighting for his beliefs — an almost supernatural belief in himself. "Had I started with the money that other cannabis companies started out with, we wouldn't even be talking about other cannabis companies right now," he tells me, and though he'd steered $2 billion of investor money into his company, he still felt outgunned when the pandemic began and his stock wouldn't stop sinking. He said that every institution that ever put money into Hexo had made money.

"That's how I keep power," he says. "Making people money."

While he traded at $31 a share in April 2019, he was now at $1.89, and that's how your power becomes tricky to hold. During the pandemic, amid layoffs and sinking shares, he was trying to keep his staff motivated. He had personally lost more than $80 million from Hexo's stock drop, but he kept his personal wealth at arm's length and says he kept his emotions untethered from the market.

Seven times, he says, his company — a company he started with his brother-in-law with a $35,000 line of credit and investment from family and friends — had brushed up against bankruptcy. He says he didn't falter then and he wouldn't falter now. St-Louis reconfigured the Hexo assembly lines at the grow ops to promote physical distancing and, since there were already cameras everywhere at a licensed facility, contact tracing was easy to establish.

In cannabis, the factory workers already wear personal protective equipment, so production went on full steam ahead during Covid-19. Hexo was trying to grab investor attention and St-Louis had survived this long by making big bets. When the Quebec government gave Hexo a billion-dollar contract to produce its cannabis in 2017, Sébastien signed on. He just had to build a million-square-foot facility to grow it all first. The job was supposed to take eighteen months, but Quebec needed weed; Hexo got it onto shelves in eight months. That's his legacy, says Sébastien St-Louis. That's the moxie he was relying on now. But everyone knows you can be fast, cheap, or thorough, but not all three, not at the same time. So the facility builds were expensive and Hexo was diluting its stock for capital to keep growing. He had to grow, Sébastien tells me. Doubt or fear are emotions he can't afford.

"If you go into the cage match thinking anyone other than you is going to win," he says, "you're dead already."

At Hexo, Sébastien believed the way to win was building technology to create new products. His pitch now was an extraction machine that would cut costs. He had invested more than $35 million on this gamble. Investing $35 million on a future product while your stock tanks is risky. But Sébastien wasn't thinking about the short term. He says there was a 20 percent chance his new $35 million technology investment wouldn't work. But he was betting his life on the 80 percent chance that it would.

He says, "If a man is convinced he's going to die, tomorrow he'll find a way to make it come true."

———●

The problem — well, one problem — was that at this point Covid-19 hadn't yet killed the illegal market. In August 2020, the OPP conducted Project Woolwich and raided an illegal grow in the Niagara region, not far from where the licensed producer Redecan ran its privately held, industry-leading company, famous for its pre-roll joints.

The Canadian police have obviously always had a strange relationship with marijuana. First, they were adamantly against pot, with former OPP commissioner Julian Fantino decrying legalizing pot as akin to legalizing murder. Most officers didn't feel quite as strongly — and most didn't go on to open $100 million licensed producers — but there has been confusion among members of the police force. That was why Linton's plane was stopped in Kelowna and why the RCMP had to call Health Canada when they busted Mat Beren's grow.

This was all before legalization, of course; the laws change fast and cops are human. Since the Cannabis Act was passed, the police have been trying to mature in their arresting. In January 2018, two officers in Toronto busted an illegal dispensary and, after making their arrests, sampled the products. One officer, feeling the effects of an illegal edible, ended up climbing a tree and getting stuck up there. He had to call in for backup. Stories like these created an almost farcical environment for launching an industry.

But during the pandemic, illegal large-scale indoor and outdoor grows were still a real concern for organized crime bureaus across the country. In Barrie, Ontario, an entire Molson production facility was turned into a large-scale, organized illegal grow op, with police insinuating there was no way the property managers couldn't have known about the true work being done in their shuttered facility.

To hear the police describe the illicit market in our first Covid summer, these weren't hippies making edibles for their family and friends. "These were criminal organizations looking to help fund their entire illegal operation based, in part, on illegal weed," a deputy with Ontario's Organized Crime Enforcement Bureau told me, adding that the majority of his officers believed the legalization experiment was successful — kids weren't being rushed to the ER and the reefer madness epidemic never occurred. Wide swaths of kids weren't suddenly dropping out of school and turning to crime; the legal pot shops hadn't created red-light districts in the neighbourhoods where they operated. In fact, with restaurants and bars closing during the summer of 2020, pot shops became some of the only commercial real estate worth investing in.

Criminals, however, remain in crime, and crime is dangerous, even in marijuana, even during the pandemic. The group busted in Project Woolwich had cocaine and rocket launchers and $2.5 million in cash. One constable told me that thousands of pounds of illegal pot were being funnelled from Ontario into the United States at the Buffalo border. That pot, the constable said, returns washed into Canada in the form of fentanyl and guns. At the Woolwich bust, illegal producers revealed designated growers' licences, easily bought online by "patients" receiving licences from unscrupulous "doctors" writing scripts for both consumers and producers, which provide a cloak of respectability to an illegal business. Since day one, this designated grower system has been abused. Removing this was the idea behind legalization, yet it's nearly impossible to stamp out. Consulting companies help illegal operators get an address, buy a farm, push out the farmers, and grow — in the case of the Project Woolwich bust — more than $40 million worth of illegal weed. "Medical-designated grow areas are out of control and seizures of illegal pot in the U.S. have gone up one thousand percent since 2019," said the detective, the nightmare scenario that doomsday analysts in the U.S. predicted would happen.

———•

Trevor Fencott worried about the mom-and-pop retailers opening up during the pandemic without corporate financing. They had a difficult path before them in legal marijuana. Sure, they were his competition, but he says that when these new store owners first submitted their licence applications, competition was scarce and the shops were cash cows: Hunny Pot sold $1 million per week of legal marijuana, and the problem it faced was keeping its shelves stocked. But as the pandemic raged, waves of stores in Ontario opened, twenty at a time in some months, and directly beside one another. Since they sold the same thing, and had, by law, blacked-out front windows, there was almost no way for a store to differentiate. As the price of legal pot dropped, the margins kept getting worse. The discount brand Original Stash by Hexo helped usher in a trend: the price of pot kept dropping alongside the wave of new stores. Bruce Linton was going to napalm the industry by selling cheap bud, but the bud got cheap anyway, making it even harder for any facet of the industry to turn a profit.

The new shop owners, meanwhile, who had received their licences, secured their spaces, and celebrated their grand openings, still couldn't have customers enter their stores. Click-and-collect cannabis pickup would last months. Plus, as Fencott always points out, they were competing not only with one another, but also with the Ontario Cannabis Store, which offered delivery at a discounted rate on the exact same products that the new legal weed stores were trying to sell. The OCS would be the most profitable cannabis company in the country by spring 2022.

"The system can't work!" Fencott says. "All the way up to Doug Ford, cannabis distribution in Ontario is based on cronyism, not good business, and private enterprise can't thrive when there's government monopoly."

Meanwhile, one in two pot smokers say their cannabis usage went up during the pandemic.

In May, for US$40 million, Aurora acquired Reliva, an American CBD company led by CEO Miguel Martin, a former Altria executive. It says everything about the Canadian market that a month after buying Reliva for U.S. distribution, Aurora fired seven hundred people in Canada and shut down Terry Booth's production facilities in Ontario, Saskatchewan, Alberta, and Quebec.

I checked in with Booth, who says he was riding out the pandemic with his wife and small kids in Edmonton. "I got up to two-twenty during Covid. The fattest I've ever been in my life," Terry says. "I'm not moving off the couch. Honey, pass me my phone — can you grab me a beer?"

On September 8, 2020, Aurora named Miguel Martin as its new CEO. Martin lived in Virginia, so now Aurora and Canopy both had American CEOs. Tilray's CEO lived in Seattle. Aphria's CEO lived in New York. At Aurora, they never arranged a conversation between Booth and Miguel Martin, who began his job by firing almost one thousand Canadians.

CHAPTER 20

Merge or Die

"Get rid of your fucking potheads!"

Cole Cacciavillani

Tilray was American Brendan Kennedy's Canadian juggernaut from the medical marijuana days. After its IPO in September 2018, it spent a few crazy hours trading at $300 per share. In a world of crazy drug money stories, Tilray's stock price is the craziest, the apex of a market out of control. Largely fuelled by retail investors, Tilray would cost short sellers roughly $600 million on a single day, September 19, 2018, Kennedy told CNBC, when retail investors rallied behind his shares on Robinhood — as they would later do for GameStop and Aurora. Cannabis stocks were considered "meme stocks" (youth-led block investments that could move the markets without traditional, institutional alignment) before GameStop went viral. This notion of the stoned nerd army taking on the hedge funds was manifest in Tilray: retail investors got high and bought marijuana and stock in companies that sold weed.

Kennedy, a Seattle-based venture capitalist, was ready, initially, for the ride. A Blessed 13 company, Tilray listed on the Toronto Stock Exchange and was worth, in 2018, more than $26 billion (a comical valuation that could never last). By offering limited numbers of shares and by graduating from the TSX to become the first weed brand listed on the Nasdaq, Tilray was an outlier, which had nothing to do with the quality or quantity of its cannabis. In a world of contradictions, Tilray, the juggernaut, wholesaled most of the cannabis it sold. Their biggest supplier? Aphria. Cole Cacciavillani says Tilray's engineers inspected his grows from the earliest days of both companies' being among the Blessed 13.

"I told those guys, 'Get rid of your fucking potheads!' They can grow good weed, but you need sustainable production, and you get that through science, through calcium levels and nitrogen, not pink shirts and fucking reggae music," says Cacciavillani, who nonetheless enjoyed the early close relationship between the two companies. He says back in the day, the early companies had no problem sharing information. Especially when other farmers marvelled at what Cacciavillani had built. "Tilray never could believe me because while they were growing grams with costs as high as four dollars per gram, I could do it at fifty cents, even as low as twenty cents per gram. Of course Brendan and his boys always saw the value there."

Unlike most licensed producers, Tilray had no identity. The company was an empty vessel that could be moulded into anything. And so, after locking up a joint venture worth $100 million with Anheuser-Busch, the company and Kennedy became industry outliers in a frenzied field, steady operators with a venture capital background in a world of promotion and hype. By wearing a suit, not erecting fake walls to hide plants, or acquiring untested properties overseas, Tilray's prominence, among investors, grew.

However, after legalization, and by Christmas 2020, Tilray, like everyone else, had sunk like a stone. Trading around seven dollars, it had been stripped of its halo and seen its stock carry that foul cannabis stink.

Tilray lost 96.4 percent of its value. Still, the company had assets, including a Canadian medical marijuana business and a production facility in Portugal. It also owned a CBD business called Manitoba Harvest that operated in the U.S. After seven long years in the business — especially the last two — Tilray's operators were rumoured to want out. The Aphria leadership, now led by sharp-tongued Irwin Simon, wanted out, too. Simon is a Glace

Bay, Nova Scotia, son of a grocery man who cut his teeth on organic foods at Hain Celestial, which he ran for twenty-seven years. At Hain, Simon saw sales peak at $2.89 billion in 2016, selling consumer packaged goods and partnering with Heinz. In 2018, Simon left Hain under a cloud of a Security and Exchange Commission investigation and was semi-retired — like Vic before him — when the Aphria board gave him a call.

Taking the helm in January 2019, Simon unwound the Neufeld deals in South America and the Caribbean and increased Aphria's Canadian market share while continuing to advance its low-cost indoor grow. Aphria had a market cap of $2.8 billion in December 2020. Tilray had a $2 billion market cap. In the merger that would fulfill Sébastien St-Louis's prophecy and turn the weed world upside down, Kennedy exited and Simon became CEO of the new company. Now, with a combined market cap of close to $5 billion, Canadian brands in recreational and medical, operations in Europe and headquarters in New York, the new company, which would be called Tilray (shedding Aphria's sketchy skin), would leap-frog Canopy. There was a new largest cannabis company in the country.

Sébastien St-Louis says he was ready for war.

Always haughty, he levelled up during Covid-19 and leaned on his dad; while Sébastien fought the competition, his father battled cancer. Jean St-Louis, Sébastien's father, who he describes as a "warrior poet," had been in the fight of his life against his failing health since 2017, but had broadened his worldview in the process. At first, Jean had no taste for his son's line of work. Jean St-Louis had crusaded for French language schools in Sturgeon Falls, in northern Ontario, at seventeen years old taking his fight all the way to Pierre Trudeau. His dad, Sébastien told me, was stubborn and hard, but also composed music and wrote poetry. He was the ideal man in his young son's eyes. At first, his father had negative opinions about marijuana, even though Sébastien didn't touch the stuff until he was twenty-four. Sébastien says pot was everywhere when he was growing up, and he even considered selling it when he dropped out of high school at sixteen. That would have been 1999, two years before the MMAR laws were passed by Prime Minister Jean Chrétien. "I knew there was demand and talk of it going legal but, ultimately, I was late to the party," he says.

Sébastien St-Louis wouldn't begin to meet that demand until 2013, with his licensed medical producer Hydropothecary, which he later called Hexo. If Jean didn't quite get what Sébastien was attempting at the beginning, eventually he began to grasp the scope of his son's vision and came to admire the extent of his business dream. Once enthralled, he followed Sébastien's company as one would follow a hockey team.

"With my father, I didn't leave anything on the table," St-Louis tells me, adding that it was cold comfort that they managed to spend emotional, vulnerable time together during the pandemic, breaking Covid protocol. In May 2020, while he was running the company without his brother-in-law Adam, laying off staff, closing facilities, and seeing his stock fall, Sébastien, alongside his mother, began to feel himself recharging. In his book, *Billion Dollar Start-Up*, authored with his brother-in-law and dedicated, in part, to his dad, Sébastien wrote, "He never did anything he did not want to do." In the obituary later published in the *Globe and Mail*, Sébastien, interviewed by his uncle, says Jean taught him "to think, lead and, when necessary, fight."

The fighting spirit, now aimed at Tilray, would infuse Sébastien's new year.

———•———

At the end of 2020, the capacity of Aurora Sky, Terry Booth's eight-hundred-thousand-square-foot greenhouse monstrosity at the Edmonton Airport, had been reduced by 70 percent, and nearly ten cannabis companies faced bankruptcy. St-Louis saw opportunity. Companies he couldn't have touched in 2015 or 2019, he could now own. Looking across the country at his competitors reeling in a buyer's market, he assumed any property could be his — "Everyone knows Hexo is the best operator," he tells me. He turned down acquisition inquiries for his company as he began to feel more powerful in his leadership role. Sébastien never held the microphone in Canadian weed. There were no profiles on him in *Report on Business*. His brother-in-law had the better personal story to share on BNN. Sébastien St-Louis was a French-speaking high-school-dropout outsider who now could add survivor to the attributes that would prepare him for war. "The recognition was never there and still isn't," St-Louis tells me. "Bruce had the rock star thing going on, and I was never the most fun, but I'm not afraid of the spotlight, the big moment. It might be time for me."

In January 2021, St-Louis received a call from bankers representing the Supreme Cannabis Company, now on its third CEO since they axed John Fowler in 2019. There was talk of the company being in play for $260 million, and St-Louis declined. Six months later, Canopy Growth picked up the property — for $435 million. St-Louis couldn't reconcile the price tag on the acquisition. But he came to understand how Canopy borrowed $750 million of private equity to go shopping. Canopy was declaring that, even without Bruce Linton, they were still fighting to be the biggest bully on the block and would take on Tilray. Sébastien, who prides himself on being a quick learner, was taking notes. How would he respond? Canopy got a stock bump from their acquisition. Irwin Simon — now running the beefed-up Tilray — stepped into Bruce Linton's shoes as a quote machine. St-Louis was going to be aggressive. "If you make no decisions," he tells me, "you're dead."

"Would you take on nearly a billion dollars of private equity debt to make your own purchase?" I ask him. "We never had institutions behind us," he answers, "but if you take five billion and blow through three billion [an allusion to Canopy], you have trouble." But was the trouble worth it?

Didn't Hexo have to grow? "I'm not afraid to be defiant," he says. "Maybe it's the French revolutionary in my genes."

Sébastien St-Louis plotted to put Hexo in Tilray's shoes. He was negotiating with Zenabis Global, a company in British Columbia founded by Monty Sikka that, when it listed on the TSX in January 2019, had a market cap close to $1 billion. Zenabis, like Tilray, was representative of the industry. It had lost nearly 70 percent of its value by the time Hexo began kicking its tires for a deal. Sikka invested more than $400 million into the Zenabis indoor grow in Delta, BC — and was floundering. St-Louis, thinking of his hub-and-spoke model, and perhaps of what Canopy got from Supreme, saw Zenabis as ripe for the picking. Since Canadian companies were moving into the States and Europe, the Zenabis education centre in England and production facility in Malta were valuable. Plus, their BC greenhouse could still pump out premium weed. This was what Canopy got from Supreme: a fancy cannabis product that connoisseurs would consume. The goal at Zenabis was to make a premium strain of pot above 30 percent THC. And so Zenabis could help with Canadian market share while also adding flavour to St-Louis's international pitch for more money on Bay Street. While Hexo increased product categories and sales in Canada, it needed capital infusions to continue to grow. Hexo, led by Jean St-Louis's boy, wasn't backing down from Canopy or Tilray. Sébastien was still hungry for his recognition and success.

———————

During a lull between Covid's third and fourth waves, in the fall of 2021, St-Louis tells me all of these things, taking his time over a plate of french fries. He says that earlier that year when Sundial came after Zenabis in a hostile takeover, he played white knight and swooped in for the largest acquisition in his company's history — paying $235 million for a funded capacity of 110,000 kilograms of marijuana, with facilities in New Brunswick and Nova Scotia, in addition to their flagship greenhouse in BC. St-Louis was feeling talkative and proud; he showed up for lunch alone, with no media attendant or assistant, as if wondering why more people hadn't been beating down his door. He tells me that Zenabis added market share and revenue to Hexo's bottom line and his stock jumped 20 percent after the deal, but quickly levelled off, peaking around nine dollars per share. The pandemic, along with quitting drinking, seeing original founders get axed, and saying goodbye to his father, had St-Louis emboldened, taking chances. Chief executive officers were exiting marijuana. Covid-19 reinforced his mantra: no fear.

"I told my people, 'If you get Covid, I'll get Covid right next to you.' Leadership isn't sitting in an office in an ivory tower." St-Louis was still young in 2021 — thirty-eight years old — and he had grown up in his office. He tells me that he was able to fix Zenabis and bridge the culture gap between C-suite and grower at the company because, he believes, his

French Canadian background helped him live in two worlds. As the child of teachers, he held resentment for the stuffed shirts and Deloitte, and he says he never was condescending to the farmers; he wore a chip on his shoulder under the black Under Armour T-shirts he wore when he sized up financiers. He didn't flinch, he says, back when the value proposition for a medical marijuana company grew to $100 million from $10 million back in 2013. St-Louis was outside Bay Street when he started and stayed there, preferring rural Quebec to Toronto. If he had started out with the connections of Irwin Simon, Brendan Kennedy, or Bruce Linton, "nobody would have heard of any of them," he says.

As CEO, St-Louis spent time in the greenhouse, worked in defoliation, got his hands dirty, and kept his common touch. It differentiated him. "Management you can't see on a spreadsheet," he says. "If you're a CEO on Bay Street all friggin' day, you have no clue how your business runs."

There's a graveyard filled with executives who couldn't see how their businesses ran. Cannabis was no exception. For Terry Booth, too large a gap formed between him and his investor relations team. He had also invited Nelson Peltz into his home. Bruce Linton was a celebrity. He ceded control for money, and his ego made him not meet the Constellation bosses on their terms. Linton spent too much too quickly, so it was no surprise he found himself beaten up by Constellation's board, which he himself had brought into his mix. If you buy companies and don't know how anything works, St-Louis says, you'll be caught flat-footed when costs soar and integration becomes four people for each job, with the C-suite taking bonuses and everyone else getting canned and Canadian properties being foreclosed. It had been that way since Brent Zettl opened a greenhouse beneath a lake. Aurora wanted Zettl's company. Booth spent $1 billion, and his hostile takeover cost Jay Wilgar his deal. But what did CanniMed do for Aurora and the people who worked there? Layoffs, closures, and bad weed thrown in the trash.

St-Louis wanted to learn from what came before him. There had to be a reason that he was the only Canadian founder left. Every cannabis executive wanted to be Elon or Bezos. Hexo, says St-Louis in 2021, is Amazon.

Walk down Queen Street West in Toronto or West Fourth in Vancouver today and there are more pot shops than convenience stores or craft breweries. It's gotten to the point where a plant store on Queen Street West in Toronto — a store that sells flowers, not actual weed — has a sign out front saying "I can't believe it's not a weed store!" There are seven pot shops on the north side of Queen between Ossington Avenue and Gladstone. All of the stores are clean. All of the budtenders are friendly. Lorne Gertner's dream of cannabis retail has happened. But due to terrible margins, the existence of too many shops, and the still-mighty presence of black market weed, many of the retailers — except chains like Gertner's old Tokyo Smoke, retailers with deep pockets — will be closed unless something changes soon.

Darren Karasiuk, the original numbers man from Deloitte, again capitalized first. In August 2020, six months after Terry Booth's ouster at Aurora, Karasiuk also left the company. He had an idea both to deal with the pot surplus and to combat the deluge of stores. In May 2019, he had joined the board of Alcanna and steered Aurora to purchase 20 percent of the company. Terry Booth hated the deal, but Darren didn't care and Terry, his capital diminished, couldn't fire him. Two years later, Darren was the CEO of Alcanna's cannabis division. It was Karasiuk who found the solution to glutted retail. He pivoted the Alcanna cannabis division into a novel concept: Value Buds. Darren, who could read the tea leaves more clearly than seemingly anyone, believed the future of cannabis retail wasn't Domino's Pizza. It was Costco.

Canada, thanks to the outdoor grows and increasing efficiencies and number of licensed producers, had too much weed in the pandemic. Big bags of pot, that's what consumers wanted. Not expensive drinks with low THC, CBD oils, or gimmicky marijuana lubes. The 20 percent of people who bought 80 percent of the pot weren't coming into stores to snap a picture for Instagram. Beverages, once the hope of Cannabis 2.0, accounted for less than 3 percent of legal cannabis sales.

When Nova Cannabis opened Value Buds in 2020, sales climbed 800 percent. The product flying off shelves, says Sébastien St-Louis, was Hexo's

Original Stash. The market was dictating to the cannabis licensed producers. It was Winners, not Gucci, where the consumer wanted to shop. St-Louis thought that with Original Stash selling and his acquisition of Zenabis complete, he could hit consumers' tastes whether they shopped high or low. He drew inspiration from his partner Molson, who purchased Creemore Springs for $25 million in 2005 to get into the craft beer category. Sébastien made cheap weed in Quebec; now he could also make the good stuff in BC.

Craft and bulk, plus he had Alison Gordon's 48North, so he could also serve women with a female-focused cannabis brand. St-Louis says that the success of Value Buds played into his Zenabis deal. St-Louis could feel himself growing during the pandemic. He shaved his head. He lifted weights. "Earlier, I couldn't swallow Zenabis. I wasn't strong enough, but I got strong enough," he says.

He loved describing the Zenabis deal. "They poured $400 million into their indoor grow, a thousand dollars per square foot, and we picked up the whole company for $160 million," he says, and adds that he revamped the entire Zenabis facility within the first thirty days of his acquisition. He says the company had been so short on cash that they had to cut corners, and there were safety risks alongside deteriorating cannabis quality. "I needed more capacity so it was 'build or acquire,' and we knew Zenabis was so screwed up from capital markets that it was an incredible value."

One company was going to control 40 percent of the Canadian market, St-Louis believed, and that would translate into sales all over the world. "It's about winning. We're going to make the whole industry look like a joke," Sébastien tells me, and it sounds pretty good to my ears.

I let Sébastien pick up our lunch.

CHAPTER 21

Last Dance with Mary Jane

"The largest bribe I've said no to was $40 million."

Sébastien St-Louis

It was in this headspace that Sébastien St-Louis made the last deal of his cannabis life.

Though he insists his deal was already months in the works before Aphria-Tilray, St-Louis bought Redecan at the end of August 2021, for nearly $1 billion. The deal closed at $925 million, with $525 million in stock and $400 million in cash, and suddenly St-Louis wasn't only the world's longest-serving marijuana CEO. He also might have been — *might have been* — the best. He tells me, "I don't see Redecan as a billion-dollar acquisition. I see Redecan as holding IP that nobody can touch."

Despite the lofty valuations all around them, Redecan, the seven-year-old licensed cannabis producer, never went public. The company, which grew its cannabis in the Niagara escarpment, had massive market share and was known for its technology around a very particular brand of pre-rolls, toothpick-sized spears more similar to a Virginia Slim than anything resembling a Bob Marley joint. It was founded by the Thrower family of farmers.

It was financed by the Montours, an Indigenous family with generational business roots and some ongoing lawsuits over taxation. The Montours were owners of the fourth largest cigarette manufacturer in the world. The company had a shrouded legacy.

Operating on its own jurisdiction — Indigenous land — for the purposes of tax laws, Redecan was long thought to be a no-go for acquisition because, given its ties, the company existed outside of the legal industry regulations. While the other legal companies decried their taxation — which could eat up either one dollar per gram or ten percent of a product's value — Redecan played by different rules. While Bruce Linton and Terry Booth made it a point to kick the tires of every operator for possible acquisition, both men told me Redecan — and only Redecan — was never in play. Intentionally, the company stayed out of the spotlight. It sold millions of identical pre-rolls and had technology from its cigarette manufacturing, which approached widgetizing the valuable pre-roll sector of the cannabis industry.

The plan for Redecan was in play, St-Louis says, before the Zenabis deal.

Redecan, believed Sébastien, was the final piece of the puzzle that would turn him into Bruce.

It was the second day of our October 2021 interviews and we were huddled on a black leather couch in Hexo's boardroom, facing each other, our knees touching. We were eating steamies, little French hotdogs, on a snowy afternoon in Gatineau, Quebec.

St-Louis tells me he's mapped out his plan. "If weed's going to be a $300 billion business and retail manufacturers take a $100 billion slice of it, if you can have thirty percent global market share — and that's what we're playing for — you're a $30 billion company," he says. "Now put a four times sales multiple on that and Hexo has a $120 billion market cap. That was at the front end of Zenabis. That's where I want to take this. That's what we're playing for."

Hearing Sébastien talk like this over hot dogs, even after spending so much time with Terry Booth and Bruce Linton, I was still blown away. Even over tequila shots and edibles, the numbers never got that high. A market cap of $120 billion, in weed? But Sébastien passionately told his story and I think that's why he wanted to do these interviews. He wanted to tell somebody, like there was a story in his brain that he wanted to get off his chest. No one was saying how smart he was.

And there was something else bugging him, that he made references to during our two days together before coming out with it right at the end of our last session. It's no secret that cannabis, once legal, had a difficult time completely shedding its criminal connections. St-Louis, however, made the most radical claims I'd ever heard.

"The largest bribe I've said no to was $40 million," he tells me, and he says that other CEOs in cannabis have accepted that kind of money. They've done that, he says, mostly to get something done that would go against the interest of their shareholders — while pocketing cash themselves. A cannabis executive could be bribed to purchase an asset, or to ignore a potential deal, or perhaps to make a sweetheart arrangement with a rival company. The numbers were high and the industry was new, and since pot growers had once been illegal, there was an element to the industry that made it different from selling raincoats or shoes.

Of course, you hear stories like this not only in cannabis, but all over the business world. Yet legal cannabis, like the smell of a joint on a blazer, has never been able to shake its illegal past. And all of the founders had their stories of dangerous criminal incidents. Terry Booth told his partners, when they were going into dispensaries in 2012, "If a gun flashes, hit the ground." Tom Flow travelled with a notorious crowd before MedReleaf. The Ascent Industries CEO, Blair Jordan, told me he couldn't stand by a window at his office in Maple Ridge, because he was afraid of drive-bys.

Bruce Linton told me his story of being spooked. In 2015, the Canadian Cannabis Corporation (CCC) tried to buy Hexo and also tried to buy Canopy Growth. Back then, Linton checked out of the company on a Sunday to go talk to these potential partners and didn't tell anyone where he was. Not out of secrecy. It just slipped his mind. However, when he walked into the building north of Toronto, Linton said, it was the first time in the industry when he actually felt scared. He was in an empty warehouse with people he didn't know, talking about big money and — even if it was just weed, it was still drugs. Who were these people?

St-Louis tells me he had signed a definitive agreement deal with CCC, but backed out when they missed a payment. He considered himself lucky because the principals at CCC were eventually accused of misusing millions of dollars in investor funds. And that was just the tip of the iceberg. There were also two high-profile murders in Toronto in 2017 tied to CCC. St-Louis didn't specifically call out CCC in our conversation or mention what company he was referring to in terms of the $40 million bribe, but he did add insight into a closed-door world.

"The black market doesn't come with bats and threaten kneecaps. Organized crime comes up from behind and they compromise you. Set you up for blackmail. They come as friends," Sébastien says. "Often you piss off a shareholder block that wants to do something that hurts other shareholders." In the telling of the story, St-Louis went from the general to the more personal, as if catching his train of thought. "My political capital goes down — they have it out for me. That happens a lot. But I'm uncompromising."

I can't help thinking St-Louis, stoned on hero worship, was echoing his father when describing his legacy. Did you ever take a bribe? I ask him. How close did you come? "I'm squeaky clean," he says. "I would never do it any other way."

Sébastien St-Louis closed on Redecan on August 30, 2021. I spoke with him on October 7 and 8. Newspapers later reported, after our interviews were through, that on September 26, a Redecan lead adviser had written a letter to the Hexo board accusing Sébastien of "dilutive financings ... misalignment with shareholders, and a lack of basic business skills to lead." On October 20, 2021 — twelve days after our interviews and three days after the third anniversary of legal weed — the company announced Scott Cooper would be taking the reins of Hexo, the company Sébastien St-Louis founded. Cooper was the former Denver-based chief innovation officer at Molson Coors and subsequent leader of Truss, the joint venture between Hexo and Molson. Sébastien's former COO, it was announced in the same Hexo press release, would also be stepping down.

When we spoke, St-Louis must have known that all of this was transpiring, but he never mentioned any of it. Afterward, the former CEO who had been so candid stopped returning my calls. He still has not returned them to clarify what transpired.

The following month, with Hexo trading below two dollars per share, a tabloid in Quebec ran a front-page story on Redecan's ties to the Hells Angels. It was nothing more than some Instagram pictures, but rumours swirled of an investigation by the RCMP, who wouldn't comment for this book, and neither would anyone from the Redecan team, even though I'd interviewed them before for an advertorial — paid editorial content — about their vapes.

Trevor Fencott says he always had a good relationship with Redecan and Will Montour was always friendly at the cannabis conferences, but while the Redecan gossip swirled in the media, a pot convention was held that fall in downtown Toronto. I met a financier through Bruce Linton who handed me a manila folder inside an envelope. We met by a hot dog stand in front of the Toronto Convention Centre. My contact wore gloves to hand off the papers, lest there be fingerprints. The documents were a series of questions without context that looked into allegations and associates of Hexo and the Redecan group.

The papers mentioned gambling, Hells Angels, the Bahamas, other licensed producers, investment firms in Canada, and individuals and banks called out by name. I have more experience with writing paid endorsements for cannabis-infused chocolate chip cookies than with revealing the Panama Papers, but I tried to follow up on the leads.

And found nothing.

John Fowler doesn't put much stock into this stuff. He was also at the cannabis convention in Toronto, speaking alongside Alison Gordon. He says the allegations might have just been a ploy to beat up Hexo's stock price so the next group of financiers could pick up the company on the cheap. It's not against the law to have bad friends — most cannabis companies have some associations with people who trafficked marijuana before it crossed to the other side of the street of the law. Once a company goes legit, Fowler tells me, the legacy ties don't just disappear.

Sébastien St-Louis announced he was leaving the board of Hexo on November 19, 2021, and has remained quiet since. The last thing he told me in our interviews was "I will be a billionaire — maybe, but I'm not chasing that. I'm chasing the win."

EPILOGUE

The Last Drag

The idea behind Canadian legalization wasn't to create a frozen Silicon Valley, an industry that would sell Canadian weed all over the world. It was supposed to rectify bad laws that, from inception, were systemically racist. Legalization enriched people who already had every advantage, who needed no assistance because they were already rich. Justin Trudeau, when he started, seemed to represent such hope for a progressive society but, when he got down to it, became just another politician working angles to survive the next vote.

The end of cannabis prohibition is a good thing; we didn't need a war on drugs to tell us that. Billions of dollars have been invested into the Canadian economy from cannabis taxes, and tens of thousands of jobs have been created. There is Canadian intellectual property in marijuana growing and distribution all over the world. Countries, including the U.S., can look at our pot laws and see for themselves that weed doesn't lead to the end of the world. In Canada today there are far fewer Black and Indigenous lives being destroyed for the simple possession of weed.

On the last Friday in March 2023, four years after we first became friends, I asked Terry Parker, the victor of the medical cannabis suit back in 2001 that sent pot hurtling toward where we are today, if he'd ever heard of Terry Booth or Bruce Linton, Irwin Simon or Sébastien St-Louis, whose company would eventually be purchased by Tilray for $229 million (less than what St-Louis had paid for Zenabis when he first went on his ill-fated buyer's spree). He had no idea who any of these people were. He knew Jodie Giesz-Ramsay, who had finally been granted a dispensary licence the previous fall, and he knew Hilary Black, who David Klein at Canopy eventually fired. Terry still grows his own pot in the closet of his fourth-floor Parkdale apartment, the place where he grew the weed that would end up changing so many lives.

After Rosie Rowbotham passed away and Lorne Gertner offered to pay for his gravestone, and after the Smiths Falls Canopy location was shuttered in February 2023 and bought back by Hershey (who has announced exactly zero plans to sell edibles), Terry and I walk into a Fire & Flower near where we live. Trevor Fencott is now out of his company — he accepted an award for retailer of the year after he was fired, and now he works in private equity. He still hates the Ontario Cannabis Store, the government entity he competed against that was 2023's highest-earning cannabis company, while Fire & Flower, currently under Companies' Creditor Arrangement Act protection, has lost more than $200 million since 2018. Trevor says he never wanted to be Bruce Linton, who remains a friend and stays at the Marriott when he comes to Toronto, even if he no longer can buy the companies making the hotel's soap. He's on the board of the Canadian Olympic Foundation, and when I ran into trouble, he put his lawyer on my case.

Terry Booth is sober and dating and says any claims that his Aurora weed was terrible are bullshit. He thinks his stock at Audacious is undervalued and he still wants Bruce to invest.

Bruce says he still may.

Inside the Fire & Flower with Terry, there are few Canopy or Aurora products on the shelves. Instead, it's all buzzy new craft cannabis brands. There are more than one thousand licensed Canadian marijuana producers, and Ontario has almost seventeen hundred weed stores. By the time you read this, many of them will be closed. Cannabis is legal. But more people still prefer to buy craft beer and coffee, Tylenol and Gatorade. You can get a legal edible for five dollars, an ounce for a hundred bucks, and an Olli gummy with a juicy centre, like a weed fruit blast that tastes like bubble-gum. Terry Parker, of course, isn't recognized by the friendly sales staff. I give him a copy of *KIND* magazine — Lenny Kravitz is on the cover — and offer to buy him anything he wants from the shelves. But the original cannabis pioneer says he doesn't want anything.

"None of this stuff would be here without you," I say, and I mean it. I wouldn't have a job if it weren't for him. "At least get some cannabis pretzels or — look at this — a diamond-infused pre-roll blunt. Try a peach iced tea with THC."

"That's okay," Terry tells me, and he buttons up his army jacket and we walk out of the store onto Queen Street.

He's going to go back to his apartment to smoke his own weed.

INDEX

Index

ABOUT THE AUTHOR

Photograph by Matthew Kaplan, in Austin, with Lester Kaplan, Dale Kaplan, Lisa Kaplan, Andy Powell, Mia Powell, and Esme. All of them were kicked out of the frame. Clothing by Josh Kessler.

Ben Kaplan is a writer, editor, and journalist, co-founder of *KIND* magazine, and the owner of *iRun*, for which he gladly runs many marathons, some not financial. A frequent contributor to the *Globe and Mail* and *Post City* magazines, Kaplan worked at *GQ*, *National Post*, *P.O.V.* (Jay, Larry, and Randall), and *New York* magazine and wrote for *Sharp*, *Spin*, *Men's Journal*, *Forbes*, *Cosmopolitan*, *Seventeen*, and, once, the *New York Times*. His first book is *Feet, Don't Fail Me Now* (2014, Greystone), and he lives in Toronto with, especially, Matthew and Esme.